THE
DOOM AND BLOOM™
MEDICAL SURVIVAL
HANDBOOK

A GUIDE TO STAYING HEALTHY
IN AN UNCERTAIN FUTURE

JOSEPH ALTON, M.D.
AMY ALTON, A.R.N.P.

DISCLAIMER

The information given and opinions voiced in this volume are for educational and entertainment purposes only and does not constitute medical advice or the practice of medicine. No provider-patient relationship, explicit or implied, exists between the authors and readers. This handbook does not substitute for such a relationship with a qualified provider. As many of the strategies discussed in this volume would be less effective than proven present-day medications and technology, the authors and publisher strongly urge their readers to seek modern and standard medical care with certified practitioners whenever and wherever it is available.

The reader should never delay seeking medical advice, disregard medical advice, or discontinue medical treatment because of information in this book or any resources cited in this book.

Although the authors have researched all sources to ensure accuracy and completeness, they assume no responsibility for errors, omissions, or other inconsistencies therein. Neither do the authors or publisher assume liability for any harm caused by the use or misuse of any methods, products, instructions or information in this book or any resources cited in this book.

Copyright 2012 Doom and Bloom™, LLC
All rights reserved.

Printed in the United States of America

ISBN: 0615563236
ISBN 13: 978-0615563237

JUL - - 2014

THE
DOOM AND BLOOM™
MEDICAL SURVIVAL
HANDBOOK

DEDICATIONS

This book is dedicated to my wife Amy, whose positive attitude and sunny disposition truly puts the "Bloom" in "Doom and Bloom". She is the person who first made it clear to me that this book was both possible to write and needed by those who want to be prepared in times of trouble.

JOSEPH ALTON, M.D.

I dedicate this book to my husband Joe, whose selfless attitude and compassion for his patients over the years has never wavered. He is unceasing in his efforts to help those who want to learn how to keep their loved ones healthy, in good times or bad.

AMY ALTON, A.R.N.P.

Additionally, we both dedicate this book to those who are willing to take responsibility for the health of their loved ones in times of trouble. We salute your courage in accepting this assignment; have no doubt, it will save lives.

JOSEPH ALTON, M.D. AND AMY ALTON, A.R.N.P.

"DO WHAT YOU CAN, WITH WHAT YOU HAVE, WHERE YOU ARE."

THEODORE ROOSEVELT

ABOUT JOSEPH ALTON, M.D. AND AMY ALTON, A.R.N.P.

Joseph Alton practiced as a board-certified Obstetrician and Pelvic Surgeon for more than 25 years before retiring to devote his efforts to preparing your family medically for any scenario. He has been a Fellow of the American College of Obstetrics and Gynecology and the American College of Surgeons for many years, served as department chairman at local hospitals and as an adjunct professor at local university nursing schools. He has been a speaker at various survival and preparedness conferences on the subject of medical readiness in austere times. A member of MENSA, Dr. Alton collects medical books from the 19th century to gain insight on off-the-grid medical protocols.

Amy Alton is an Advanced Registered Nurse Practitioner and a Certified Nurse-Midwife. She has had years of experience working in large teaching institutions as well as smaller, family-oriented hospitals. Amy has extensive medicinal herb and vegetable gardens and works to include natural remedies into her strategies.

Dr. and Ms. Alton are both Master Gardeners for their state. They also are devoted aqua culturists (currently raising tilapia) and aquaponic, raised bed and container gardening experts. Additionally, they have been regular contributors to Survivalist Magazine. As "Dr. Bones and Nurse Amy", they host a blog and radio program under the Doom and Bloom™ label. Dr. and Ms. Alton are firm believers that, to remain healthy in hard times, we must use all the tools at our disposal. Their goal is to promote integrated medicine; in this way, their readers will have the most options to keep their loved ones healthy in a collapse situation.

PREFACE

✚ ✚ ✚

WHEN THE "BUCK" STOPS WITH YOU

Most outdoor medicine guides are intended to aid you in managing emergency situations in austere and remote locations. Certainly, modern medical care on an ocean voyage or wilderness hike is not readily available; even trips to the cities of underdeveloped countries may fit this category as well. There are medical strategies for these mostly short term scenarios that are widely published, and they are both reasonable and effective. An entire medical education system exists to deal with limited wilderness or disaster situations, and it is served by a growing industry of supplies and equipment.

The basic premise of wilderness/disaster medicine is to:

- Evaluate the injured or ill patient,
- Stabilize their condition, and…
- Transport the individual to the nearest modern hospital, clinic, or emergency care center.

This series of steps makes perfect sense; you are not a physician and, somewhere, there are facilities that have a lot more technology than you have in your backpack. Your priority is to get the patient out of immediate danger and then ship them off; this will allow you to continue on your wilderness adventure.

Transporting the injured person may be difficult to do (sometimes very difficult), but you still have the luxury of being able to "pass the buck" to those who have more knowledge, technology and supplies.

One day, however, there may come a time when a pandemic, civil unrest or terrorist event may precipitate a situation where the miracle of modern medicine may be unavailable. Indeed, not only unavailable, but even to the point that the potential for access to modern facilities no longer exists. We refer to this type of scenario as a "collapse". In a collapse, you will have more risk for illness and injury than on a hike in the woods, yet little or no hope of obtaining more advanced care than you, yourself, can provide. It's not a matter of a few days without modern technology, such as after a hurricane or tornado. Help is NOT on the way; therefore, you have become the place where the "buck" stops for the foreseeable future, at least when it comes to your medical welfare.

Few are prepared to deal with this harsh reality. To go further, very few are willing to even entertain the possibility that such a tremendous burden might be placed upon them. Even for those willing, there are few, if any, books that will consider this drastic turn of events.

Almost all handbooks (some quite good) on wilderness survival will usually end a section with: "Go to the hospital immediately". Although this is excellent advice for modern times, it won't be very helpful in an uncertain future when the hospitals might all be out of commission. We only have to look at Hurricane Katrina in 2005 to know that even modern medical facilities may be useless if they are understaffed, under-supplied, and overcrowded.

When you are the end of the line with regards to the medical well-being of your family or group, there are certain adjustments that have to be made. Medical supplies must be accumulated and expanded. Medical knowledge must be obtained and assimilated. These medical supplies and knowledge must then be adjusted to fit the mindset that you must adopt in a collapse: That things have changed for the long term, and that you are the sole medical resource when it comes to keeping your people healthy. As Theodore Roosevelt once said, "You must do what you can, with what you have, where you are".

This is a huge responsibility and many will decide that they cannot bear the burden of being in charge of the medical care of others. Others will find the fortitude to grit their teeth and wear the badge of collapse "medic". These individuals may have some medical experience, but most will simply be fathers and mothers who understand that someone must be appointed to handle things when there are no doctors. If this reality first becomes apparent when a loved one becomes deathly ill, the likelihood that you will have the training and supplies needed to be an effective medical provider will be close to zero.

This volume is meant to educate and prepare those who want to ensure the health of their loved ones. If you can absorb the information here, you will be better equipped to handle 90% of the emergencies that you will see in a power-down scenario.

All the information contained in this book is meant for use in a post-apocalyptic setting, when modern medicine no longer exists. If your leg is broken in five places, it stands to reason that you'll do better in an orthopedic hospital ward than if I make a splint out of two sticks and strips of my T-shirt. The strategies discussed here are not the most effective means of taking care of certain medical problems. They adhere to the philosophy that something is better than nothing; in a survival situation, this "something" might just get you through the storm.

Hopefully, societal destabilization will never happen; if not, this book will still have its uses. Natural catastrophes will tax even the most advanced medical delivery systems. Medical personnel will be unlikely to be readily available to help you if they are dealing with mass casualty events. Even a few days without access to health care may be fatal in an emergency. The information provided here will be valuable while you are waiting for help to arrive.

An important caveat: In most locales, the practice of medicine or dentistry without a license is against the law, and none of the recommendations in this book will protect you from liability if you implement them where there is a functioning government and legal system. Consider obtaining formal medical education if you want to become a healthcare provider in a pre-collapse society. All it takes is your time, energy, and motivation.

Although you will not be a physician after reading this volume, you will certainly be more of a medical asset to your family, group, or community than you were before. You will have:

- Learned to think about what to do when today's technology is no longer at your fingertips.

- Considered preventative medicine and sanitation.

- Looked at your environment to see what plants might have medicinal value.

- Put together a medical kit which, along with standard equipment, includes traditional medications and natural remedies.

Most importantly, you will have become medically prepared to face the very uncertain future; and after all, isn't that what you wanted to accomplish when you first picked up this book?

TABLE OF CONTENTS

✚ ✚ ✚

INTRODUCTION

✚ ✚ ✚

ARE YOU NORMAL?

Excuse me, sir, may I ask you something: Are you normal?

Seems like such a simple question, doesn't it? There aren't too many people who think they're abnormal, are there? The truth, however, is that it's not as simple as it seems.

Okay, then, let's talk about "normal" people. Normal has several definitions, but we'll focus on two:

1. "Standard, average or conforming to the group", and…
2. "sane".

"Normal" people have certain characteristics: They need a level of organization in their life. They don't want a lot of clutter, so they make sure to keep no more than 3 days' supply of food in the pantry. They wait until the gas tank is nearly empty to re-fill it, and have no medical supplies other than a few Band-Aids and some aspirin. Whenever there's a crisis, whether it's national (like the 9/11 attacks) or personal (like losing a job), they see before them just a bump on the road. When they stumble, they pick themselves up, brush the dirt off, and continue on their mer-ry way as if nothing had happened.

Normal folk don't feel that there are lessons to be learned. This is because they expect others to resolve the problem for them. They pay taxes, so they believe the government will step in and give them a helping hand whenever they need it. The help they expect could be in the form of food stamps in hard finan-cial times, or in swift emergency responses in natural calamities, or in efficient and effective intervention in areas of civil unrest. Various surveys prove that this is the "normal" thinking of most people in civilized countries. Given the definition of "normal" listed above, this attitude certainly is "standard" and conforms to the group, but is it "sane"?

Let's take the case of essential personnel for any municipality. This would include police officers, firefighters, emergency medi-cal techs, etc. These are the emergency responders that "normal" folks expect to get them out of a crisis. But what would really happen? In surveys performed in several cities' police precincts and fire stations, many essential personnel have indicated that they will not report in case of a serious catastrophe, such as a societal collapse.

Unthinkable? To some, perhaps. However, these people that we depend upon to rescue us in times of trouble also have wives, husbands, parents, and children. Who do you think they will be rush to protect in a truly horrendous emergency, you or their own families?

In the aftermath of Hurricane Katrina, the New Orleans Police Department surveyed those law enforcement officials who did not report for duty. Although some were victims of the catastrophe, most cited their families as the reason for their absence. To expect them to do their duty and, at the same time, leave their own loved ones at risk might be standard and "normal" in our society, but it certainly isn't "sane".

So how do "normal" people become "sane" people? By realizing that society can be fragile and there are events that may occur to send the world awry. Once things happen that knock us off-kilter, a downward spiral will make life difficult. Certainly, it will be a challenge for all, but less so for that small minority known as "Preppers".

Preppers are what we call people who stockpile food and supplies for use in a societal upheaval. Preppers also take time to re-learn skills largely lost to modern urbanites/suburbanites; skills that would be useful if modern conveniences are no longer available.

What types of events could cause such a collapse to happen? There are various scenarios that could lead to times of trouble: Flu pandemics, terrorist attacks, solar flares, and economic collapse are just some of the possible calamities that could befall a community or even a country. The likelihood of any one of these life-changing occurrences may be very small, but what is the chance that NONE of these events will occur over the course of your lifetime?

Preppers see the writing on the wall; unlike the oblivious majority, they face perilous circumstances with a "can-do" attitude. Instead of facing an uncertain future with fear and desperation, they are using this opportunity to learn new skills. Many of these skills were common knowledge to their ancestors, such as growing food and using natural products for medicinal uses. By learning things that are useful in a power-down situation, they increase the likelihood that they and their loved ones will succeed if, heaven forbid, everything else fails. If a calamitous scenario transpires, they will be prepared for the worst, even while hoping for the best.

This is not to say that Preppers are eagerly waiting for some terrible series of events to bring society down. They want nothing more than to die at age 100, with their grandchildren whispering in their ear: "Gee, Grandpa, what the heck are we going to do with all these supplies?" They view their preparations as insurance. You buy health insurance, but that doesn't mean you want to get sick; you buy life insurance, but you certainly don't want to die. Being prepared is insurance as well. Instead of paying money for something that isn't tangible, you're buying food, medical supplies, and other things that will ensure that you and your loved ones will do well regardless of what slings and arrows life may throw at you.

The road to self-reliance is a long and winding one. It will take some of your time and some of your energy to become self-sufficient. It will take some of your money, as well, to accumulate things that will be useful in obtaining a head start to success in dark times. This can be done frugally; a 50 pound bag of rice, for example, is still under $20 at the time of this writing.

Many of the products that will be useful in a collapse scenario can also be improvised. A bandanna and a stick will be almost as good a tourniquet as a high-tech, commercially manufactured one. Look at what you have in your home and consider the ways that an item can be used in a survival situation. A realistic assessment of your storage will give you a good idea of how prepared you are for an unforeseen event. Where are you deficient? What purchases or improvisations will offer you the best opportunity to be ready? What skills would be useful to learn?

Benjamin Franklin once said: "When the well is dry, we learn the worth of water". The same can be said of many aspects of modern technology. If you are thrown into a situation where there is no electric power, how many items in your house will be useless?

Consider the ways that you will get power. For most people, there are a few un-rechargeable batteries in a drawer somewhere. This may get you a few hours' worth of flashlight or radio use, but what then? It's important to have a strategy that will give you a steady supply of at least minimal power. Switch to rechargeable batteries, and get a solar battery charger so that you can keep a renewable power source in your possession at all times. Consider the various other options, such as propane gas, wind power and solid solar panels with marine batteries. You don't have to be an industrial engineer or an extremely wealthy person to put these together; just some motivation and perhaps a little elbow grease, and you'll be on your way.

This volume is meant to help you on your way to medical preparedness. You won't be a physician after reading this. I promise you, however, that you will know more about assuring your family's medical well-being and be more of an asset than a liability to those you care about. If you begin to prepare for difficult times, and maintain a positive attitude, you will be an example for others in your family or community to emulate. If they see that preparing just makes good old common sense, they might start to prepare as well. Imagine that, an entire community, nation or even the world ready to deal with life's untoward events. If that were the case, "normal" would truly mean "sane".

SECTION 1

✦ ✦ ✦

PRINCIPLES OF MEDICAL PREPARDNESS

Public Perception of Preparedness (L) vs. Actual Preparedness (R)

DOOM AND GLOOM VS. DOOM AND BLOOM

✚ ✚ ✚

There are a variety of reasons that the majority of the population chooses not to prepare for hard times. One reason relates to the perception that those that store food and other items are full of "Doom and Gloom". Many in the general public still see the old-time camouflage-clad survivalists when they think of preparedness. The term "Doom and Gloom" itself is filled with the worst connotations; synonymous with despair and inaction, very few are willing to identify with what they consider to be a personality flaw. I don't blame them. Placing oneself into a category that always sees the negative in a situation is an unattractive option.

Yet, events are occurring in rapid succession. Our quality of life is being eroded even as we speak. The downward spiral may be starting, and it's difficult for many to escape a negative attitude when they consider the future of our society. The problems are many, and the solutions are few (and they are painful, as well). It is easy to choose the despair and inaction that goes with being a "Doom and Gloom-er"; there's not a lot of sweat involved in sitting in front of a television or computer, bemoaning the ills of modern-day civilization. You don't have to study or learn new skills; you don't have to change your current lifestyle. You can just sit there and watch soap operas and reality shows. Although there's not a lot to like about the term "Doom and Gloom", plenty of people are just fine with the apathetic, do-nothing attitude that goes along with it.

These are dangerous times. There are many (very many) who are in denial of this fact. These people could be cured of this denial simply by examining current events. Besides them, there are the "Doom and Gloomers", fully aware of the situation but apathetically waiting for the apocalypse in a morose stupor. They will be no better off than the oblivious majority in times of trouble; worse, really, as they have been miserable for a longer time.

Furthermore, their negativity has soured the general public on the idea of preparedness. For the future of our society, this is probably the worst legacy of the "Doom and Gloom" mindset. The less prepared our citizens are for hard times, the more difficult it will be for there to be a future at all.

There is hope, however. The preparedness community understands that there are storm clouds on the horizon. They see the signs of the deterioration that have begun to erode the civilization that we have enjoyed for so long. Facts do not cease to exist just because they are ignored, and we may be on the brink of a meltdown. So, why do today's Preppers have an advantage over everyone else in terms of their potential for success in the future? Because, unlike the "Doom and Gloom" crowd, they have evolved a new, more positive philosophy: "Doom and BLOOM".

Adherents of the "Doom and Bloom" philosophy view negative current events with an unblinking eye. There is neither denial nor sugarcoating of the factors that might send things south, perhaps in a hurry. This is, if you will, the "Doom" part. Instead of despair and inaction, however, Preppers have hope and determination. They see the danger, but also the opportunity: The opportunity to become truly self-reliant. This is the "Bloom" part. They see the challenges of today as a wake-up call. It might be an alarm, but it's also a call to action.

Unlike others, the Prepper Nation is positive that there are ways to succeed in the coming hard times. They look to what has worked before there was high technology. They see how their grandparents and great-grandparents succeeded, and they are learning skills that their ancestors had; skills that modern society has lost, somewhere along the way. "Doom and BLOOMERS" see the silver lining in those storm clouds, and are learning how to grow their own food, take care of their own health, and provide for their common defense. There's a learning curve, to be sure, but every bit of knowledge that they can absorb will mean a better future for themselves and their loved ones. They are applying lessons from the past to assure themselves that future.

If the public's perception of the preparedness community is one of "Doom and Bloom" rather than "Doom and Gloom", the association would be one with positivity and "can-do", instead of negativity and inertia. This would allow Preppers to serve as ambassadors of hope. With the acceptance of a positive viewpoint, a rebirth of a collapsed society would not only be possible, but would be inevitable. Armed with knowledge and skills to function in a power-down society, "Doom and Bloomers" would be the vanguard for the establishment of a self-sustainable community.

It is not just wishful thinking. It may be seem daunting to you, but it is well within your potential. It has been said that a 1000 mile journey begins with the first step. Take that first step today, and you'll be ahead of the crowd in terms of assuring your survival and that of your loved ones.

BAD NEWS
AND GOOD NEWS

✚ ✚ ✚

A good percentage of the population has an uneasy feeling about the future. They have heard all the dire predictions of the last 50 years: The Soviet Union and the U.S. will destroy the world in a nuclear war. Y2K will make the entire grid shut down. It seems that, every year, there is a Doomsday prediction, and, every year, it fails to come to fruition (whew!). A new series of predictions, even more dire, for the coming years are also out there. Yet, because we have cried "Wolf" so many times without an actual collapse event happening, the general public has become jaded. Apathy mixed with inertia is their response. This is a dangerous attitude, as the wolf really may show up, eventually.

Have we reached the high water mark as a civilization? There are some signs that we have. One sure sign of the decline of a civilization is the inability to reproduce the technological achievements of its past. Although we are still moving forward technologically in some areas, this sign is now visible. For example, we no longer have the capability or desire to put a man on the moon. The end of the Space Shuttle and International Space Station programs now confines the human race to our own planet. This is not the best course of action for a planet with limited resources and a burgeoning population. Resources that were once earmarked for space travel, however, now are needed simply to keep people fed and the infrastructure in place.

This has happened many times before, with many (now-extinct) cultures. Take Rome, for instance. The Romans were able to develop indoor-plumbing, systems of aqueducts, realistic art, etc. As the civilization went into decline, these advances were unable to be maintained, let alone expanded upon. At one point, collapse of the entire culture occurred. There were still "Romans", but they were at a loss to understand how their ancestors were able to produce such miracles. This period was called a "dark age". We could find ourselves on the road to a dark age, also.

In a recent poll, 65% of American citizens felt that the country was in decline. Indeed, the prominence of the United States has been in jeopardy for some time from far-away nations such as China and India. The American Century may be coming to a close. By 2026, the United States is projected to be surpassed by China economically, and by India around 2050. Our leadership in science and technology (especially military) will be challenged between 2020 and 2030. This descent has been projected to be gentle and gradual; yet, many of us remember the shocking rapidity of the collapse of the Soviet Union. Why are we immune to that fate?

The "end of the world" can be objective, as in a large asteroid striking the planet, or subjective, as in the internet going down for an online business. Why is this subjective? Well, not so very long ago, there wasn't an internet at all. We didn't have mobile phones. There were no microwave ovens or televisions and our cars didn't have computers or cruise control. Most of us would consider the loss of these and other items the "end of the world", but life went on without these things just a few decades ago.

Life went on without credit cards, as well. If you didn't have the funds for an item, you went without it. This would be considered cruel and unusual punishment in today's culture. Taken together, the possibility of the loss of these modern conveniences is heinous to the general population. So heinous, indeed, that they reject the idea of a collapse simply by refusing to even think about the future and preparedness.

What are the issues that could tip a fragile society into dark times? To fully delineate every scenario that can befall us would require a lot more paper and ink than we have, but let's discuss some of them now.

The most likely, in my opinion, is economic collapse. There are at least three major factors in the decline of the United States economically. They are: Trade deficits, the loss of the dollar as the world's currency, and the decline in our status as the world's technological innovator.

Once the world's biggest exporter of goods, the U.S. is now behind China and the European Union. The outsourcing of jobs, especially in manufacturing, has been constant and leaves the nation with less and less products that other countries need. For example, at the time of this writing there are no cellular phones produced in the United States at all. There seems to be no end to this trend, and the rising unemployment rate attests to it.

China and Russia are no longer using the dollar to transact business with each other, instead using their own currencies. The indiscriminate printing of more and more money to pay our debts has the entire world uneasy. Increasingly, we are seeing calls for an alternative to the current system.

A country's technological prowess is dependent on its ability to educate its citizens and to attract the best and brightest that are not yet citizens. Our ranking in math and science education is dropping in every survey. Although we are still attracting students from other countries to our universities (50% of math and science graduate students are from elsewhere), they are no longer planning to live here after they graduate. They see better opportunities in their own countries.

All of the above, combined with an astronomical debt and near-default, have left the United States as a fading superpower unable to pay its debts. Once the world ceases to use the dollar as its trade currency, no one will want to buy the treasury notes that have served as our way to pay interest on the debt. The costs of imports will rise as a result. To pay for all these rising costs, less money will go to repairing infrastructure, research, and military defense. Do you see where this is headed?

In all likelihood, this will be a gradual downward spiral. The average person will find it more difficult each year to pay his or her bills. Mortgage payments will be behind and more people will find themselves less able to fill up their gas tank or pay for their kids' day care or college tuitions. We will all slowly become poorer than we were. Unemployment or under-employment will further rise, and more adult children will find themselves living at their parent's house. This is already a reality for many folks.

Oil is another major factor where the United States is at a disadvantage. Consumption of foreign oil has risen to 66% in 2007, up from 36% 30 years earlier. The failure of the U.S. to develop alternative sources of energy leaves the country at the mercy of others. Only 12% of our energy use comes from alternative (solar, hydro, wind, etc.) methods. As other countries, such as China, continue to increase their energy use, the demand for oil rises and so does the price. As the dollar weakens, oil-producing nations may begin to demand payment by other means than U.S. dollars. This will further raise the price; as low-cost oil becomes a thing of the past, the cost of travel (and export) will skyrockets. Trade will be seriously affected. As winter approaches, the economy stagnates as more and more money is required to simply heat the house. The logical endpoint is bankruptcy, universal poverty and the civil unrest it portends, and eventually, collapse.

This scenario is not the only road to perdition. Influenza viruses, with their ability to mutate, are outpacing vaccines. With the ability to travel around the world in a day, outbreaks that would have been localized can become worldwide in a matter of weeks. Widespread use of antibiotics in livestock is producing super-bacteria that can beat drugs that were effective against them previously. Electro-Magnetic Pulses (EMPS), either natural (solar flares) or man-made (terrorism) have the potential to shut down the power grid for decades. Military adventures by various countries might ignite larger conflicts that could destabilize the world. Any number of "acts of God", such as hurricanes, earthquakes, tsunamis, etc., might wreak their havoc. Of course, the likelihood of any one of these situations occurring is small, but what is the likelihood that NONE of these scenarios will occur sometime in the future?

Ok, enough Doom, how about some Bloom? If any of the above actually happens, there will be turmoil. However, after a rocky (perhaps very rocky) period, there will be a transition to a steady state. This transition will probably be gradual with fitful starts and stops. The world may no longer be affluent, but it will be more self-sustainable. The economy will be an insular one providing the essentials to local communities, using local materials. You might not be able to buy bananas in Montana during the winter, but you will be eating organically, and you will be able to grow that food yourself.

Towards that goal, you'll replace your water-guzzling lawn with vegetable gardens, fruit trees, and berry bushes. Water is just too precious to waste on a putting green. Any remaining grassy areas will become pasture land for goats, cows, etc. We will all become accomplished homesteaders or have skills that pertain to homesteading.

Self-sufficiency will be the order of the day. If something breaks, you will have learned how to repair it or will barter with someone who does. If you get sick, much of your medicine is already growing in your herb garden. Every family will have someone with the healing touch that will take responsibility for medical well-being in the absence of modern medical care.

Is this a lot to swallow in one sitting? Sure it is. It's a challenge, to be sure, but it's a challenge your great grandparents accepted. You're just as smart as they were. You probably know even more about preventative medicine than they did, or at least have the resources today to learn. All you need is a little motivation and a positive attitude.

What's the end result of all this? Your children will cease wanting to grow up to be runway models and rock stars, and will want to take up truly useful trades that make them an asset to their community. You might wind up living in a larger group; an extended family means more hands to share in the chores. Your children will spend a lot more time interacting with the rest of the family than they do now. Without a computer in front of them, they will actually get to know their loved ones, at last.

Also, there will be a sense of accomplishment. You will have seen that seed that you planted become a plant, and produce something that you can actually eat! And it's there because YOU planted and cared for it. Society is so used to specialization today that most people feel like just another cog in a very big machine. In a self-sufficient world, you and your family will likely be the whole ball of wax, from beginning to end. It's a lot of responsibility, but the satisfaction you will have in a job well done will be something you rarely experience today.

So, not so bad, is it? Nobody's anxious for society to start collapsing, but we can be ready for it and have a rewarding life no matter what happens. Keep a quiet determination and a positive outlook with regard to the present, get some skills under your belt, and you will guarantee yourself a future.

HISTORY OF PREPAREDNESS

✚ ✚ ✚

Some say that preparedness has its origin in the animal kingdom. Squirrels, foxes, chipmunks, and various other animals store or bury food which they dig up in the winter to get through lean times. Even though it is instinctual behavior for them, they are assuring their survival in a fashion that we can all learn from. When human beings realize that tough times are on the way, a relatively small percentage will start preparing, and these people are the ones that will be successful in times of trouble.

Preparedness is just the human way to store those nuts for the coming winter. It is our effort to prepare ourselves and our families for any eventuality. We prepare, as mentioned before, to ensure that there will be food, medical supplies, and all the other things we need to survive. In a collapse situation, most of these necessities will be hard or impossible to obtain. By putting some time, effort and money into accumulating tangible items, we will be able to ensure our well-being if the worst happens. We certainly don't want disasters to occur, but we want to be ready to withstand hard times. It's a sign of intelligence to be prepared and it's an achievable goal. Anyone, regardless of their station in life, can work towards that goal.

We all, in the back of our minds, are concerned about the massive calamity: The perfect storm, solar flares, terrorist attacks, economic collapse, and any of a number of events that could turn our fragile civilization into a nightmare for our citizens. We call it "the end of the world as we know it". These events are horrific, to be sure, but "the end of the world" doesn't have to be nationwide or worldwide; it can just as easily be personal. The loss of a family member or one's employment can easily throw a family into disarray. By storing food and other essential items, the "personal apocalypse" can be a bump in the road instead of the end of the road.

The preparedness community has a long history; as far back as biblical times, in fact. When the Hebrew Joseph was in the Egyptian Pharaoh's jail, he was known for his ability to interpret dreams. After hearing about this ability, Pharaoh sent for the young man, and asked him about a recurring dream that the Egyptian leader was having. In the dream, there were 7 fat, healthy cattle. There then came along 7 thin, diseased cattle and they devoured the healthy ones. Joseph took this to mean that Egypt would experience 7 years of plenty followed by 7 years of famine. So he recommended that the Pharaoh spend the next 7 bountiful years accumulating grain; in that way, the people would be fed during the subsequent lean years. This was done, and Egypt was prosperous during a famine that left all of its neighbors destitute and starving. This was the very first recorded instance of "prepping"! By following Joseph's recommendation to prepare, we can be a prosperous Egypt instead of its unfortunate neighbors.

In the millennia since the time of Joseph, there have been many instances in which disaster has been averted in times of trouble by the concept of preparedness. Farmers stored grain by erecting silos and "cribs". Every army crossing into enemy territory stockpiled supplies in advance; if they didn't, they would find themselves starving and out of ammunition in a hostile land. In every instance, those who prepared for times of crisis had a head start on everyone around them. Out of this, the modern survival community was born.

The modern survival community has people with varied skills but of like minds. These people are in the minority, but you will find them scattered everywhere: In cities, suburbs and rural areas. They are diverse: Liberals concerned about global warming prepare and so do conservatives concerned about excessive government. They might disagree on some issues and they may not always be on the same page, but they are committed to the same goal. That goal is the continuation of the species, and a life for everyone in the group that is worth living. These are the people that will rebuild a society after a catastrophe.

MEDICAL PREPAREDNESS

✚ ✚ ✚

After gathering food and building a shelter, many people in the preparedness community consider personal and home defense to be the next priority in the event of a societal collapse. Certainly, defending oneself is important, but have you thought about defending your health?

In a situation where power might be down and normal methods of filtering water and cleaning food don't exist, your health is as much under attack as the survivors in the latest zombie apocalypse movie. Infectious diseases will be rampant in a situation where it will be a challenge to maintain sanitary conditions.

Simple chores, such as chopping wood, commonly lead to cuts that could get infected. These minor issues, so easily treated by modern medical science, can easily become life-threatening if left untreated in a collapse scenario.

Don't you owe it to yourself and your family to devote some time and effort to obtain medical knowledge and supplies? The difficulties involved in a grid-down situation will surely put you at risk for sickness or injury. It's important to seek education so that you can treat infectious disease and the other ailments that you'll see. There will likely be a lot more diarrheal disease than gunfights at the OK corral. History teaches us that, in the Civil War, there were a lot more deaths from dysentery than there were from bullet wounds. Some say "Beans, Bullets and Band-Aids", but I say "Beans and Band-Aids, then Bullets". I suppose, as a physician, that's not too surprising.

If you make the commitment to learn how to treat medical issues and to store medical supplies, you're taking a genuine first step towards assuring your family's survival in dark times. The medical supplies will always be there if the unforeseen happens, and the knowledge you gain will be there for the rest of your life. Many medical supplies have long shelf lives; their longevity will one of the factors that will give you confidence when moving forward.

It's important to know some illnesses will be difficult to treat if modern medical facilities aren't available. It will be hard to do much about those clogged coronary arteries; there won't be many cardiac bypasses performed. However, by eating healthily and getting good nutrition, you will give yourself the best chance to minimize some major medical issues. In a collapse situation, an ounce of prevention is worth, not a pound, but a ton of cure. Start off healthy and you'll have the best chance to stay healthy.

When I say to obtain medical knowledge, I am also encouraging you to learn about natural remedies and alternative therapies that may have some benefit for your particular medical problem. I cannot vouch for the effectiveness of every claim that one thing or another will cure what ails you; suffice it to say, that our family has an extensive medicinal garden and that it might be a good idea for your family to have one, also. Many herbs that have medicinal properties grow like weeds, so a green thumb is not required to grow them. Many of them do not even require full sun to thrive.

I'm not asking you to do anything that your great-grand-parents didn't do as part of their strategy to succeed in life. In a collapse situation we'll be thrown back, in a way, to that era. We should learn some lessons from the methods they used to stay healthy. I won't dwell too much on natural remedies in this chapter, as there are chapters devoted to the subject in other parts of this manual.

The non-prepper members of my family wonder why I spend all my time trying to prepare people medically for a collapse situation. They tell me that I can't turn everyone into doctors, so why I should try?

Am I trying to turn you all into doctors? No, there's too much to learn in one lifetime; even as a physician, I often come across things I'm not sure about. That's what medical books are for, so make sure that you put together a library. You can refer to them when you need to, just as I do. I AM trying to turn you into something, however: I'm trying to make you a better medical asset to your family and/or survival community than you were before. If you can absorb the information I'll provide in this handbook, I will have succeeded in my mission.

THE CONCEPT OF
INTEGRATED MEDICINE

✚ ✚ ✚

On a regular basis, I receive comments from both those in the traditional medical profession and also from herbalists, homeopaths and other practitioners of alternative medicine. Medical doctors are known as Allopathic Physicians and learn standard medical theory and the use of modern technology and pharmaceuticals to treat illness. Alternative practitioners use herbal teas, essential oils and other substances to deal with disease. Both traditional and natural healthcare providers seem to have very polarized views on their opposite number. Allopathic physicians believe that few, if any, natural medicines have benefits for their patients. Herbalists often feel that most, if not all, standard methods of treatment are part of a scheme on the part of physicians and pharmaceutical companies to make a buck. Both are suspicious of the other.

In a collapse situation, it is clear to me that we must use all of the tools available to us if we wish to remain healthy. Traditional M.D.s must recognize that the vast majority of their drugs and technology will be non-existent if the power goes down. Who will manufacture antibiotics and blood pressure medications? How will a physician be able to access X-rays or CAT scans in a scenario where there might not even be electricity? How will someone who has spent their career reading MRIs in a hospital radiology department be able to serve their community? With great difficulty, I would imagine.

My example of a radiologist also points out another issue with conventional medicine: The tendency to over-specialize. To take another example, OB/GYNs can decide to obstetricians, gyne-cologist, infertility specialists, high risk pregnancy specialists or cancer specialists. Whatever happened to the idea of treating the whole patient? These doctors have to take their own family members to other physicians because it's been so long since they treated anything other than their sub-specialty. Conventional doctors can take a lesson from their natural healer counterparts in how to deal with a patient holistically.

Allopathic physicians will also have to learn some things they haven't paid attention to since medical school: Hygiene, nutrition, and sanitation. Without knowledge of basic strate-gies to keep their survival community healthy, that radiologist or infertility specialist will be of little use to their own families, much less society in general.

A new focus will be required to function as a medical resource in times of trouble. They will have to learn what medicinal properties exist in the plants around them. Aloe Vera can help treat a burn, pine needles have Vitamin C, and aspirin-like substances exist in the under bark of willows and poplar trees. They will have to understand how to grow and process herbs that have medicinal benefits, because all of the commercially manufactured drugs will no longer be available.

Having said that, alternative healers must also understand that not all traditional medicine is harmful. Infected wounds really do get better with Amoxicillin; Insulin really does lower a diabetic's blood sugar. It's difficult to treat a major hemorrhage without tourniquets and hemostatic agents such as Quikclot or Celox. Don't delay life-saving treatment just to spite the American Medical Association.

Alternative healthcare providers have important knowledge: Which herbs and essential oils might have a benefit for various conditions, and what are the possible benefits of colloidal silver or even acupuncture. This is knowledge that will help them become effective medics for their community, but knowledge of how to use a SAM splint to set a broken bone or how to suture a laceration is important as well.

Having an inflexible attitude towards one branch of medicine or another is harmful to your family or survival group. As such, this book is not just geared towards standard medical treatment, but includes other natural healing options. It is not, however, a book solely on alternative medicine either. Those of you that are wholly against one or the other will probably be unhappy with it; you should examine why you are so dead set against one or the other.

This intransigence is akin to entering a fistfight with one hand tied behind your back. We must integrate medicine to include all methods if we are serious about maintaining the health of our people. The tools are there, so why not take advantage of all of them and not just some?

Besides having more options, you have more flexibility. Your approach to a patient can change, based upon what the problem is how serious it is. If you break your arm, for example, you will first turn to traditional medicine to set the bone and splint it. Afterwards, however, you might add other approaches to strengthen your immune system to speed the healing process; holistic practices that help you recover from the mental stress associated with your injury as well as the physical.

Don't forget the part that spirituality plays in the recovery from an injury or illness. Studies show that those cancer patients with a positive attitude obtained through spiritual means survive longer and have a better quality of life. Never underestimate the power of positive thinking and spiritual peace when considering the health of your loved ones.

I say this not to endorse a specific religion or ritual, but to encourage you to reach inside yourself. There is an inner strength there that many folks don't know they have. Consider it just another tool you'll want in your medical arsenal.

If we ever enter truly bad times, we will have to do a lot of improvising. If the bad times last long enough, our stockpiled drugs will eventually run out. Unless we have the skill to distill essential oils from plants, they will run out also. Both alternative and traditional medical professionals should have respect for and encourage cooperation with each other; together, they can work to ensure a healthy post-collapse society.

WILDERNESS MEDICINE VS. LONG TERM SURVIVAL MEDICINE

✚ ✚ ✚

Wilderness Medicine

Survival/Collapse Medicine

W hat is wilderness medicine? I define it as medical care rendered in a situation where modern care, training and facilities are not readily available. Wilderness medicine would involve medical care rendered during long hikes, maritime expeditions, and sojourns in underdeveloped countries. The basic assumption is that trained doctors and hospital care exist, but are unavailable at the time that medical care is required (perhaps for a significant period of time). You, as temporary caregiver, will be responsible for stabilizing the patient. That means not allowing the injury or illness to get worse. Your primary goal will be the evacuation of the patient to modern medical facilities, even though they might be hundreds of miles away from the location of the patient. At that point, your responsibility to the sick or injured individual is over, and you can go on your merry way.

This is different from what I would call "survival" or "collapse" medicine". In a societal collapse, there is no access to modern medical care, and there is NO potential for accessing such care in the foreseeable future. As President Harry Truman used to say, "The buck stops here".

As a result of this turn of events, you go from being a temporary first-aid provider to being the caregiver at the end of the line. This fact will lead you to make adjustments to your medical strategy. You will have to obtain more knowledge and have more supplies, if you intend to maintain the well-being of your family or survival community.

Wilderness medical classes, Emergency Medical Technician and even Military Medical Corps training presupposes that you are rendering care in the hope of later transporting your patient to a working clinic, emergency room or field hospital. This training is very useful to have; it's more likely that you'll experience a short term deficit of medical assistance than a long term one.

Despite this, you must plan for the possibility that you will be completely on your own one day. That includes medically, so your health strategy must be modified for a day when intensive care units and emergency rooms are going to be inaccessible. You won't have the luxury of passing the sick or injured individual to the next healthcare provider, so you must learn how to deal with medical problems from start to finish.

You will also have to understand how to treat certain chronic medical conditions. Many of these conditions are treated with high technology that will no longer be available in a collapse, so you must learn methods that will work even in a power-down scenario. Using a combination of prevention, improvisation, and prudent utilization of supplies, you will be able to treat the grand majority of problems you will face in a collapse situation.

I'm not trying to scare you. In fact, I hope to impart enough information in this handbook to make you more confident. That confidence will come as a result of having planned for both short term disasters and long term ones. When you know what to do in any scenario, you will feel that quiet resolve that comes with the knowledge that you can do the job. You'll be up to the challenge before you, and you'll know it.

THE TASMANIAN WOLF: GONE AND FORGOTTEN

+ + +

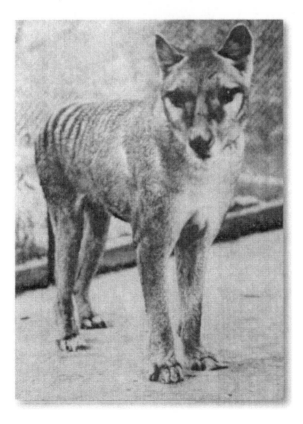

The very first way to help assure your medical well-being is very basic. Don't be a lone wolf! The forlorn creature in the above photograph is a Tasmanian wolf. Why did I choose this animal instead of a majestic red or gray wolf? I chose it because the Tasmanian wolf is extinct, and, if you try to go it alone in a collapse situation, you will be too.

The support of a survival group, even if it's just your extended family, is essential if you are to have any hope of keeping it together when things fall apart. Daily chores, growing and hunting food, keeping watch and all the other day-to-day activities that you will be required to perform are taxing. Being the sole bearer of this burden will negatively impact your health and decrease your chances of long-term survival. Exhausted and sleep-deprived is no way to go through life! Division of labor and responsibility will make a difficult situation more manageable.

Now is the time to communicate, network and put together a group of like-minded people. The right number of able individuals to assemble will depend on your retreat and your resources. Look for those with skills that you don't possess, such as medical training, experience in homesteading, or animal husbandry. There are many online forums that pertain to preparedness, such as the American Preppers Network. Start there and I guarantee you will find others like you.

It's not enough to just be in a group. The people in that group must have regular meetings, decide on priorities, and set things in motion! Put together Plan A, Plan B, and Plan C and work together to make their implementation successful. Preparedness means having a plan; have several plans in place for different turns of events. Keep lines of communication open so that all your group members are kept informed.

The second way to assure your medical well-being is an essential part of preparedness, yet is rarely emphasized. That is to optimize your health PRIOR to any catastrophe occurring. To do this, you must accomplish the following goals: Maintaining a normal weight for your height and age, eating a healthy diet, and keeping fit, and managing chronic medical issues in a timely fashion.

It's important to "tune up" any chronic medical problems that you might have. You'll want to have that blood pressure under control, for example. If you have a bum knee, you might consider getting it repaired surgically so that you can function at maximum efficiency if times get tough.

Dental problems should also be managed before bad times make modern dentistry unavailable. Remember how your last toothache affected your work efficiency? If you don't work to achieve all of the above goals, your preparations will be useless.

In a collapse situation, you will be building shelters, walking long distances to find food, tending fires, and many other activities that will test you physically. Getting fit now will prepare you to accept those challenges. Also, make sure you get good nutrition and watch those calories. Doctors say to eat well and exercise for a reason. This doesn't mean that you have to run marathons. Even just a daily walk around the block is going to help keep you active and mobile.

This philosophy also is pertinent for your mental health and acuity as well. You can't go for long without food and water, but many people will go without a new thought for years on end. Just doing crossword puzzles or reading a newspaper will help keep your mind sharp. Remember that a mind is a terrible thing to waste. Don't waste yours.

If you have bad habits, work to eliminate them. If you damage your heart and lungs by smoking, for example, how will you be able to function in a situation where your fitness and stamina will be continually tested? If you drink alcohol in excess, how can you expect anyone to trust your judgment in critical situations?

Paying careful attention to hygiene is also an important factor for your success in times of trouble. Those who fail to maintain sanitary conditions in their retreat will have a difficult time stay-ing healthy. Infections that are usually seen only in underdeveloped countries will become commonplace. As such, an essential part of your supply storage will be simple items such as soap and bleach.

These two basic strategies, fostering community and practic-ing preventive medicine/fitness, will take you a long way in your journey to preparedness. They don't cost anything to speak of, and will give you the best chance of succeeding if everything else fails.

SECTION 2

✚ ✚ ✚

BECOMING
A MEDICAL RESOURCE

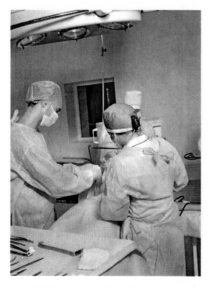

What You Won't Have

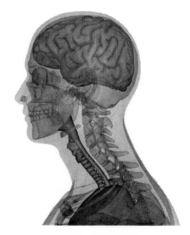

What You Will Have

THE SURVIVAL MEDIC

✚ ✚ ✚

When there is no doctor, someone in your group should be assigned the responsibilities of group medic. Some people feel that this is a daunting task, and it certainly will be a challenge to accumulate adequate medical stores and obtain the medical knowledge necessary to be a healthcare provider. Those who are willing to step up and take responsibility for the medical well-being of their loved ones will be special individuals, with a special mission.

If you have chosen to pick up the flag, your first assignment is to get some training. Some of it will be book learning, and some will be hands-on; the more you learn the better. Study basic first aid and have a good book on family medicine. A good start is to learn as much anatomy and physiology as possible. Anatomy is the blueprint of the body, and physiology is the operating manual. With a working knowledge of these two subjects, you're in a better position to understand disease and injury. They're essential for you to become a successful medic for your group.

The most important asset needed to become a competent healthcare provider for your group is just having common sense. A sensible person with good medical supplies, a few medical books and a willingness to learn will be an effective medical resource.

It helps to have a calm demeanor, as sick or injured people need comforting and a caregiver with a level head. Another useful attribute of a good medic is the dedication to teach other members of his/her group some of the skills that he/she learned. You can't be everywhere at once, and the basics aren't that hard to teach. Cross-training is important, as the medic may one day need a medic!

Confidentiality is another important factor to success as a medical resource. You will have to interview your group members so that you have all the information you need to keep them healthy. Sometimes that information includes things that your patient doesn't want to be made public. You must never disclose anything that would make others see you as untrustworthy.

There is one last essential characteristic of the successful medic: Self-preservation! This may sound strange to you, but you are an indispensable resource to your entire group. If you place yourself frequently in harm's way, you will eventually find yourself as the patient more often than you or anyone else would like. Always assess the scene of an injury to determine if you can care for the victim without placing yourself in undue danger. If someone has a gunshot wound, it stands to reason that there's a guy with a gun out there! Always remember that you do a disservice to your survival community by becoming the next casualty.

THE STATUS ASSESSMENT

✚ ✚ ✚

The first thing that the group medic should perform in
preparation for a collapse situation is a status assessment.
You will be asking yourself, among other things, the
following questions:

What will my responsibilities be?

It goes without saying that, as group medic, you will be responsible for the medical well-being of your survival community. But what does that mean? It means that, as well as being the healthcare provider, that you will be:

Chief sanitation officer: It will be your duty to make sure that sanitary conditions at your camp or retreat don't cause the spread of disease among the members. This will be a major issue in a collapse situation, and will cause the most medical issues in any survival group. Some of your responsibilities will relate to latrine placement and construction, others will relate to appropriate filtering and sterilization of water and cleaning of food, others to maintaining personal and group hygiene. In areas of extreme climate, it is important to ensure that all members have adequate shelter. Careful attention to these details will be part of a preventative program that will keep your survival community healthy.

Chief dental officer: Medical personnel in wartime or in remote locations report that patients arriving at Sick Call complained of dental problems as much as medical problems. Anyone who has had a bad toothache knows that it affects concentration and, certainly, work efficiency. You will need to know how to deal with dental issues if you are going to be an effective medic.

Chief counselor: It goes without saying that any societal collapse would wreak havoc with peoples' mindsets. You will have to know how to deal with depression and anxiety as well as cuts and broken bones. You will have to sharpen your communication skills as much as your medical skills. A good healthcare provider also understands the importance of confidentiality in all their patient contacts.

Medical quartermaster: You've done your job and accumulated medical supplies, but when do you break them out and use them? When will you dispense your limited supply of antibiotics, for example? In a collapse situation, these items will no longer be produced, due to the complexity of their manufacture. Careful monitoring of supply stock and usage will give you an idea of your readiness to handle unexpected medical emergencies.

Medical Archivist: You are in charge of writing down the medical histories of the people in your group. This will be useful to remember all the medical conditions that your people have, their allergies, and medications that they might be taking. Also, your histories of the treatments you have performed on each patient are important to put into writing. One day, you might not be there to render care; your archives will be a valuable resource to the person that is in charge when you're not available. Until that day, however, these histories must remain confidential.

Medical education resource: You can't be in two places at once, and you will have to make sure that those in your group have some basic medical knowledge. It's important that they can take care of injuries or illness while you're away. Also, providing some basic education in preventing injuries and decreasing the chance of infectious disease will give you a head start towards having a healthy survival community.

These responsibilities may be modified somewhat by the makeup of your group. If you have a pastor or other clergy in your group, they can take some of the burden of psychological counseling away from you. If you have someone skilled in engineering, water treatment, or waste disposal, they might be able to use their knowledge to help maintain sanitary conditions at the retreat, or assure healthy filtered water.

What scenario am I preparing for?

It's important to accumulate medical supplies and knowledge that will work in any collapse situation, but what are you actually expecting to happen? Your preparations should be modified to fit the particular situation that you believe will cause modern medical care to be unavailable. There are many possible scenarios that could cause times of trouble, and each of them requires some specialized planning.

If you feel that we are on the verge of an economic collapse, you probably believe that the reliable transport of food from farms to the public will no longer exist (nobody is paying the truckers). In that case, malnutrition will be rampant. Your responsibility as medic would be to make sure that your group's food storage includes everything required to give good nutrition. Stockpiling vitamin supplements, commercial or natural, would be a good strategy in this situation. Even if not taken daily, vitamin supplements may be helpful in preventing deficiencies.

Knowledge of what nutrients are present in local plant life will be useful. Take the following historical example: In the 1500s, a Spanish exploration party was dying of scurvy (Vitamin C deficiency) in the middle of a pine forest. Native Americans came upon them and took pity on their situation. They walked to the nearest pine tree and picked some pine needles. They made a tea out of them and nursed the Spaniards back to health. They knew that pine needles were rich in Vitamin C. That knowledge will be helpful for you as well.

Are you concerned about civil unrest? In that case, tailor your supplies and training to equip you to deal with possible traumatic injuries. Stock up on bandages and antiseptics. How about a pandemic? If you're worried about a "super flu" descending on your area, stock up on masks and gloves as well as antiviral drugs. How about a nuclear reactor meltdown? To take this to extremes, perhaps you live near an army base, a large city or a nuclear plant and you're concerned about a terrorist group setting off a nuclear bomb. In that scenario, you'll have to know how to protect your group from radiation, and how to build an effective shelter. You'll want medications like Potassium Iodide to counteract some of the long-term effects on the thyroid gland. So, you can see that your supplies and training change somewhat, depending on the course of events.

How many people will I be responsible for?

Your store of medical supplies will depend somewhat on the number of persons that you will be responsible for. If you have stockpiled 5 treatment courses of antibiotics, it might be enough for a couple or a sole individual, but it will go fast if you are taking care of 20 people.

Remember that most of those people will be out performing tasks that they aren't used to doing. They will be making campfires, chopping wood and toting gallons and gallons of water. You'll see more injuries like sprains and strains, fractures, lacerations, and burns among those people in a collapse situation.

It only makes sense to accumulate as many supplies as you possibly can. You might wind up dealing with more survivors than you expected; in reality, you almost certainly will, so you can never have too many medical supplies. Excess items (is there such a thing?) will always be highly sought after for barter purposes. You might spend your money on buying physical silver and gold, but you won't be able to set a broken bone or wrap a sprained ankle with "precious" metals. Food and medical items will be more valuable than mining stocks in hard times.

The bottom line is simple: Always have more medical items on hand than you think are sufficient for the number of people in your group.

What special needs will I be required to care for?

The special issues you will deal with depend on who is in your group. The medical needs of children or the elderly are different from an average adult. Women have different health problems than men. You will have to know if group members have a chronic condition, such as asthma or diabetes.

Be certain to interview all of your group members, so that you won't be surprised that this person has thyroid problems, or that person has high blood pressure. All of these variables will modify the supplies and medical knowledge you must obtain. Encourage those with special needs to stockpile materials that will help keep them well.

What physical environment will I live in?

Is your retreat is a cold climate? If so, you will need to know how to keep people warm and how to treat hypothermia. If you're located in a hot climate, you will need to know how to treat heat stroke. Is your environment wet and humid? People who are chronically wet generally don't stay healthy, so you will have to have a strategy to keep your group members dry. Are you in a dry, desert-like environment? If you are, you will have to provide strategies for providing lots of clean water. These considerations might even be a factor in where you would choose to live if a collapse situation is imminent.

How long will I be the sole medical resource?

Some catastrophes, such as major damage from tornadoes or hurricanes, may limit access to medical care for a relatively short period of time. A societal collapse, however, could mean that there is no availability of advanced medical care for the foreseeable future.

The longer you will be the healthcare resource for your group, the more supplies you will have to stockpile and the more varied those supplies should be. If the catastrophe means a few weeks without medical care, you probably can get away without, for example, equipment to extract a diseased tooth. If it's a true long-term collapse, however, that equipment will be quite important. Spend some time thinking about all the possible medical issues you might face and prepare a plan of action to handle each one.

How do I obtain the information I will need to be an effective healthcare provider?

A good library of medical, dental, survival and nutritional books will give you the tools to be an effective medic. Even if you were already a doctor, let's say a general practitioner, you would need various references to learn how to perform surgical procedures that you ordinarily would send to the local surgeon. If you're a surgeon, you would need references to refresh your knowledge of the treatment of diabetes. Even the most resourceful Prepper can't know everything! Luckily, medical reference books are widely available, with tens of thousands on sale at online auction sites like EBay or retail sites like Amazon.com on any given day. Often, they are deeply discounted. If money is tight, many libraries have a medical section and many local colleges have their own medical library.

Don't ignore online sources of information. Take advantage of websites with quality medical information; there are thousands of them. By printing out information you believe will be helpful to your specific situation, you will have a unique store of knowledge that fits your particular needs. I recommend printing this information out because you never know; one day, the internet may not be as accessible as it is today.

The viral video phenomenon, at sites like YouTube, has thousands of medically oriented films on just about every topic. They range from suturing wounds to setting a fractured bone to extracting a damaged tooth. You will have the benefit of seeing things done in real time. To me, this is always better than just looking at pictures.

I have compiled a list of reference books and useful videos at the back of this book. Review them and consider adding them to your library.

How do I obtain medical training?

There are various ways to get practical training. Almost every municipality gives you access to various courses that would help you function as an effective healthcare provider.

EMT (Emergency Medical Technician) Basic: This is the standard for providing emergency care. The courses are set out by the U.S. Department of Transportation, and are offered by many community colleges. The course length is usually several hundred hours.

I know that this represents a significant commitment of time and effort, but it is the complete package short of going to medical or nursing school for four years. You will receive an overview of anatomy and physiology, and an introduction to the basics of looking after sick or injured patients. It is based around delivering the patient to a hospital as an end result. It's not perfect for a collapse situation, but you will still learn a lot of useful information.

It should be noted that there are different levels of Emergency Medical Technician. EMT-Basic is the primary course of study, but you can continue your studies and become a Paramedic. Paramedics are taught more advanced procedures, such as placing airways, using defibrillators, and placing intravenous lines. In remote areas, they might take the place of physicians and nurses to give injections, place casts or stitch up wounds. These skills are highly pertinent during a disaster situation.

Most of us will not have the time and resources to commit to such an intensive course of training. For most of us, a Red Cross First Responder course is the ticket. It covers a lot of the same subjects in much less detail, and would certainly represent a good start on your way to getting trained. The usual course length is 40-80 hours. A number of community outreach groups also offer the course.

Of course, the American Heart Association and others provide standard CPR (cardio-pulmonary resuscitation) courses and everyone in the entire survival community should take these.

There are a number of "specialty" courses provided by private enterprises which might be helpful. Wilderness EMT/Tactical EMT courses are programs meant to teach medical care in a potentially hostile environment. Sometimes, they have a prerequisite of at least EMT-Basic. There are many wilderness "schools" out there, however, that will offer some practical training that might be useful in a collapse situation. At least, they are cognizant that a collapse scenario could exist and that your goal of transporting the patient to modern medical facilities might not be a valid option. It pays to research the schools that provide this training, as the quality of the learning experience probably varies.

LIKELY MEDICAL ISSUES YOU WILL FACE

✚ ✚ ✚

It is important to tailor your education and training to the probable medical issues you will have to treat. In a post-collapse setting, it might be difficult to predict what these might be. It's helpful to examine the statistics of those who provide medical care in underdeveloped areas. Looking at one healthcare provider's experience over an extended time in a remote area is a good way to identify likely medical issues for the collapse medic. It wouldn't be unusual to see the following:

- Minor Musculoskeletal injuries (sprains and strains)
- Minor trauma (cuts, scrapes)
- Minor infections (cellulitis, "pinkeye", urinary infections)
- Allergic reactions (some severe)
- Respiratory infections (pneumonia, bronchitis, influenza, common colds)
- Diarrheal disease (minor and major)
- Dental issues (toothache, loose crowns and lost fillings)
- Major traumatic injury (fractures, occasional knife and/or gunshot wounds)
- Burn injuries (all degrees)
- Pregnancy (!) and Birth Control

A short aside here: If you have purchased this volume, you probably have done some research into collapse scenarios which could lead to society unraveling. You have probably been given a great deal of advice as to what to do in this situation or that, but you have never been given this advice:

If you want to be fruitful, don't multiply; at least in the early going of a major collapse. You are going to need all of your personnel at 110% efficiency. Anyone who has been pregnant knows that there may be a "glow" associated with it, but you sure aren't at peak performance. Even experienced Preppers often forget that pregnancies happen, and don't plan ahead for them.

Pregnancy is relatively safe these days, but there was a time in the not too distant past where the announcement of a pregnancy was met as much with concern as joy. Complications such as miscarriage, postpartum bleeding and infection took their toll on women, and you must seriously plan to prevent pregnancy, at least until things stabilize. Condoms are fine, but will become brittle after two or three years.

Consider taking the time to learn about natural methods of birth control, such as the Rhythm method. This is a simple method that predicts ovulation by taking body temperatures, and is relatively effective. A discussion of this will take place later in this book.

Don't misunderstand me: I am not saying that you should not rebuild our society and follow your personal or religious beliefs. I just want you to understand that your burden, in a collapse, will be heavier if you don't plan for every possibility.

MEDICAL SKILLS YOU WILL WANT TO LEARN

+ + +

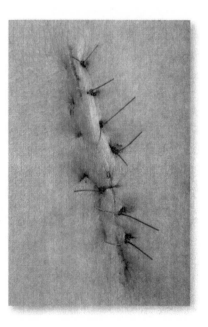

A very reasonable question to ask is "What exactly will I be expected to know?" The answer is: As much as you're willing to learn! Using the previous list will give you a good idea what skills you'll need. You can expect to deal with lots of ankle sprains, colds, cuts, rashes, and other common medical issues that affect you today. The only difference will be that you will need to know how to deal with more significant problems, such as a leg fracture or other traumatic injury. Here are the skills that an effective medic will have learned in advance of a collapse situation:

- Learn how to take vital signs, such as pulses, respiration rates and blood pressures.
- Learn how to place wraps and bandages on injuries
- Learn how to clean an open wound
- Learn how to treat varying degrees of burns
- Learn the indications for use of different medications, essential oils and alternative therapies. As well, know the dosages, frequency of administration, and side effects of those substances. You can't do this on your own; you'll need resources such as the Physician's Desk Reference. This is a weighty volume that comes out yearly and has all the information you'll need to use both prescription and non-prescription drugs. Also consider purchasing a good book on home remedies and alternative therapies as well.
- Learn how to perform a normal delivery of a baby and placenta.
- Learn how to splint, pad and wrap a sprain, dislocation, or fracture.
- Learn how to identify bacterial infectious diseases (such as Strep throat, etc.)
- Learn how to identify viral infectious diseases (such as influenza, etc.)
- Learn how to identify parasitic/protozoal infectious diseases (such as Giardia, etc.)
- Learn how to identify and treat head, pubic, body lice, and ticks

- Learn how to identify venomous snakes and treat the effects of their bites
- Learn how to identify and treat various causes of abdominal, pelvic and chest pain
- Learn how to treat allergic reactionsand anaphylactic shock
- Learn how to identify and treat sexually transmitted diseases
- Learn how to evaluate and treat dental disease (replace fillings, treat abscesses and perform extractions)
- Learn how to identify and treat skin disease and rashes
- Learn how to care for the bedridden patient (treating bedsores, transport considerations)
- Learn basic hygiene, nutrition and preventive medicine (this couldn't be more important)
- Learn how to counsel the depressed or anxious patient (you will see a lot of this in times of trouble)
- learn how to insert an IV (EMT classes teach this),
- Learn how to place sutures in a wound.

Actually, more important that knowing how to suture is knowing WHEN to suture. Most wounds that will occur in a power down situation will be dirty wounds, and closing such an injury will lead to bacteria being locked into the tissues, causing infection. See our discussion on this topic later in this book.

I know, this is a lot to absorb, but don't feel that learning this information is impossible, or that you can't of benefit if you only learn some of the above. The important thing to do is to learn enough that you can treat some of the more common medical issues. Once you've learned the basics, you'll be able to take care of 90% of the problems that are brought before you in a collapse. After that, any additional information you learn will just make you even more effective as a medical resource. Knowledge is power!

MEDICAL SUPPLIES

✚ ✚ ✚

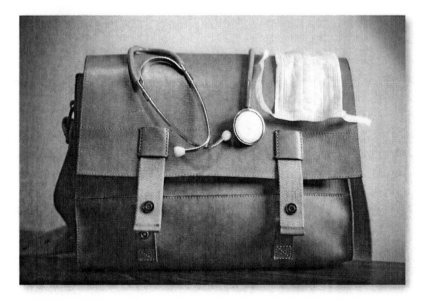

For anyone to properly do their job, they have to have the right equipment. Imagine a carpenter having to use a steak knife as a saw, or a hunter using a pea shooter instead of a rifle. The same goes for the medic. The successful healthcare provider has spent a lot of time and energy (and some money) on accumulating a good amount and variety of medical supplies.

The more the better, since you don't know how long you might have to function without access to modern medical care.

It's important to note that the value of many medical supplies depends largely on the knowledge and skill that the user has obtained through study and practice. Additionally, many items can be improvised; a bandanna may serve as a triangular bandage, an ironing board as a stretcher or thin fishing line and a sewing needle might be useful as suturing equipment. A careful inspection of your own home would probably turn up things that can be adapted to medical use. Look with a creative eye and you'll be surprised at the medical issues you are already equipped to deal with.

Sterile Vs. Clean

A significant factor in the quality of medical care given in a survival situation is the level of cleanliness of the equipment used. You may have heard of the terms "sterile" and "clean", but do you have more than a vague idea of what they mean?

When it comes to medical protection, "sterility" means the complete absence of microbes. Sterile technique involves hand washing with special solutions and the use of sterile instruments, towels, and dressings. When used on a patient, the area immediately around them is referred to as a "sterile field". To guarantee the elimination of all organisms, a type of pressure cooker called an autoclave is used for instruments, towels, and other items that could come in contact with the patient.

Clean techniques concentrates on prevention by reducing the number of microorganisms that could be transferred from one person to another by medical instruments, or other supply such as gloves. Meticulous hand washing with soap and hot water is important.

Disinfectants are substances that are applied to non-living objects to destroy microbes. This would include surfaces where you would treat patients or prepare food. Disinfection does not necessarily kill all bugs and, as such, is not as effective than sterilization, which goes through a more extreme process to reach its goal.

Disinfection removes bacteria, viruses, and other bugs and is sometimes considered the same as decontamination. Decontamination, however, may include the removal of noxious toxins and could pertain to the elimination of chemicals or radiation. The removal of radiation would not be called disinfection.

It's useful to know the difference between a disinfectant, an antibiotic, and an antiseptic. While disinfectants kill bacteria and viruses on the surface of non-living tissue, antiseptics kill microbes on living tissue surfaces. Antibiotics are able to destroy microorganisms that live inside the living human body.

Medical Kits

Most commercial first aid kits are fine for the family picnic or a day at the beach, but we will talk about serious medical stockpiles here. There are three levels of medical kits that we will identify. The first kit is a "nuclear family bag" that anyone with a basic knowledge of first aid can utilize. This kit is mobile, with the items packable in a standard backpack, and will suffice as a medical "bug-out" bag for a couple and their children. The second kit is a "medic at camp" kit, one that the person responsible as medical resource for the group would be expected to carry or maintain in an away camp. The third kit is the "community clinic", or everything that a successful medic will have stockpiled for long term care of his/her survival family or group.

Don't feel intimidated by the sheer volume of supplies in the clinic version; it would be enough to have a reasonably well-equipped field hospital and few of us have the resources or skills to purchase and effectively use every single item. If you can put together a good nuclear family bag, you will have accomplished quite a bit!

Nuclear Family Bag

Quantities are dependent on the number of people to be cared for.

First aid reference book
Antibacterial Soap/Hand Sanitizers
Antiseptic/Alcohol Wipes
Gauze pads-(4" x 4" – sterile and non-sterile)
Gauze rolls-(Kerlix, etc.)
Non-Stick pads (Telfa brand)
Triangular bandages or bandannas
Safety Pins (large)

Adhesive Band-Aids (various sizes/shapes)
Large absorbent pads (ABD or other brand)
Medical Tape – (Elastoplast, Silk, Paper varieties), 1 inch, 2 inch
Moleskin or Spenco Second Skin Blister kit
Sawyer Extractor kit for Snakebite
Cold Packs/Heat Packs (reusable if possible)
Cotton Eye Pads, Patches
Cotton Swabs (Q-tips), Cotton Balls
Disposable Nitrile Gloves (hypoallergenic)
Face Masks (surgical and N95)
Tongue Depressors
Bandage Scissors (all metal is best)
Tweezers
Magnifying Glass
Headlamp or Penlight
Kelly Clamp (straight and curved)
Needle Holder
2-0, 4-0 Silk Sutures
Styptic pencil (stops bleeding from superficial cuts)
Saline Solution (liter bottle or smaller)
Steri-Strips/butterfly closures - thin and thick sizes
Survival Sheet/Blanket
Thermometer (rectal or ear)
Antiseptic Solutions (Betadine, Hibiclens, etc.)
3% Hydrogen Peroxide
Benzalkonium Chloride wipes
Rubbing Alcohol
Witch Hazel
Antibiotic Ointment
Sunblock
Lip balms
Insect Repellant
1% Hydrocortisone Cream
2.5% Lidocaine cream (local anesthetic)

Acetaminophen/Ibuprofen/Aspirin
Benadryl (Diphenhydramine)/Claritin (Loratadine)
Imodium (Loperamide)
Pepto-Bismol (Bismuth Subsalicylate)
Oral Rehydration Packs (or make it from scratch)
Water Purification Filter or Tablets
Gold Bond foot powder
Silvadene Cream (burns)
Oral Antibiotics
(or natural equivalents of all the above)
Birth Control Accessories (condoms, birth control pills, cervical caps, etc.)
Herbal Teas, Tinctures, Salves, and Essential Oils

Dental Tray:
Cotton pellets
Dental mirror
Dental pick, toothpicks
Dental floss
Oil of cloves (anesthetic for toothache)
Zinc Oxide (make a paste with oil of cloves and you get temporary dental cement), or...
Commercial dental kits (Den-Temp, Cavit)
Extraction equipment (forceps and elevators)

The Medic Bag at Away Camp

All of the above in larger quantities, plus:

Medical reference book(s)
Combat Dressings (Israeli bandages aka The Emergency Bandage)
"Bloodstopper" dressing (inexpensive multipurpose dressing)
Tourniquet
Quik-Clot or Celox dressings (these are impregnated with substances that help stop bleeding) or powder
Extra-Large gauze dressings

Neck Collar
Eye cups, eye wash
Ammonia inhalants
Head Lamp
Slings
Splints
Irrigation Syringes (30 ml– 60 ml is good)
Needle Syringes (various sizes- 20 gauge, 6 ml is common)
Surgical scissors (Mayo or Metzenbaum)
Needle holders and clamps, (enough to do basic minor surgery)
Scalpel and disposable blades (lots)
Sawyer Extractor kit (for removal of snakebite venom)
Emergency Obstetric Kit (comes as a pack)
Vicryl or Silk 2-0, 3-0, 4-0, 5-0 suture material (very fine nylon fishing line will work if necessary)
Suture removal tray
Fels-Naptha/Zanfel Soap (poison ivy, oak and sumac)
Saline solution- for irrigation of open wounds (sterilized water will also be acceptable for this purpose)
Cidex solution-for cleaning instruments
1% or 2% (Lidocaine) (local anesthetic in injectable form-prescription medication)
More varied supply of antibiotics (prescription)
Zofran (for nausea and vomiting-prescription)
Tramadol (stronger pain medicine- prescription)
Oral Rehydration powder (this can be made using home ingredients as well)
Epinephrine (Epi-pen, prescription injection for severe allergic reactions)
Rid lotion/Nix Shampoo (lice/scabies treatment)
Terconazole cream (antifungal)
Fluconazole 100 or 150mg tablets (prescription antifungals)
Wart removal cream/ointment/solution
Hemorrhoid cream/ointment
Tincture of Benzoin ("glue" for bandages)

The Community Clinic Supply List

All of the above in larger quantities, plus:
Extensive medical library
Treatment Table
Plaster of Paris cast kits (to make casts for fractures) (4in/6in)
Oropharyngeal airway tubes (to keep airways open)
Nasal airways (keeps airways open))
Resuscitation facemask with one-way valve
Resuscitation bag (Ambu-bag)
Endotracheal tube/ Laryngoscope (allows you to breathe for patient)
Portable Defibrillator (expensive)
Blood Pressure cuff (sphygmomanometer)
Stethoscopes
CPR Shield
Otoscope and Ophthalmoscope – (instruments to look into ears and eyes)
Urine test strips
Pregnancy test kits
Sterile Drapes (lots)
Air splints (arm/long-leg/short-leg)
SAM splints
Scrub Suits
IV equipment, such as:
Normal Saline solution
Dextrose and 50% Normal Saline IV solution
IV tubing sets - maxi-sets + standard sets
Blood collection bags + filter transfusion sets
Syringes 2/5/10/20 mL
Needles 20/22/24 gauge
IV kits 16/20/24 gauge
Paper tape (1/2 in/1in) for IV lines
IV stands (to hang fluid bottles)
Saline Solution for irrigation (can be made at home as well)
Foldable stretchers

Surgical Tray (extremely ambitious)

Sterile Towels
Sterile Gloves
Mayo scissors
Metzenbaum scissors
Small and medium needle holders
Bulb syringes (for irrigating wounds during procedures)
Assorted clamps (curved and straight, small and large)
Scalpel Handle and blades (sizes 10, 11, 15) or disposable scalpels
Emergency Obstetric Kit (includes cord clamps, bulb suction, etc.)
Obstetric forceps (for difficult deliveries)
Uterine Curettes (for miscarriages, various sizes), Uterine "Sound" (checks depth of uterine canal)
Uterine Dilators (to open cervix; allows removal of dead tissue)
Bone saw (for amputations)
Sutures, such as:
Vicryl; 0, 2-0, 4-0 (absorbable)
Chromic 0, 2-0 (absorbable)
Silk or Prolene 0, 2-0, 4-0(non-absorbable)
Surgical staplers and staple removers
Chest decompression kits and drains – various sizes for collapsed lungs
Penrose drains (to allow blood and pus to drain from wounds)
Foley Catheters – Sizes 18, 20 for urinary blockage
Urine Bags
Nasogastric tubes (to pump a stomach)

Additional Prescription Medications

Medrol dose packs, oral steroids
Salbutamol inhalers for asthma/severe allergic reactions
Antibiotic, anesthetic eye and ear drops
Oral Contraceptive Pills

Metronidazole, oral antibiotic and anti-protozoal
Cephalexin, oral antibiotic
Ciprofloxacin, oral antibiotic
Doxycycline, oral antibiotic
Ceftriaxone, IV antibiotic
Diazepam IV sedative
Oxytocin (Pitocin) IV for post-delivery hemorrhage
Percocet, (oxycodone with paracetamol/acetaminophen),
strong oral pain medicine
Morphine Sulfate or Demerol, strong injectable analgesic

I'm sure there is something that I might have missed, but the important thing is to accumulate supplies and equipment that you will feel competent using in the event of an illness or an injury. Some of the above supplies, such as stretchers and tourniquets, can be improvised using common household items.

It should be noted that many of the advanced items are probably useful only in the hands of an experienced surgeon, and could be very dangerous otherwise. These items are essentially a wish list of what I would want if I was taking care of an entire community.

You should not feel that the more advanced supply lists are your responsibility to accumulate alone. Your entire group should contribute to stockpiling medical stores, under the medic's coordination. The same goes for all the medical skills that I've listed. To learn everything would be a lifetime of study that even few physicians can accomplish. Concentrate on the items that you are most likely to use on a regular basis.

NATURAL REMEDIES

✚ ✚ ✚

I've just spent the last chapter telling you to stock up on all sorts of high-tech items (even defibrillators!) and, indeed, many of these things are indispensable when it comes to dealing with certain medical conditions. Unfortunately, you probably will not have the resources or skills to stockpile this medical arsenal.

Even if you are able to do so, there are concerns. Your supplies will last only a certain amount of time. Depending on the number of people you are medically responsible for, you can expect to be shocked at the rapidity in which your precious medications and other items dwindle away. Tough decisions may have to be made.

One solution is to grossly overstock on commonly used medical supplies, but this is costly and doesn't really solve your problem; even large stockpiles will eventually be used up. There must be some strategy that will allow you to provide medical care for the long run: Something that might allow you to produce substances that will have a medical benefit without having a pharmaceutical factory at your disposal.

Well, there is: The plants in your own backyard or nearby woods. You might ask yourself, "I thought I was reading a book by a medical doctor. What's all this plant stuff?"

To answer this, we have to look at the history of medicine. Physicians have occupied different niches in society over the ages, from priests during the time of the pharaohs, to slaves and barbers in imperial Rome and the dark ages, and artists during the Renaissance. For all of these starkly different people, there was one thing they had in common: They knew the use of natural products for healing purposes. If they needed more of a plant substance than occurred in their native environment, they cultivated it. They learned to make teas, tinctures and salves containing these products and how best to use them to treat illness. If modern medical care is no longer available one day, we will have to take advantage of their experience.

Salicin is a natural pain reliever found in the under bark of Willows, Poplar and Aspen trees. In the 19th century, we first developed a process to commercially produce Aspirin from these trees commonly found in our environment. Today, most artificially produced drugs involve many different chemicals in their manufacture. To make Insulin or Penicillin, for example, so many chemicals are used that it would be impossible to reproduce the process in any type of collapse scenario. Do we even know what effect all of these ingredients have on our health? Despite this, we have gone so far in our ability to synthesize medications that we use them far too often in our treatment of patients.

Even organized medicine is realizing that we are too fast and loose in our utilization of pharmaceuticals. Medical journals now call for physicians to focus on prevention instead of reflexively reaching for the prescription pad. Doctors are now being asked to prescribe only one drug at a time, due to the interactions that multiple medications have with each other. There's a new skepticism that might just be healthy regarding all this new technology.

Having said this, not all pharmaceuticals are bad. Some of them can save your life. Natural remedies, however, should be integrated into the arsenal of anyone willing to take responsibility for the well-being of others. Why not use all the tools that are available to you? At one point or another, the medicinal herbs and plants you grow in your garden may be all you have.

Natural substances can be used medically via several methods:

Teas: A hot drink made by infusing the dried, crushed leaves of a plant in boiling water.

Tinctures: a plant extract made by soaking herbs in a liquid (such as water, grain alcohol, or vinegar) for a specified length of time, then straining and discarding the plant material. (also known as a decoction)

Essential Oils: highly concentrated aromatic liquids of various mixtures of natural compounds obtained from plants. These are typically made by distillation.

Salves: A highly viscous or semisolid substance used on the skin (also known as an ointment, unguent, or balm).

Some of these products may also be ingested directly or in irrigation solutions. Most of these substances will have fewer side effects than commercially produced drugs. It is the obligation of the group medic to obtain a working knowledge of how to use and, yes, grow these plants. Consider learning the process of distillation to obtain concentrated versions for stronger effect. A number of reference books are available on the subject of natural remedies, and are listed in the appendix of this book.

Another alternative therapy thought by some to boost immune systems and treat illness is colloidal silver. Colloidal silver products are made of tiny silver particles, silver ions, or silver combined with protein, all suspended in a liquid — the same type of precious metal used in jewelry and other consumer goods. Silver compounds were used in the past to treat infection before the development of antibiotics. Recently, laboratory studies at the department of Biochemistry at Jiaxing College, China, have shown that "silver-containing alginate fibers" provide a sustained release of silver ions when in contact with samples of wound drainage, and are "highly effective against bacteria".

Colloidal silver products are usually marketed as dietary supplements that are taken by mouth. Colloidal silver products also come in forms that can be applied to the skin, where they are thought to improve healing by preventing infection. Continuous use of silver, especially internally, may result in a condition known as Argyria. This rare condition causes your skin to turn blue; this is mostly a cosmetic concern.

Ionic silver (Ag^+) and silver particles in concentration has been shown to have an antimicrobial effect in certain laboratory studies. Physicians use wound dressings containing silver sulfadiazine (Silvadene) to help prevent infection. Wound dressings containing silver are being used more and more often due to the increase in bacterial resistance to antibiotics. A study under the aegis of the Hull York Medical School found that a dressing containing silver was "a highly effective and reliable barrier to the spread of MRSA into the wider hospital." As a topical agent, Silvadene has been used on burn injuries for many years.

Less evidence is available from traditional medical sources regarding ionic silver solutions for internal use. Silver ions are like members of the lonely hearts club; they are desperately looking to bond with another ion. Once inside our body, they have a willing partner in the form of the Chloride from our cells. Once bonded as Silver Chloride, they are essentially inert. As such, it is uncertain how much benefit that internal use of Silver will give you.

Despite this, there are many prominent naturopaths who strongly support its use. Home ionic silver generators are available for sale at a multitude of sites.

Silver proteins bind organic materials to Silver, so they are not ionic silver. Unless suspended in a gelatin base, they have a tendency to drop to the bottom of the bottle (this is called "precipitation") and lose their antimicrobial effect. The larger the Silver particle, the more likely this will occur. In rare circumstances, the presence of organic matter in the compound could lead to contamination.

It is important to understand that colloidal effectiveness is determined by particle surface area. Large silver particles tend to precipitate, so smaller is better. Since the smallest silver particles do not require a protein to be suspended in the solution, more surface area will be available for antimicrobial effects. Seek out products that will produce the smallest silver particles in their solutions.

I have to mention that the FDA has banned colloidal silver sellers from claiming any therapeutic or preventive value for the product. As a result, the product is a dietary supplement by status, and cannot be marketed as preventing or treating any illness.

ESSENTIAL OILS

✦ ✦ ✦

Nature may, one day, be our pharmacy. The knowledge of herbal remedies had been passed down generation after generation. In a situation where regular medications are no longer produced, it is imperative to learn the medicinal benefits of plants that you can grow in your own garden. Essential oils are distilled from whole plant material, not a single ingredient; therefore, every oil has multiple uses.

Essential oils are highly concentrated and should be used sparingly. A reference book or two about essential oils would be a great addition to your medical library; see the medical reference section in the back of this book.

The following are some essential oils (EO) that should be considered for your medical storage:

1. Lavender- An analgesic (pain reliever), antiseptic (antimicrobial substance applied to living tissue/skin to reduce the possibility of infection) and immune stimulant. Good for skin care and to promote healing: burns, bruises, scrapes, acne, rashes and bug bites. Has a calming effect, and is used for: insomnia, stress and to relieve depression. Also is used as a decongestant through steam inhalation (1 drop per cup of steaming water). Lavender is also available as a tea for internal use.

2. Tea Tree- A powerful anti-fungal, antibacterial, antiseptic and analgesic. It can be used "neat" or with a carrier oil (CO), like coconut or olive for dilution in a 1:9 ratio of EO:CO. Good for acne, athlete's foot, skin wounds and irritations, cuts, warts, cold sores, and insect bites. Tea Tree oil also serves as an anti-parasitic and insecticide, good for lice and scabies, and also in the garden as a pest and disease spray. It is an expectorant (loosens respiratory congestion), decongestant (relieves sinus congestion) and immune stimulant when used as inhalant with or without steam. Not for internal use. Tea tree oil may be mixed with lavender, lemon, thyme, rosemary and ginger.

3. German Chamomile- An anti-inflammatory (decreases swelling, redness, irritation) and analgesic. When mixed with a CO, use for insect bites, burns, diaper rash, eczema, psoriasis, and many other skin conditions. Relaxing effect; use EO as an inhalant to help with insomnia, nervousness, anxiety and cramps, also available as a tea for internal use. EO hot or cold compress good for headaches and menstrual pains, apply externally to affected area.

4. Blue Tansy (Tanacetum anuum)- EO is an antihistamine (relieves allergies), analgesic, and anti-inflammatory. This herb may be used for skin inflammation and itching. Use to treat allergies, rashes, burns, swelling. Calming effects help decrease stress and relax tense muscles. Can be used externally either "neat" (undiluted) or may be blended with carrier oil for massage or application to skin conditions.

5. Helichrysum (italicum)- An analgesic, antibacterial and one of the strongest anti-inflammatory EOs. Known for "deep healing" properties and for tissue "regeneration"; increases circulation of blood and lymph systems. Good for bruises, chronic pain relief including fibromyalgia, arthritis, tendonitis, and carpel tunnel syndrome. Helichrysum is often used for irritated skin conditions. Use for massage neat or blended with lavender, clary sage, German chamomile, or geranium.

6. Peppermint- An antiseptic, antibacterial, decongestant, and anti-emetic. Also helps with digestive disorders such as IBS (irritable bowel syndrome), heartburn, and abdominal cramping. Apply EO daily every morning to the bottom of feet for prevention and treatment of chronic conditions. Good for headaches (massage 1 drop EO to temples). For sudden abdominal conditions, achy muscles or painful joints: massage weak and diluted EO externally onto affected area. For heartburn relief, apply 1 drop EO to tongue.

7. Eucalyptus- An antiseptic, antiviral, decongestant, and excellent insect repellent; "Cooling" effect on skin. Aids with all breathing issues and boosts immune system, use for flu, colds, sore throats, coughs, sinusitis, bronchitis, and hay fever. Best used as a preventative of viruses when exposure is expected. Eucalyptus may be used in massages, steam inhalation, and as a bath additive. Apply EO directly to the chest for respiratory problems. Also helps acne. Use this oil only externally.

8. Clove Oil- Considered the most diverse universal medicinal remedy! It is anti-fungal, antimicrobial, antiseptic, antiviral, analgesic, anesthetic, and sedative. Clove oil combats, prevents and treats external infections naturally instead of using antibiotics. Natural pain killer and sedative used for toothaches. A toothpaste can be made by combining clove oil and baking soda. Mix clove oil with geranium for open wounds, cuts, abrasions and burns.

9. Rosemary- Antibacterial, anti-fungal, anti-parasitic, antispasmodic (relaxes muscles), disinfectant, and enhances mental clarity. Use a few drops with water for a disinfectant mouthwash. Inhalation either cold or steam for congested or constricted respiratory problems. Mix equal amount essential oil with a carrier oil for massage to treat headaches, muscle pain and soreness.

10. Geranium- Antibacterial, antioxidant, antispasmodic, anti-inflammatory, hemostatic (stops bleeding), and anti-fungal. Apply undiluted essential oil 2-4 drops apply directly to wound, cuts, or burns and loosely cover. Undiluted EO also used for irritated or inflamed skin conditions such as eczema, ringworm, psoriasis and acne. Care must be taken, as geranium may lower blood sugar.

11. Thyme- Highly antimicrobial (kills harmful bacteria), anti-fungal, antiviral, expectorant and anti-parasitic and insecticide. Use, mixed with carrier oil in a 1:4 dilution on cuts and lacerations to decrease infection risk and cure infections; also treats ringworm and athletes foot. Thyme relaxes spasms in the respiratory tract, nerves, muscles, intestines and other organs when used as an external massage. Loosens congestion with colds and coughs as inhalation therapy.

12. Lemon- Antiseptic, disinfectant and immune stimulant (increases white blood cells) and powerful antioxidant.

Inhaling vapors improves memory, concentration and relaxation and may have antidepressant effects. For wound treatment mix a 1:1 dilution with carrier oil, and apply to injury. Lemon oil is commonly used as a household disinfectant.

13. Wintergreen- Anticoagulant (reduces blood clotting), antispasmodic, highly anti-inflammatory, analgesic, and reduces blood pressure. Massage, mixed in 1:1 dilution with carrier oil, for conditions with intact skin, such as: muscle aches, arthritis, and nerve pain. Use a few drops of EO mixed in Epsom's salts then added to hot bath water for a relaxing treatment.

14. Hyssop- Strong antiviral, antiseptic, antibacterial, expectorant, decongestant, and anti-inflammatory, Use EO mixed with equal amount of carrier oil for inhalation therapy to help with congestion and coughs. Also use the same dilution for skin conditions such as: wounds, bruises and eczema.

15. Frankincense- Immune stimulant, antiseptic, antispasmodic, expectorant, and sedative. Direct application to wounds, cuts and scrapes helps regeneration of tissue and decreases infections. Hot or cold vapors, or even direct applications are disinfectants to surfaces and air. Cold or steam inhalant used for lung and nasal congestion.

16. Clary sage- Antioxidant, anticoagulant , anti-fungal, antiseptic, anti-inflammatory, antispasmodic, anesthetic, and sedative. Inhalation or massage is beneficial for nervousness, stress, muscle cramps and aches, insomnia, and irritated skin. May be beneficial to treat PMS and menopausal symptoms. Has a "cooling" action for inflammations.

17. Thieves Essential Oil Blend- Contains: Clove, lemon, cinnamon bark, eucalyptus and rosemary essential oils.

Cinnamon bark is strongly antibacterial, antiviral, and anti-fungal. This is a strong and multi-purpose essential oil. Some actions include: expectorant, decongestant, antiseptic, antiviral, antibacterial, anti-fungal, disinfectant, and anti-inflammatory. There are a great number of uses for thieves blend EO.

There are many more essential oils out there; it's important to perform your own research on these products and come to your own conclusions. Remember that, unless you learn how to distill these oils from plants, your supplies may eventually run out. Learn this process now if at all possible.

THE PHYSICAL EXAM

✚ ✚ ✚

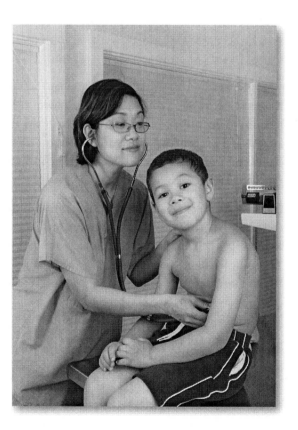

Whenﾠevaluating a patient, it is important to perform an organized and systematic exam. Sometimes the problem is obvious; other times, you will have to examine the entire body to determine the problem. During an exam, always communicate to your patient what you are doing and why. Never force movement beyond its normal range.

Basic information is obtained by checking the vital signs. This includes the following;

- Pulse rate – this can be taken by using 2 fingers to press on the side of the neck or the inside of the wrist (by the base of the thumb). A normal pulse rate at rest is 60-100 beats per minute. You may choose to feel the pulse for, say, 15 seconds and multiply the number you get by 4 to get beats per minute. A full minute would be more accurate, however.

- Respiration rate – this is best evaluated for an entire minute to get an accurate reading. The normal adult rate at rest is 12-18 breaths per minute, somewhat more for children. Note any unusual aspects, such as wheezing or gurgling noises.

- Blood pressure – blood pressure is a measure of the work the heart has to do to pump blood throughout the body. You're looking for a pressure less than 140/90 at rest. A very low blood pressure may be seen in a person who has hemorrhaged or is in shock. Instructions on how to take a blood pressure can be found in the chapter on high blood pressure, also called "hypertension".

- Mental status – You want to know that your patient is alert and, therefore, can respond to questions and commands. Ask your patient what happened. If they seem disoriented, ask simple questions like their name, where they are, or what year it is. Note whether the patient appears lethargic or agitated. Some patients may appear unconscious, but may respond to a spoken command. For example: "Hey! Open your eyes!" If no result, determine if they respond to a stimulus, such as gentle pressure on their breastbone. If they don't, they are termed "unresponsive" and something very serious is going on.

- Take the person's temperature to verify that they don't have a fever. A normal temperature will range from 97.5 to 99.0 degrees Fahrenheit. A significant fever is defined as a temperature above 100.4 degrees (38 degrees Celsius).

Once you've taken the vital signs, remain calm and evaluate the patient from head to toe. Touch the patient's skin; is it hot or cold, moist or dry? Is there redness, or is the patient pale? Examine the head area and work your way down. Are there any bumps on their head, are they bleeding from the nose, mouth, or ears? Evaluate the eyes and see if they are reddened and if the pupils respond equally to light.

Have the patient open their mouth and check for redness, sores, or dental issues with a light source and a tongue depressor. Check the neck for evidence of injury and feel the back of the head and neck, especially the neck bones (vertebrae).

Take your stethoscope and listen to the chest. This is called "auscultation". Do you hear the patient breathing as you place the instrument over different areas of each lung? Are there noises that shouldn't be there? Practice listening on healthy people to get a good idea of what clear lungs should sound like. Listen to the heart and see if the heartbeat is regular or irregular in rhythm. Check along the ribs for rough areas that might signify a fracture. Check the armpits (also known as the axilla) for masses. Perform a breast exam by moving your fingers in a circular motion over the breast tissue, starting from the periphery near the axilla and ending at the nipple.

Press on the abdomen with your open hand. Is there pain? Is the belly soft or is it rigid and swollen? Do you feel any masses? Use your stethoscope to listen to the gurgling of bowel sounds. Lack of bowel sounds may indicate lack of intestinal motility; excessive bowel sounds may be seen in some diarrheal disease. Place your open hand on the different quadrants of the abdomen and tap on your middle finger. This is called "percussion". The abdomen will sound "hollow" normally, but dull where there might be a mass. Press down on the right side below the rib cage to determine if the liver is enlarged (you won't feel it if it isn't). An enlarged spleen will appear as a mass on the left side under the rib cage.

Check along the patient's spine for evidence of pain or injury. Pound lightly with a closed hand on each side of the back below the last rib; this is where the kidneys are, and injury or infection would cause this action to be very painful.

Check each extremity by feeling the muscle groups for pain or decreased range of motion. Make sure that there is good circulation by checking the color on the tips of the fingers and toes. Poor circulation will make these areas white or blue in color. Check for sensation by lightly tapping with a safety pin. Place your hands on their thighs and ask them to lift up, to check for normal tone. Ask them to grasp your fingers with each hand; then try to pull your hand away. If you can't, that's good. The strength on each side should be about equal.

Human beings are what we call "symmetrical bilaterally". This means that, if you are uncertain whether a limb is injured or deformed, you can compare it to the other side.

These are just some basics. Certainly, there's a lot more to a physical exam than what you've just read, but practicing exams on others will give you experience. As time goes by, you'll get the feel of what is normal and what isn't. Your efforts now will prepare you for making a diagnosis if we find ourselves without access to modern medical care.

PATIENT TRANSPORT

✚ ✚ ✚

As we mentioned earlier, the main goal of a medic in a survival situation is to transfer the injured or ill person to a modern medical facility. These facilities will be non-existent in the scenarios that this book deals with. As such, you will have to make a decision as to whether your patient can be treated for their medical problem where they are or not. If they cannot, you must consider how to move your patient to where the bulk of your medical supplies are.

Before deciding whether to move a patient, stabilize them as much as possible. This means stopping all bleeding, splinting orthopedic injuries, and verifying that the person is breathing normally. If you cannot assure this, consider having a group member get the supplies needed to support the patient before you move them. Have as many helpers available to assist you as you can. The most important thing to remember is that you want to carry out the evacuation with the least trauma to your patient and yourself.

An important medical supply in this circumstance is a stretcher. Many good commercially-produced stretchers are available, but improvised stretchers can be put together without too much effort. An ironing board makes an effective transport device. A person with a spinal injury should be rolled onto the stretcher without "bending" them.

Other options include taking two long sticks or poles and inserting coats or shirts through them to handle the weight of the victim. If the rescuer grasps both poles, a helper could pull the coat off. This automatically moves the coat onto the poles. Lengths of Paracord or rope can also be crisscrossed to form an effective stretcher.

If you must pull a person to safety, grasp their coat or shirt at the shoulders with both hands, allowing their head to rest on your forearms. You could also place a blanket under the patient, and grasp the end of the blanket near their head and pull. If you are uncertain about the extent of any spinal injuries, do your best to not allow much bending of the body during transport.

If your patient can be carried, there are various methods available. The "Fireman's Carry" is effective and keep's the victim's torso relatively level and stable. In a squatting or kneeling position, you would grasp the person's right wrist with your left hand and place it over your right shoulder. Keeping your back straight, place your right hand between their legs and around the right thigh. Using your leg muscles to lift, rise up and you should their torso over your back and the right thigh resting over your right shoulder. Their left arm and leg will hang behind your back if you have done it correctly. Adjust their weight so as to cause the least strain.

Another option is the "Pack-Strap Carry". With your patient behind you, grasp both arms and cross them across your chest. If squatting, keep your back straight and use your back muscles to lift the victim. Bend slightly so that the person's weight is on your hips and lift them off the ground.

If you have the luxury of an assistant, you might consider placing your patient on a chair and carry using the front legs and back of the chair. This constitutes a sitting "stretcher". Another two person carry involves one rescuer to wrap their arms around the victim's chest from behind while the second rescuer (facing away from the patient) grabs the legs behind each knee. This is done in a squatting position, using the leg muscles to lift the patient.

It's important to remember this simple acronym when pulling or carrying a person: B.A.C.K.

- Back Straight – muscles and discs can handle more load safely when the back is straight.
- Avoid Twisting – joints can be damage when twisting.
- Close to body – reaching to pick up a load causes more strain on muscles and joints.
- Keep Stable – the more rotation and jerking, the more pressure on the discs and muscles.

Be sure to check the YouTube page at the back of this book to see some of these methods being used in real time.

SECTION 3

✚ ✚ ✚

HYGIENE AND SANITATION

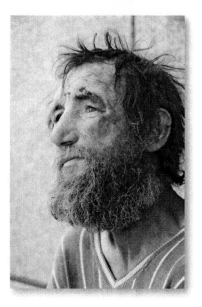

HYGEINE-RELATED MEDICAL PROBLEMS

✚ ✚ ✚

In nature, many animals make specific efforts to preen and groom themselves. Their instinctual tendency to remain clean keeps them healthy. Although not instinctual, the human urge to be clean has done its job to keep us healthier. When humans are under stress, their attention to hygiene suffers.

Body odors occur when sweat mixes with bacteria, and we all know that bacteria can lead to disease. It is up to the medic to ensure that hygiene issues do not put the survival group at risk.

In the situation where there is no longer access to common cleansing items such as soap or laundry detergent, the goal of good hygiene is difficult to achieve (Hint: stockpile these items). Cleanliness issues extend to various important areas, such as dental care and foot care. With the increase of physical labor that we will be required to perform, we will get sweaty and dirty. The dirtier and wetter we get, the more prone we will be to problems such as infections or infestations. With careful attention to hygiene, we can decrease our chances of dealing with these illnesses.

LICE, TICKS, AND WORMS

✚ ✚ ✚

L ice

A common health problem pertaining to poor hygiene is the presence of lice. There are three types: Head, Body and Pubic. Lice are species specific, which means that you cannot get lice from your dog, like you could get fleas. You get them only from other humans.

Head lice cause itching and sometimes a rash. However, this type of lice is not a carrier of any other disease. Kids, with their less developed immune systems, sometimes don't even know they have them, but adults are usually kept scratching and irritated unless treated.

Pubic lice, also known as scabies, usually starts in the pubic region but may eventually extend anywhere there is hair, even the eyelashes. They are most commonly passed by sexual contact. Severe itching is the main symptom. Although they are sometimes seen in a patient that has other sexually transmitted diseases, pubic lice do not actually transmit other illnesses.

Body lice are latecomers compared to head lice, probably appearing with the advent of humans wearing clothes. As the concept of cleaning clothes occurred quite later, the constant contact with dirty garb caused frequent infestations. This is a common issue with the homeless today, but will likely be an epidemic in a collapse situation. Body lice are slightly larger than head lice, and live on dirty clothes. They go to the human body only to feed. They are sturdier than their cousins, and can live without human contact for 30 days or so.

Removal and, preferably, destruction of the infested clothing is the appropriate strategy here. Sometimes, using medication is unnecessary as the lice left with the clothes (don't bet on it, however). Body lice, unlike head lice, ARE associated with infectious diseases such as typhus, trench fever and epidemic relapsing fever. Continuous exposure to body lice may lead to areas on the skin that are hardened and deeply pigmented.

The diagnosis is made by identifying the presence of the louse or nits (their eggs). Nits are more easily seen when examined using a "black light". This causes them to fluoresce as light blue "dots" attached to the hair shafts near the scalp. As "black lights" will be rare in a collapse, a fine-tooth comb run through the hair will also demonstrate adult lice and nits. Special combs are used to remove as many lice as possible before treatment and to check for them afterwards.

Nix lotion (permethrin) will kill both the lice and their eggs. Rid shampoo will kill the lice, but not their eggs; be certain to repeat the shampoo treatment 7 days later. This may not be a bad strategy with the lotion, as well. Ask your physician for a prescription for Kwell (lindane) shampoo to stockpile. It is a much stronger treatment for resistant cases. It may cause neurological side-effects in children, so avoid using this medicine on them.

Wash all linens that you don't throw away in hot water (at least 120 degrees). Unwashable items, such as stuffed animals, that you cannot bring yourself to throw out should be placed in plastic bags for 2 weeks (for head lice) to 5 weeks (for body lice), then opened to air outside. Combs and brushes should be placed in alcohol or very hot water.

Natural remedies for lice have existed for thousands of years. For external use only, mix a blend of salt, vinegar, Tea Tree oil and Neem oil and apply daily for 21 days. Alternatively, Witch Hazel and tea tree oil applied daily after showering for 21 days has been reported as effective against hair lice.

A triple blend of tea tree, lavender, and Neem oil applied to the public region for 21 days may be effective in eliminating Scabies. Witch Hazel and tea tree oil, again, may be helpful for lice in this region as well. Some have advocated bathing with ½ cup of Borax and ½ cup of hydrogen peroxide daily for 21 days.

Ticks

Ticks are not as clearly associated with poor hygiene. The American dog tick carries pathogens for Rocky Mountain spotted fever, and the blacklegged tick, also known as the deer tick, carries the microscopic parasite that's responsible for Lyme disease. Some tick-borne illness is similar to influenza with regards to symptoms; it is often missed by the physician. Lyme disease has a tell-tale rash, but other tick-related diseases may not.

Most Lyme disease is caused by the larval or juvenile stages of the deer tick. These are sometimes tough to spot because they're not much bigger than a pinhead. Each larval stage feeds only once and very slowly, usually over several days. This gives the tick parasites plenty of time to get into your bloodstream. The larval ticks are most active in summer. Although most common in the Northeast, they seem to be making their way further West every year.

Ticks don't jump like fleas do; they don't fly like, well, flies, and they don't drop from trees like spiders. The larvae like to live in leaf litter, and they latch onto your lower leg as you pass by. Adults live in shrubs along game trails (hence the name Deer Tick) and seem to transmit disease less often.

Many people don't think to protect themselves outdoors from exposure to ticks and other things like poison ivy, and many wind up being sorry they didn't. If you're going to spend the day outdoors, you should be taking some precautions. Be careful about leaving skin exposed below your knee. Wear thick socks, and consider tucking your pants into them to prevent an avenue for the tick to reach your skin. Good high-top boots are also protective. Of course, a good bug repellant is going to improve your chances of avoiding bites, so always have some on hand. Citronella can be found naturally and is related to plants like lemon grass; just rub the leaves on your skin. Soybean oil and oil of eucalyptus will also work.

The important thing to know is that your risk of Lyme disease or other tick-spread illness increases the longer it feeds on you. The good news is that there is generally no transmission of disease in the first 24 hours. After 48 hours, though, you have the highest chance of infection, so it pays to remove that tick as soon as possible. This is how you do it....

Take the finest set of tweezers you have and try to grab the tick as close to your skin as you can. Pull the tick straight up; this will give you the best chance of removing it intact. The mouthparts sometimes remain in the skin, which might cause an inflammation at the site of the bite. Fortunately, it won't increase your chances of getting Lyme disease. Afterwards, disinfect the area with Betadine or triple antibiotic ointment. I'm sure you've heard about other methods of tick removal, such as smothering it with petroleum jelly or lighting it on fire. No method, however, is more effective that pulling it out with tweezers.

Luckily, only about 20% of deer ticks carry the Lyme disease or other parasite. If you get a rash that looks like a bulls-eye, along with flu-like symptoms that are resistant to medicines, you'll need further treatment. Oral antibiotics will be useful to treat early stages. Amoxicillin (500 mg 4x/day for 14 days) or Doxycycline (100mg 2x/day for 14 days) should work to treat the illness. These can be obtained without a prescription in certain veterinary medications. See the chapter in this book titled "stockpiling medications".

Parasitic Worms

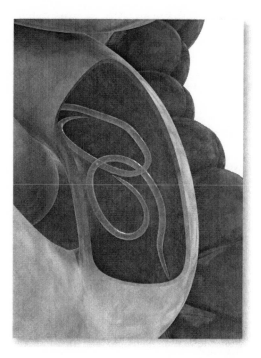

In a collapse situation, you can bet that you will be exposed to some pretty strange diseases and infestations. Simply being outside more often will expose you to mosquitos that carry illness. As well, your food and water may be contaminated or poorly cooked; this is yet another vector to allow infection to enter your body. The organisms involved might be bacteria, viruses, or even parasites. Even walking barefoot can cause you to pick up one of these organisms. You gardeners know that nematodes (a type of roundworm) live in and on the soil.

Parasitic worms (also known as helminthes) are what we call internal parasites, because they live and feed inside your body. This differentiates them from external parasites such as lice or ticks, which live and feed on the outside of your body. When infected or infested, you are called a "host" (lucky you).

There are three types of parasitic worms: tapeworms, roundworms, and flukes. They range in size from microscopic to almost a foot long, depending on the species. The most common infection we'll see in the U.S. is the tiny Pinworm, which affects 40 million Americans. Underdeveloped countries in Africa and Asia have the highest incidence, but it is thought that over a quarter of the world's population has one type of worm or another in their system. Children are especially vulnerable, and parasites account for stunted growth and poor development.

Worms attach themselves mostly to the intestinal tract, although some flukes infect the liver and lungs as well. Worm eggs or larvae enter through the mouth, nose, anus or breaks in the skin. Many helminthes are dependent on the acid in the stomach to dissolve the egg shell, and cannot hatch without it. The worm itself, however, is immune to the effects of stomach acid.

Many infections are asymptomatic or just involve some itching in the anal area (especially Pinworms); with some species, however, you can get a large concentration of organisms which cause serious problems. Some symptoms include stomach pains, nausea and vomiting, diarrhea, fatigue, and even intestinal obstruction. In rare cases, an obstruction can cause so much damage to the bowel that the patient may die. Organisms that invade the liver or lungs can even cause respiratory distress or weakened metabolism.

Your body knows when it has been invaded, and sets up an immune response against the worm. It is unlikely to kill it, however, and all the energy put into defending the body may weaken the ability to fight other infections. As such, people with worms are more prone to other infections, and those infections are harder to fight off.

Some worms actually compete with your body for the food that you take in. Ascaris, for example, will eat partially digested food that comes its way, preventing you from absorbing the nutrients effectively. Anemia and malnutrition may result. This may not matter much now, when you have access to as much food as you want. In a collapse, you will not have this luxury. Mixed with diarrhea, you could be at a significant nutritional deficit.

There are various drugs such as Vermox, which are called vermicides. These are effective in killing the worms inside your body, and might be a good choice to stockpile if you're in an area that has seen parasitic worm infections before. It is thought that overuse or multiple uses of these drugs may eventually cause the organism to become resistant. This is especially becoming an issue with livestock. Natural anti-helminthic plants also exist. Wormwood, Clove, and Plumeria have been reported as effective. Interestingly, tobacco will also help eliminate worms.

Parasitic worm infections are contagious in that they can be passed through contact with the infected individual. Careful attention to hygiene and, among medical providers, strict glove use will decrease this likelihood. Hand washing is considered important in preventing a community-wide epidemic, especially before preparing food. Scratching during sleep may transmit eggs to fingernails, so be certain to wear clothing that will prevent direct hand contact with the anus. Known worm patients should wash every morning to remove any eggs deposited overnight in that area.

It's important to realize that unusual illnesses and infections will be problems that the survival medic may have to deal with. Obtaining knowledge of which organisms exist in your area, even if they are not major problems today, will be key in keeping your loved ones healthy.

DENTAL ISSUES

✚ ✚ ✚

The stages of tooth decay

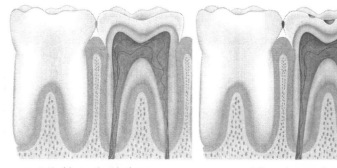

1. Healthy tooth with plaque

2. Decay in enamel

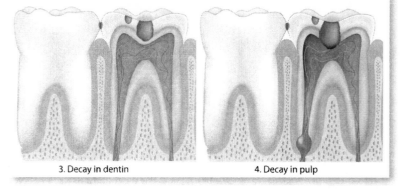

3. Decay in dentin

4. Decay in pulp

I've always said that an ounce of prevention is worth a pound of cure, and this is never truer than when it comes to your teeth. Doctors who provide care in remote areas care for as many dental issues as they do general medical issues. In a collapse situation, so will you.

Most dental disease is caused by bacteria. Your mouth is full of them, so anything that decreases the amount of bacteria there will reduce the chances of having dental disease. By keeping up their oral hygiene, a person will decrease their risk of an appointment at the collapse dental office. A daily brushing routine is essential, but at one point or another you will run out of toothbrushes and toothpaste. As an alternative, you can use your finger, or a piece of cloth; these methods will work in a pinch. You can also chew on the end of a twig until it gets fibrous and use that to clean your teeth.

No toothpaste? Consider Baking soda. Baking soda is less abrasive to dental enamel than commercially prepared silica-based toothpaste. It is an excellent alternative, and it doesn't have Fluoride. Fluoride is sometimes useful as a direct treatment for those under 12 years old, but adults really get very little benefit from it. There is even a school of thought that there are major medical risks associated with long term exposure to it.

Every time you eat a meal and especially before going to bed, you should be brushing your teeth or at least rinsing your mouth with water or a good antibacterial rinse. A good option would be to use ½ water and ½ 3% hydrogen peroxide. Most Preppers don't include mouth rinses as part of their storage, but this is a great way to prevent tooth issues.

Another method of preventing tooth decay is faithful flossing. It may be inconvenient for some, but a lot of bacteria like to accumulate between your teeth. You can prove this by flossing and then smelling the floss. Unless you're flossing regularly, it will have a foul odor. This is due to the large amounts of bacteria you just flossed out.

So how does bacteria cause tooth disease? Bacteria live in your mouth, and they colonize your teeth, usually in the crevices on your molars and at the level where the teeth and gums meet. When you eat, these bacteria also have a meal; they digest the sugars you take in and produce a toxic acid. This acid has the effect of slowly dissolving the enamel of your teeth (the outside of the tooth that's shiny). This commonly happens around areas where you've had dental work already, like the edges of fillings and under crowns or caps.

Once the enamel is broken down, you have what is called a cavity. This could take just a few months to cause problems or could take 2-3 years. Once the cavity becomes deep enough to approach the soft inner part of the tooth (the pulp), the process speeds up and, because you have nerves in each tooth, starts to cause pain. If the cavity isn't dealt with, it can lead to infection once the bacteria make it deep enough into the nerve or the surrounding gum tissue.

Inflamed gums have a distinctive appearance: They'll bleed when you brush your teeth and appear red and swollen. This is called "gingivitis", and is very common once you reach adulthood. As gingivitis worsens, it could easily lead to infection. A particularly severe infection is called an abscess. This is an accumulation of pus and inflammatory fluid that can be quite painful. Once you have an abscess, you will need antibiotic therapy and/or perhaps a procedure to drain the pus that has accumulated.

A diet that is high in sugar causes bacteria to produce the most acid. The longer your mouth bacteria are in eating mode, the longer your mouth has acid digging into your teeth. The two most important factors that cause cavities are the number of times per day and the duration of time that the teeth are exposed to this acid.

Let's say you have a can of soda in your hand. If you drink the entire thing in 10 minutes, you've had one short episode in which your mouth bacteria are producing high quantities of acid. The acid level drops after about 30 minutes or so. If you nurse that soda, however, and sip from it continuously for hours, you've increased both the number of exposures to sugar and the amount of time it's swishing around in there. The acid level never really gets a chance to drop, and that leads to decay.

Toothache

Treatment of a toothache starts with finding the bad tooth. First, you will carefully look around for any obvious cavity or fracture. If there is nothing that you can see, you may still have serious decay between teeth or below the gums.

So how do you tell which tooth is the problem if you don't see anything obvious? Do this: Touch the teeth in the area of the toothache with something cold. The bad tooth will be very sensitive to cold. Now touch it with something hot. If there is no sensitivity to heat, the tooth is salvageable. A tooth that's beyond hope will cause significant pain when you touch it with something hot, and will continue to hurt for 10 seconds or so after you remove the heat source. This is because the nerve has been irreversibly damaged. Once the nerve is actually dead, you won't feel either hot or cold. It will, however, be painful to even the slightest touch.

The basis of modern dentistry is to save every tooth if at all possible. In the old days (not biblical times, I mean 50 years ago), the main treatment for a diseased tooth was extraction. If we find ourselves in a collapse situation, that's how it will be in the future. If you delay extracting a tooth because it "isn't that bad yet", it will likely get worse. It could cause an infection that could spread to your bloodstream (called "sepsis") and cause major damage.

The important thing to know is that 90% of all dental emergencies can be treated by extracting the tooth. There are numerous viral videos on sites like YouTube that demonstrate the procedure. An interesting one is listed in the back of this book.

Besides a dental pick and mirror, what else needs to be in the group medic's dental kit? Gloves are one item that you should have in quantity. Don't ever stick your hands in someone's mouth without gloves; hat they say about human bites isn't too far from the truth. Instead of latex, buy nitrile gloves, as they will not irritate someone who is allergic to latex. Other items that are useful to the survival dentist are:

- Dental floss, Toothbrushes.
- Dental or orthodontic wax as used for braces; even a candle will do in a pinch.
- A Rubber bite block to keep the mouth open. This will help you see the dentition and prevent yourself from getting bitten. One of those large pink erasers would serve the purpose just fine.
- Cotton pellets, Q tips, gauze sponges.
- Temporary filling material such as Tempanol, Cavit or Den-temp
- Oil of cloves (eugenol), a natural anesthetic. Commercial toothache medications that have this include Red Cross Toothache Medicine containing 85% eugenol, Dent's Toothache Drops containing benzocaine, another anesthetic, and eugenol in combo, and Orajel or Hurricaine containing benzocaine. This might come in a kit that includes dental tweezers and cotton pellets that you'll need for placement. It's important to know that Eugenol burns the tongue, so never touch anything but teeth with it.
- Oil of oregano, a natural antibacterial.
- Dental tweezers and a dental pick or toothpicks.

- Extraction forceps. These are like pliers with curved ends. They come in versions specific to upper and lower teeth.
- Elevators, one small, one medium. These are thin but solid chisel-like instruments that help with extractions (some parts of a Swiss army knife might work in a pinch).
- Pain medication and antibiotics.

If a collapse situation lasts long enough, you will come across people who have lost fillings or have loose caps or crowns. Temporary filling material like Den-Temp or Cavit will be useful, although you will have to replace the filling from time to time.

A more economical way to get temporary filling material is to make it yourself. Take a drop of Oil of Cloves (Eugenol) and mix it with Zinc Oxide powder until you make a paste. Apply this to the area and it will harden, relieving pain at the same time.

The loss of a tooth is called an avulsion, especially if caused by trauma. A tooth can sometimes be saved by picking it up by the enamel (not the root), cleaning it with antiseptic solution and replacing it gently. If it's replaced in less than 30 minutes, there's a chance it might heal. After that time, the body usually ceases to recognize the tooth as part of itself.

RESPIRATORY INFECTIONS

✚ ✚ ✚

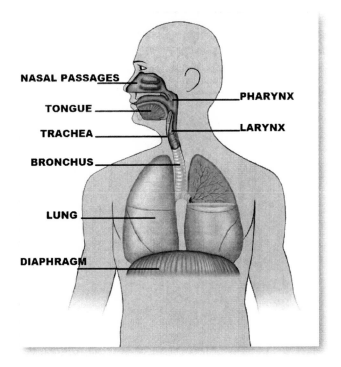

NASAL PASSAGES

TONGUE

TRACHEA

BRONCHUS

LUNG

DIAPHRAGM

PHARYNX

LARYNX

Even with today's modern medical technology, most of us can't avoid the occasional upper respiratory infection. Without strict adherence to sanitary protocol, it would be very easy in a collapse situation for your entire community to come down with colds, sinusitis, influenza or even pneumonia. Respiratory infections are spread by viral particles, and the organisms that cause these infections can live for up to 48 hours on common household surfaces. Contagious viral particles can easily travel 4 to 6 feet when a person sneezes.

Respiratory issues are usually divided into upper and lower respiratory infections. The upper respiratory tract is considered to be anything at the level of the vocal cords (larynx) or above. This includes the nose, throat, sinuses, voice box, epiglottis, and even the tonsils. The lower respiratory tract includes the lower windpipe, the airways (taken together, called "bronchi") and the lungs themselves. Respiratory infections are the most common cause of infectious disease in developed countries.

Upper respiratory tract infections (URIs) include tonsillitis, pharyngitis (sore throat), laryngitis, sinusitis, some types of influenza, and the common cold. Symptoms can include fever, cough, sore throat, runny nose (also called rhinitis), nasal congestion, headaches, and sneezing. Symptoms of lower respiratory infections include cough (with phlegm, it is referred to as a "productive" cough), high fever, shortness of breath, and weakness/fatigue. Most respiratory infections start showing symptoms 1 to 3 days after exposure to the causative organism and last for 7 to 10 days if upper and somewhat longer if lower.

There are differences between the common cold and influenza that are helpful to make a diagnosis:

Symptoms	Cold	Influenza
Fever	Rare, Low	Common, High
Headache	Rare	Common
Nasal Congestion	Common	Occasional
Sore Throat	Common	Occasional
Cough	Mild	Severe
Aches and Pains	Common	Severe
Fatigue	Mild	Severe

Symptomatic relief as described later in this chapter will improve most cold symptoms without an issue. For influenza, the addition of antiviral medications such as Tamiflu or Relenza will shorten the course of the infection.

Both upper and lower respiratory infections are different than asthma, which is a condition where the airways become constricted in a type of spasm, causing a particularly vocal kind of breathing called a "wheeze". Asthma may occur as an allergic response, or may be associated with some respiratory infections, such as childhood "croup". The treatment of asthma involves different medicines, such as antihistamines and epinephrine, than those used in treating respiratory infections.

Most upper respiratory infections are caused by various viruses, although some sore throats may be caused by a bacterium called Beta-Streptococcus (Also known as Strep Throat). These patients will often have white spots on the back of their throat and/or tonsils, and are candidates for antibiotics. In most cases, however, it is not appropriate to use antibacterial agents such as antibiotics for upper respiratory infections. Antibiotics have been overused in treating these problems, and this has led to resistance on the part of some organisms to the more common drugs.

There are anti-viral drugs effective against influenza and other viral diseases. The most commonly used is Tamiflu, which is best utilized in the first 2 days of the illness. It may even be used as a preventative agent upon being exposed to a sick patient.

The best course of action for upper respiratory infections is treating the specific symptoms. Decongestants for runny nose, lozenges or gargles for sore throat, and Ibuprofen or Acetaminophen for muscle ache and fever are commonly used to make the patient feel better. Steam inhalation and good hydration also give some symptomatic relief. Various natural remedies are also useful to relieve symptoms, which we will discuss later.

Lower respiratory infections, such as pneumonia, are the most common cause of death from infectious disease in developed countries. These can be caused by viruses or bacteria. The more serious nature of these infections leads many practitioners to use antibiotics more often to treat the condition. Most bronchitis is caused by viruses, however, and will not be affected by antibiotics. Antibiotics may be appropriate for those with a lower respiratory infection that hasn't improved after several days of treatment with the usual medications for upper respiratory infections.

These patients will appear to have worsening shortness of breath or thicker phlegm over the course of time despite the usual therapy. There is a school of thought that recommends more liberal use of antibiotics in sick persons over the age of 60 or those with other serious medical conditions. This population has a higher risk of death because of decreased resistance to secondary bacterial infections.

Effective antibiotics for bacterial infections can be obtained in veterinary form (without a medical license). Good examples are Doxycycline, Keflex, and Amoxicillin. This information is relevant only in a post-collapse setting; contact a certified healthcare provider for these medications in normal situations.

Good respiratory hygiene is important to prevent patients with respiratory infections from transmitting their infection to others. This is what needs to be done:

- Sick individuals should cover their mouth and nose with tissues and dispose of those tissues safely
- Use a mask if coughing. Although others caring for the sick individual may wear masks (N95 masks are best for healthcare providers), it is most important for the afflicted person to wear one.
- Have caregivers perform rigorous hand hygiene before and after contact. Wash with soap and warm water for 15 seconds or clean your hands with alcohol-based hand product if they do not appear soiled.
- Sick persons should keep at least 4 feet away from other persons, if possible due to droplet spread.
- Wash down all possibly contaminated surfaces with an appropriate disinfectant (dilute bleach solution will do).
- Isolate the sick individual in a specific quarantine area, especially if he/she has a high fever.
- Have medical care providers wear gloves at all times when treating the patient.

There are a number of alternative remedies for various respiratory infections; they will help to stimulate the immune system. Consider these essential oils:

- Geranium
- Clove Bud
- Tea Tree
- Lavender

You would place 2-3 drops on the palm of your hand. Warm the oil by rubbing your hands together, and then bring your hands to your nose and mouth. Breathe 3-5 times slowly and deeply. Relax and breathe normally for 2 minutes, then repeat deep breaths once more. Wipe excess oil onto throat and chest. This is called direct inhalation therapy.

For internal use, consider herbal teas: Popular ones for these conditions are Elderberry, Echinacea, Licorice root, Goldenseal,

Chamomile, Peppermint, and Ginseng. Antibacterial action has been found in Garlic and Onion oil, fresh Cinnamon and powdered Cayenne Pepper. Other options include raw unprocessed honey, lemon, and apple cider vinegar.

Other than general treatments, there are several good remedies to treat specific symptoms associated with colds and flu. To treat fever, for example, consider teas made from the following herbs:

- Echinacea
- Licorice Root
- Yarrow
- Fennel
- Catnip
- Lemon Balm

Other strategies to combat fever include sponge baths with water and vinegar. It has also been reported that slices of raw onion on the bottom of the feet are effective in some cases (wear socks to hold them in place). I haven't tested this last method myself, so I can't tell you if it is effective. It's probably not very practical, however.

Others have used herbal "spritzers" Combine several drops of any of these essential oils: Chamomile, Lavender or Thyme with water and spray on the chest, back, arms, and legs. Avoid spraying the face. The cooling effect alone will be beneficial in those with fevers.

To deal with the congestion that goes along with most respiratory infections, consider using direct inhalation therapy (described above) with these essential oils:

- Eucalyptus
- Rosemary
- Peppermint
- Tea Tree

- Pine
- Thyme

Another inhalation method of delivering herbal or even traditional medication involves the use of steam. Steam inhalation is beneficial and easy to implement. Just place a few drops of essential oil into steaming water and lower your face to inhale the vapors. Cover the back of your head with a towel to concentrate the steam.

Teas that relieve congestion include: Stinging Nettles, Licorice Root, Peppermint, Anise, Cayenne Pepper, Sage and Dandelion. Mix with honey and drink 3-4 times per day as needed. Plain saline solution (nasal spray or in a neti pot) is also used by both traditional and alternative healers.

For aches and pains due to colds, try using salves consisting of essential oils of:

- St. John's Wort
- Eucalyptus
- Camphor
- Lavender
- Peppermint
- Rosemary
- Arnica (dilute)

Helpful teas include: Passionflower, Chamomile, Valerian Root, Willow bark, Ginger, Feverfew, and Rosemary. Drink warm with raw honey 3-4 times a day.

For the occasional sore throat, time-honored remedies include honey and garlic "syrups" and ginger, Tilden flower, or sage teas. Drink warm with honey and perhaps lemon several times a day. Gargling with warm salt water will also bring relief. Licorice root and honey lozenges are also popular.

FOOD AND WATER
BORNE ILLNESS

✚ ✚ ✚

I t's just makes common sense that there will be sanitation issues in a collapse situation. Any water source that has not been sterilized or any food that hasn't been properly cleaned and cooked will be an opportunity for pathogens to start their damage. As a community medic, your duty will be to assure that water is clean and that food is prepared properly.

Sterilizing Water and Food

Water can be contaminated by floods, disruptions in water service and a number of other random events. A dead raccoon upstream from where you collect your water supplies could be a source of deadly bacteria. Even the clearest mountain brook could be a source of parasites, called protozoa, which can cause disease.

If you're starting with cloudy water, it is because there are many small particles of debris in it. There are many excellent commercial filters on the market, such as the Berkey water filter or the AquaPail, that deal with this effectively. You could also make your own particulate filter by using a length of 4 inch wide PVC pipe and inserting 2 or 3 layers of gravel, sand and/or activated charcoal, with each layer separated by pieces of cloth or cotton. Once flushed out and ready to go, you can run cloudy water through it and see clear water coming out the other side.

This type of filter, with or without activated charcoal, will get rid of particulate matter but will not kill bacteria. It's important to have several ways to sterilize your water to get rid of organisms. This can be accomplished by several methods:

- Boiling: Use a heat source to get your water to a roiling boil for at least 10 minutes. There are bacteria that may survive high heat, but they are in the minority. Using a pressure cooker would be even more thorough.
- Chlorine: Bleach has an excellent track record of eliminating bacteria and 8-10 drops in a gallon of water will do the trick. If you're used to drinking city-treated water, you probably won't notice any difference in taste.
- 2% Tincture of Iodine: About 12 drops per gallon of water will be effective.

- Ultraviolet Radiation: Sunlight will kill bacteria! 6-8 hours in direct sunlight (even better on a reflective surface) Fill your clear gallon bottle and shake vigorously for 20 seconds. The oxygen released from the water molecules will help the process along and, amazingly, even improves the taste.

Anyone who has eaten food that has been left out for too long has probably experienced an occasion when they have regretted it. Properly cleaning food and food preparation surfaces is a key to preventing disease.

Your hands are a food preparation surface. Wash your hands thoroughly prior to preparing your food. Other food preparation surfaces like counter tops, cutting boards, dishes, and utensils should also be cleaned with hot water and soap before using them. Soap may not kill germs, but it helps to dislodge them from surfaces.

If you have a good supply, use paper towels to clean surfaces. Kitchen towels, especially if kept damp, really accumulate bacteria. If you ever reach a point when paper towels are no longer available, boil your towels before using them.

Wash your fruits and vegetables under running water before eating them. Food that comes from plants that grow in soil may have disease-causing organisms, and that without taking into account fertilizers like manure. You're not protected if the fruit has a rind; the organisms on the rind will get on your hand and will be transferred to the fruit once you peel it.

Raw meat is notorious for having their juices contaminate food. Prepare meats separately from your fruits and vegetables. A useful item to be certain that meats are safe is a meat thermometer. Assure that meats reach an appropriate safe temperature and remain consistently at that temperature until cooked; this varies by the type of meat:

- Beef: 145 degrees F
- Pork: 150 degrees F
- Lamb: 160 degrees F
- Poultry: 165 degrees F
- Ground Meats: 160 degrees F
- Sauces and Gravy: 165 degrees F
- Soups with Meat: 165 degrees F
- Fish: 145 degrees F

DIARRHEAL DISEASE

✚ ✚ ✚

With worsening sanitation and hygiene, there will likely be an increase in infectious disease, none of which will be more common that diarrhea. Diarrhea is an increased frequency of loose bowel movements. If a person has 3 liquid stools in a row, it is a red flag that tells you to watch for signs of dehydration. Dehydration, if bad enough, can cause a series of chemical imbalances that can threaten your life. Over 80,000 soldiers perished in the Civil War, not from bullets, but from dehydration related to diarrheal disease.

Diarrhea is a common ailment and may go away on its own simply by taking in fluids and avoiding solid food for a period of time. I would recommend 12 hours without eating solids to be safe. There are some symptoms that may present in association with diarrhea that can be a sign of something more serious. Those symptoms are:

- Fever equal to or greater than 101 degrees Fahrenheit
- Blood or mucus in the stool
- Black or grey-white stool
- Severe vomiting
- Major abdominal distension and pain
- Moderate to severe dehydration
- Diarrhea lasting more than 3 days

All of the above may be signs of serious infection, intestinal bleeding, liver dysfunction, or even surgical conditions such as appendicitis. As well, all of the above will increase the likelihood that the person affected won't be able to regulate their fluid balance.

Cholera is one particularly dangerous disease that was epidemic in the past and may be once again in the uncertain future. This infection will produce a profuse watery diarrhea with abdominal pain. Although there is a vaccination, it is not very effective and so I cannot recommend it.

Typhoid fever is another very dangerous illness caused by contaminated food or drink. It is characterized by bloody diarrhea and pain and, like cholera, has been the cause of epidemics over the centuries. In typhoid cases, fever rises daily and, after a week or more, you may see a splotchy rash and spontaneous nosebleeds. The patient's condition deteriorates from there.

The end result (and most common cause of death) of untreated diarrheal illness is dehydration. 75% of the body's weight is made up of water, and you should be aware that the average adult requires 2 to 3 liters of fluid per day. The severity of dehydration depends on the percent of water that has been lost.The thirst mechanism is activated when you have lost 1% of your total body water content. You are still functioning normally at this point. As the percent of water lost increases, you begin to see additional symptoms and increased risks. Dehydration is often classified as mild, moderate, and severe:

- Mild dehydration: 2% of water content lost. Symptoms include anxiety, loss of appetite and decreased work efficiency.
- Moderate dehydration: 4% of water content lost. In addition to the above symptoms, the patient experiences nausea and vomiting (even if they didn't before), dizziness, fatigue and mood swings.

- Severe dehydration: 6% of water content lost. In addition to the above symptoms, the patient experiences loss of coordination and becomes incoherent and delirious.
- Continued water loss begins to cause the patient to be unable to regulate their body temperature. Chemical imbalances begin to occur that just replacing water cannot repair. Organs will begin to malfunction. Once you reach approximately 20% water loss, the patient may slip into coma and die.

Fluid replacement is the treatment for dehydration. Oral rehydration is the first line of treatment, but if this fails, intravenous fluid (IV) may be needed, which requires special skills. Always start with small amounts of clear fluids. Clear fluids are easier for the body to absorb. Examples of clear fluids would be: water, clear broth, gelatin, Gatorade, Pedialyte, etc. You can produce your own homemade rehydration fluid very easily. Simply add 6-8 teaspoons of sugar and 1 teaspoon of salt to a liter of water. You can make the fluid even better by adding ½ teaspoon of salt substitute (Potassium Chloride) and a pinch of baking soda to the solution.

As the patient shows an ability to tolerate these fluids, advancement of the diet to juices, puddings and thin cereals like grits or farina (cream of wheat) is undertaken. It is wise to avoid milk as some are intolerant. Once the patient tolerates thin cereals, you can advance them to solid food.

A popular strategy for rapid recovery is the BRAT diet, used commonly in children. This diet consists of Bananas, Rice, Applesauce and plain Toast. The advantage of this strategy is that the food is very bland, easily tolerated, and slows down intestinal motility (which will slow down diarrhea). In a collapse situation, you will probably not have many bananas, but hopefully you have stored rice and/or applesauce, and have the ability to bake bread.

Of course, there are medicines that can help and you should stockpile these in quantity. Pepto-Bismol and Imodium (Loperamide) will help diarrhea. They don't cure infections, but they will slow down the number of bowel movements and conserve water. These are over the counter medicines, and are easy to obtain. In tablet form, these medicines will last for years if properly stored.

A good prescription medicine for vomiting is Zofran (Ondansetron). Doctors will usually have no qualms about writing this prescription, especially if you are traveling out of the country. Of course, ibuprofen or acetaminophen is good to treat fevers. The higher the fever, the more water is lost. Therefore, anything that reduces the fever will help a person's hydration status.

Herbal remedies such as blackberry leaf, raspberry leaf and peppermint are thought to "dry up" the mucous membranes in the intestine. Make a tea with the leaves and drink a cup every 2-3 hours.

Half a clove of crushed garlic and 1 teaspoon of raw honey 4 times a day is thought to exert an antibacterial effect in some cases of diarrhea. A small amount of nutmeg may decrease the number of loose bowels movements. Ginger tea is a time-honored method to decrease the abdominal cramps associated with diarrhea.

As a last resort to treat dehydration from diarrhea (especially if there is also a high fever), you can try antibiotics or anti-parasitic drugs. Ciprofloxacin, Doxycycline and Metronidazole are good choices, twice a day, until the stools are less watery. Some of these are available in veterinary form without a prescription. These medicines should be used only as a last resort, as the main side effect is usually...diarrhea!

FOOD POISONING

✚ ✚ ✚

I f we find ourselves in a collapse situation, everyone that doesn't have an extensive survival garden up and running will be looking to their environment for edible wild plants. It's likely we'll be less than perfect in our choice of safe, tasty greens.

What if we find ourselves getting sick soon after trying a new plant?

Most food poisoning is actually due to eggs, dairy products and meat that have been contaminated by some type of bacteria. Despite this, most animal meat is not toxic by itself (puffer fish and barracuda are exceptions that come to mind), but there are plenty of plants that have toxins that could seriously harm you. Eating the seeds of an apple, in quantity, will make you sick due to cyanide-like compounds within it. It is just as important to be aware of how to process a particular plant. Many plants that are toxic raw are edible if cooked.

It would be wise to perform some research on what plants grow naturally in your area that have potential for use as food.

Extreme caution should be taken, for example, with mushrooms and any berries that are white or red unless you have eaten them before without ill effect. Some food that are fine when cooked are inedible raw.

A test can be performed called the survival edibility; this test is controversial, with experts recommending both for and against it. It basically involves a stepwise process in which you would first rub the plant against your skin to see if you are allergic to it. Then, you would place it on your lips, in your mouth, and then swallow it in increments; wait a period of time between one step and the next.

You would make sure to try each part of the plant (leaves, flower, stem) separately, using this technique. If done properly, the whole process would take 16 hours for each part of the plant you are testing. This procedure is not foolproof, so proceed with caution. Symptoms to expect if you have food poisoning would include nausea and vomiting, dizziness, vision disturbances, confusion and palpitations.

When you suspect that you have been poisoned, wash your mouth out immediately to make sure that you don't have any plant material still to be ingested. Then purge yourself, whether it is by pressing down on the back of your tongue with 2 fingers or using a preparation like Syrup of Ipecac. Most poison control centers will advise against using Syrup of Ipecac, because it may be difficult to figure out exactly how much will work. The answer is to use the smallest amount of the concoction that will make you vomit. Drink clear fluids to dilute the toxin and help flush it out of your system.

Activated charcoal is another product that is used to treat poisoning. Activated charcoal in your stomach and intestines causes toxins to bind to it, therefore keeping them from entering your system. Some poison control centers don't want you to use this either, due to dosing issues and the fact that it could give you constipation. Take an Ex-lax when you take the charcoal to help move things along. In terms of dosing, there are various pre-measured charcoal products that you can use in liquid or capsule form. Some brand names are SuperChar, Actidote, Liqui-char, InstaChar, and Charcodote.

Prevent food poisoning by being sure what you're eating; get a good edible plant guide for your area, one with plenty of photos. Foragerpress.com has an assortment of books that might fit the bill. Remember, if there is still modern medical care available to you and you feel sick, get to an emergency room as soon as possible!

In mild cases due to contaminated food sources, you could consider this home remedy: Squeeze 4 lemons, add sugar or honey to sweeten. Take this mixture and drink it twice daily. The idea behind this remedy is to kill any offending bacteria with the acidic lemon juice. Along that same line of thinking is a remedy using 4 tablespoons of apple cider vinegar in 1 big glass of water, with or without a sweetener. Drink this mixture twice a day until improved.

SECTION 4

✚ ✚ ✚

INFECTIONS

In the last section, we discussed infections that usually come as a result of poor sanitation and hygiene, such as diarrheal disease and body lice. There are many other types of bacterial, viral, and parasitic disease that may not necessarily have sanitation and hygiene as a factor, but can be as dangerous. Appendicitis, for example, can occur in anyone regardless of their cleanliness or the conditions at their retreat. An ingrown hair may lead to a boil or abscess.

There are no organs that are immune to infections and the ability to recognize and treat these illnesses early is essential for the successful survival medic. This section will discuss some of the more common ones that you might see.

APPENDICITIS

✚ ✚ ✚

There are various infections that can cause abdominal pain, some of which can be treated medically and some which are treated surgically. One relatively common issue that could be life-threatening in a collapse situation, especially to young people, would be appendicitis.

Appendicitis can occur in anyone but most likely affects people under 40. The appendix is a tube-shaped piece of tissue several inches long which connects to the intestine at the lower right side of the abdomen. The inside of this structure forms a pouch that opens to the large intestine. The appendix was once an important organ and still is in some animals (for example, horses), but it is shrunken and serves little purpose in human beings. This is an example of a "vestigial" organ, which means that it exists but serves little useful purpose. In humans, the appendix is located in the lower right of the abdomen. It can become inflamed, infected, and fill with pus. If not treated, the appendix can burst; this causes an infection throughout the entire abdomen and become very serious.

Appendicitis (inflammation of the appendix) starts off with vague discomfort in the area of the belly button, but moves down to the lower right portion of the abdomen after a period of time.

To diagnose this condition, press down on the lower right portion of the abdomen. It will be uncomfortable, but will be even more painful when you REMOVE your hand! This is called "rebound tenderness". Nausea and vomiting and fever will often be present. In severe cases, abdominal swelling may occur.

The patient should be restricted to small amounts of clear liquids as soon as you make the diagnosis. Surgical removal of the appendix is curative here, but will be difficult to carry out without modern medical facilities. If no hope of accessing modern care exists, consider giving the patient antibiotics in the hope of eliminating the infection. Recovery, although slow, may still be possible if treatment is begun early enough.

URINARY INFECTIONS

✚ ✚ ✚

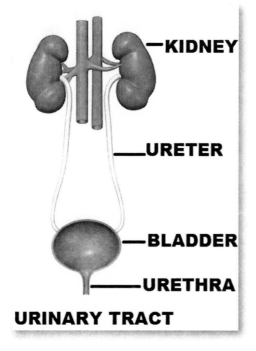

KIDNEY

URETER

BLADDER

URETHRA

URINARY TRACT

Most women, at some time of their lives, have experienced a urinary tract infection. This type of infection usually affects the bladder and urethra, the tube that drains the bladder. Although men can get a bladder infection (called "cystitis"), their urethra is much longer and bacteria are much less likely to reach the bladder.

Frequency of urination is the most common symptom, although painful urination is not uncommon. Some people notice that the stream of urine is somewhat hesitant (hesitancy) or may feel an urgent need to go without warning (urgency). If not treated, a bladder infection may possibly ascend to the kidneys, causing an infection known as "pyelonephritis".

Preventative medicine plays a large role in decreasing the likelihood of this problem. Basic hygienic method, such as wiping from front to back after urinating, is important. So is urinating right after an episode of sexual intercourse. Wear cotton undergarments to allow better air circulation in areas that might otherwise encourage bacterial or fungal growth. Adequate fluid intake, especially cranberry juice if available, is also a key to remaining free of bladder issues. Never postpone urinating when you feel a strong urge to do so.

Besides frequency of urination and a sensation of urgency, your patient may feel a burning sensation during the act. Evaluation of a urine sample might reveal it to be cloudy, blood-tinged or foul-smelling. A vague discomfort in the middle of the pelvis is also common. Once the infection reaches the kidney, other symptoms will become manifest. You will see fever and chills and an area of pain on the side of your back below the last rib. Most likely, it will be noticeable only on one side.

Treatment revolves around the vigorous administration of fluids. Lots of water, for example, will help flush out the infection by decreasing the concentration of bacteria in the affected organs. Antibiotics are another mainstay of therapy, commonly Cipro, Bactrim, or Macrodantin. An over-the-counter medication that eliminates the painful urination seen in urinary infections is Phenazopyridine (also known as Pyridium, Uristat, Azo, etc.). Don't be alarmed if your urine turns reddish-orange, it is an effect of the drug and is temporary. Vitamin C supplements are thought to reduce the concentration of bacteria in the urine, and should also be considered.

A few natural remedies for urinary tract infections include:

- Garlic or garlic oil (preferably in capsules).
- Echinacea extract or tea.
- Goldenrod tea with 1-2 tablespoons of vinegar.
- Uva Ursi (1 tablet).
- Cranberry tablets (1 to 3 pills).

Take any one of these remedies three times per day.

Another home remedy is to take one Alka-Seltzer tablet and dissolve it in 2 ounces of warm water. Pour directly over the urethral area.

One more alternative that may be helpful is to perform an external massage over the bladder area with 5 drops of lavender essential oil (mixed with castor oil) for a few minutes. Then, apply a gentle heat source over the area; repeat this 3 to 4 times daily. The combination of lavender/castor oil and warmth may help decrease bladder spasms and pain.

HEPATITIS

✚ ✚ ✚

Hepatitis is the term used for inflammation of the liver. Mostly caused by viruses, it causes the inability of the body to process toxins, and can be life-threatening. There are various types of Hepatitis, often called Hepatitis A, Hepatitis B, and Hepatitis C, etc. Hepatitis can also occur due to adverse reactions from drugs and alcohol, among other things.

I was in a quandary regarding whether to put this in the last section on hygiene and sanitation or here. I decided to place it here as some types of hepatitis may be spread by other methods, for example, sexual transmission.

The hepatitis A virus is found in the bowel movements of an infected individual. When a person eats food or water that is contaminated, they develop a flu-like syndrome that can quickly become serious. This illness could easily go through an entire community in a very short time. Even now, we are at risk; if a restaurant employee with hepatitis A doesn't wash his hands after using the bathroom, everyone that eats there may get sick. Hepatitis can also be spread by sexual contact.

The hallmark of hepatitis is "jaundice". You will find that your patient's skin and the whites of their eyes will turn yellow. Their urine becomes darker and their stools turn grey.

The liver, which can be found on the right side of the abdomen just below the lowest rib, becomes tender to the touch. There is also a sensation of itchiness that is felt all over the body. Add to this a feeling of extreme fatigue, weight loss, vague nausea, and sometimes fever. In some circumstances, people with hepatitis may have no symptoms at all and still pass the illness to others.

Hepatitis B and C can be spread by exposure to infected blood, plasma, semen, and vaginal fluids. Symptoms are usually indistinguishable from Hepatitis A, although they may lead to a chronic condition known as "Cirrhosis" that leads to permanent liver damage. The functioning cells of the liver are replaced by nodules that do nothing to help metabolism.

Possible signs and symptoms of liver cirrhosis include ascites (accumulation of fluid in the abdomen), varicose veins (enlarged veins, especially in the stomach and esophagus), jaundice, and even brain damage relating to the accumulation of toxins that are no longer processed by the damaged liver.

Other than making your patient comfortable, there isn't very much that you will be able to do in a collapse regarding this condition. Most cases of Hepatitis are self-limited, which means that they will resolve on their own after a period of time.

You can, however, practice good preventive medicine by encouraging the following among your people:

- Hand washing after using the bathroom and before preparing food.
- Wash dishes with soap in hot water.
- Avoid eating or drinking anything that may not be properly cooked or filtered.
- Make sure children don't put objects in their mouths.

There are a few "detoxifying" and anti-inflammatory herbal remedies that may help support a liver inflicted with hepatitis. Some of these supplements include artichoke, dandelion, milk thistle, green tea, red clover and turmeric. Remember these are not cures, but may be assist your other efforts.

Daily doses of 30 mg of zinc may help with an imbalance of copper and zinc levels. Avoid fatty foods and alcohol, and decrease protein intake. Increase fluid intake, especially with herbal teas, vegetable broths and diluted vegetable juices.

PELVIC AND VAGINAL INFECTIONS

✚ ✚ ✚

Less commonly, women may develop infections in their female organs. These may be common and have little effect on the rest of the body, such as vaginal yeast infections. Some infections are more internal, affecting the pelvic organs. This is referred to as Pelvic Inflammatory Disease and can be caused by a sexually transmitted disease such as gonorrhea or chlamydia.

Symptoms would include lower abdominal pain, vaginal discharge, and sometimes fever. Scarring ensues as the body tries to heal, sometimes causing infertility and chronic discomfort. Serious female infections involving the pelvis are best treated with antibiotics such as Doxycycline, sometimes in combination with Metronidazole twice a day for a week. It might be appropriate to treat sexual partners.

Vaginal yeast infections (also called Monilia) are usually not an indication of a sexually transmitted disease, however. A woman with a yeast infection will have a thick white discharge similar to cottage cheese with itching. This is often easily treated with over-the-counter creams or vaginal suppositories such as Monistat (miconazole). A prescription drug for resistant yeast infections is Diflucan (fluconazole), which comes as a pill. Non-yeast vaginal infections, those caused by bacteria or protozoa, are called bacterial vaginosis and trichomoniasis, respectively. They tend to have a foul odor and are treated with a prescription medication called Metronidazole (Flagyl), which is taken orally.

The time-honored vinegar and water douche, performed once a day, is very effective in eliminating minor vaginal infections.

Douche with 1 tablespoon of vinegar to a quart of water. Use this method only until your patient feels better. Women who douche often are, paradoxically, more likely to get yeast infections. This occurs because douching disrupts the normal balance of pH and allows naturally occurring yeast organisms in the vagina to overrun their environment.

Acidophilus supplements, in powder or capsule form, may be a good oral treatment. Cranberry juice and yogurt are good foods for vaginal infections because they change the pH of the organ to a level inhospitable to yeast.

As garlic has both antibacterial and anti-fungal action, you might consider inserting a clove of garlic wrapped in gauze and placing it in the vagina for no more than 8 hours. Make sure you leave a "tail" of gauze that you can easily reach to remove the garlic.

To relieve itching, sit in a bath of warm water with a few drops of lavender or tea tree oil for 15 minutes. Repeat as needed.

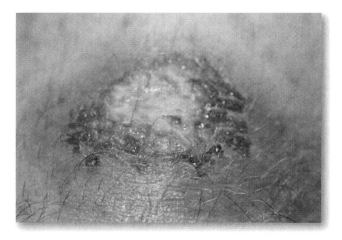

CELLULITIS

✚ ✚ ✚

Many soft tissue injuries have a degree of risk when it comes to infection. Infections from minor wounds or insect bites are relatively easy to treat today, due to the wide availability of antibiotics. With major wounds, these medications may actually save a life. In a collapse, antibiotics will be precious commodities, and should be dispensed only when absolutely necessary. The misuse of antibiotics, along with the frequent use in livestock, is part of the reason that we're beginning to see resistant strains of bacteria.

Despite your best efforts to care for a wound, there is always a chance that an infection will occur. Infection in the soft tissues below the level of the skin (epidermis) is referred to as "cellulitis". Below the epidermis, the main layers of soft tissue are the dermis (you've seen this area when you scraped your knee as a kid), the subcutaneous fat, and the muscle layers.

Cellulitis is significant to Preppers because it will be very commonly seen in a collapse. Although preventable, the sheer number of cuts, scrapes and burns will make it one of the most prevalent medical problems. This infection can easily reach the bloodstream, and, without antibiotics, can cause a life-threatening condition known as sepsis. Once sepsis has set in, inflammation of the spinal cord (meningitis) or bony structures (osteomyelitis) can further complicate the situation.

The bacteria that can cause cellulitis are on your skin right now. Normal inhabitants of the surface of your skin include Staphylococcus and Group A Streptococcus. They do no harm until the skin is broken. Then, they invade deeper layers where they are not normally seen and start causing inflammation. Cuts, bites, blisters, or cracks in the skin can all be entry ways for bacteria to cause infection that could be life-threatening if not treated. Cellulitis, by the way, has nothing to do with the dimpling on the skin called cellulite. The suffix "-itis" simply means "inflammation", so cellul-itis simply means "inflammation of the cells", appendicitis means "inflammation of the appendix" and so on...

Conditions that will be likely to cause cellulitis:

- Cracks or peeling skin between the toes
- History of varicose veins/poor circulation
- Injuries that cause a break in the skin
- Insect bites and stings, animal bites, or human bites
- Ulcers from chronic illness, such as diabetes

- Use of steroids or other medications that affect the immune system
- Wounds from previous surgery
- Intravenous drug use

The symptoms and signs of cellulitis are:

- Discomfort/pain in the area of infection
- Fever and Chills
- Exhaustion (Fatigue)
- General ill feeling (Malaise)
- Muscle aches (myalgia)
- Heat in the area of the infection
- Drainage of pus/cloudy fluid from the area of the infection
- Redness, usually spreading towards torso
- Swelling in the area of infection (causing a sensation of tightness)
- Foul odor coming from the area of infection

Other, less common, symptoms that can occur with this disease:

- Hair loss at the site of infection
- Joint stiffness caused by swelling of the tissue over the joint
- Nausea and vomiting

Although the body can sometimes resolve cellulitis on its own, treatment usually includes the use of antibiotics; these can be topical, oral or intravenous. Most cellulitis will improve and disappear after a 10 – 14 day course of therapy with medications in the Penicillin, Eythromycin, or Cephalosporin (Keflex) families. Amoxicillin and Ampicillin are particularly popular.

Many of these are available in veterinary form without a prescription (see our section on stockpiling medications later in this volume). Acetaminophen (Tylenol) or Ibuprofen (Advil) is useful to decrease discomfort. Warm water soaks have been used for many years, along with elevation of infected extremities, for symptomatic relief. Over several days, you should see an improvement. It would be wise to complete the full 10-14 days of antibiotics to prevent any recurrences.

ABSCESSES (BOILS)

✚ ✚ ✚

An abscess is a pocket of pus. Pus is the debris left over from your body's attempt to eliminate an infection; it consists of white and red blood cells, live and dead organisms, and inflammatory fluid. The body's attempt to cure an infection is a good thing; However, abscesses or boils have a tendency to wall off the infection, which also makes it hard for antibiotics to penetrate. As such, you may have to intervene by performing a procedure.

To deal with an abscess, a route must be forged for the evacuation of pus. The easiest way to facilitate this is to place warm moist compresses over the area. This will help bring the infection to the surface of the skin, where it will form a "head" and perhaps drain spontaneously. This is called "ripening" the abscess. The abscess will become less hard and have a "whitehead" pimple at the likely point of exit.

If this fails to happen by itself over a few days, you may have to open the boil itself by a procedure called "incision and drainage" First, apply some ice to the area to help numb the skin. Then, using the tip of a scalpel (a number 11 blade is best), pierce the skin over the abscess where it is closest to the surface. The pus should drain freely, and your patient will probably experience immediate relief. Apply some triple antibiotic ointment to the skin surrounding the incision and cover with a clean bandage. Alternatives to triple antibiotic ointment could be:

- Lavender essential oil
- Tea Tree essential oil
- Raw Honey

MOSQUITO BORNE ILLNESSES

✚ ✚ ✚

Unlike the stings of bees or wasps, mosquito bites are common vectors of various infectious diseases. Anaphylaxis is rarely an issue here. The increased amount of time we will spend outside in a societal breakdown will increase the chances of spreading one or more of these problems.

Malaria is caused by a microscopic organism called a protozoan. When mosquitos get a meal by biting you, they inject these into your system which then inhabit your liver. From there, they go to your blood cells and other organs. By the way, only female mosquitos bite humans.

Symptoms of Malaria appear flu-like, and classically present as periodic chills, fever, and sweats. The patient becomes anemic as more blood cells are damaged by the protozoa. With times, periods between symptoms become shorter and permanent organ damage may occur.

Diagnosis of malaria cannot be confirmed without a microscope, but anyone experiencing relapsing fevers with severe chills and sweating should be considered candidates for treatment. The medications, among others, used for Malaria are Chloroquine, Quinine, and Quinidine. Sometimes, an antibiotic such as Doxycycline or Clindamycin is used in combination with the above. Physicians are usually sympathetic towards prescribing these medications to those who are contemplating trips to places where mosquitos are rampant, such as some underdeveloped countries.

Other mosquito-borne diseases include Yellow Fever, Dengue Fever, and West Nile Virus. The fewer mosquitos near your retreat, the less likely you will fall victim to one of these disease. You can decrease the population of mosquitos in your area and improve the likelihood of preventing illness by:

- Looking for areas of standing water that are breeding grounds. Drain all water that you do not depend on for survival.
- Monitoring the screens on your retreat windows and doors and repair any holes or defects.
- Being careful to avoid outside activities at dusk or dawn. This is the time that mosquitos are most active. Wear long pants and shirts whenever you venture outside.
- Have a good stockpile of insect repellants.

Plants that contain Citronella may be rubbed on your skin to discourage bites. Lemon balm, although having a fragrance similar to citronella, does not have the same bug-repelling properties. Despite its name, lemon balm is actually a member of the mint family. When you use an essential oil to repel insects, reapply frequently and feel free to combine oils as needed. Besides Citronella oil, you could use:

- Lemon Eucalyptus oil
- Cinnamon oil
- Peppermint oil
- Geranium oil
- Clove oil
- Rosemary oil

ATHLETE'S FOOT

✚ ✚ ✚

Athlete's foot (also known as "tinea pedis") is an infection of the skin caused by a type of fungus. This condition may be a chronic issue, lasting for years if not treated. Although usually seen between the toes, you might see it also on other parts of the feet or even on the hands (often between fingers). It should be noted that this problem is contagious, passed by sharing shoes or socks and even by wet surfaces.

Any fungal infection is made worse by moist conditions. People who are prone to Athlete's foot commonly:

- Spend long hours in closed shoes
- Keep their feet wet for prolonged periods
- Have had a tendency to get cuts on feet and hands
- Perspire a lot

To make a diagnosis, look for flaky skin between the toes or fingers. The skin may appear red and the nails discolored. Your patient will complain of itching and burning in the affected areas. If the skin has been traumatized by scratching, you might see some fluid drainage.

If the condition is mild, keeping your feet clean and dry may be enough to allow slow improvement of the condition.

Oftentimes, however, topical antifungal ointments or powders such as miconazole or clotrimazole are required for elimination of the condition. In the worst cases, oral prescription antifungals such as fluconazole (Diflucan) are needed. Don't use anti-itching creams very often, as it keeps the area moist and may delay healing.

A favorite home remedy for Athlete's Foot involves placing Tea Tree Oil liberally to a foot bath and soak for 20 minutes or so. Dry the feet well and then apply a few drops onto the affected area. Repeat this process twice daily. Try to keep the area as dry as possible otherwise.

For prevention of future outbreaks of Athlete's Foot, apply tea tree oil once a week before putting on socks and shoes.

SECTION 5

✚ ✚ ✚

ENVIRONMENTAL FACTORS

The focus of your medical training should be general, but also take into account the type of environment that you expect to live in if a societal collapse occurs. If you live in Miami, it's unlikely you'll be treating a lot of people with hypothermia. If you live in Siberia, it's unlikely you'll be treating a lot of people with heat stroke. Learn how to treat the likely medical issues for the area and situation that you expect to find yourself in.

Many environmental causes of illness are preventable with some planning. If you are in a hot environment, don't schedule major outdoor work sessions in the middle of the day. If you absolutely must work in the heat, provide a canopy or other protection against the sun, and be certain that everyone involved gets plenty of water. Failure to do this could lead to dehydration (mentioned in the last section), sunburns and increased likelihood of work injury.

Likewise, those in cold environments should take the weather into account when planning outdoor activities in order to avoid hypothermia issues, such as frostbite. Youngsters especially will run out into the cold without paying much attention to dressing warmly. If an adult has had too much to drink, impaired judgment may put them in jeopardy of suffering a cold-related event. Let's discuss these issues in more detail:

HEAT-RELATED MEDICAL ISSUES: HYPERTHERMIA

+ + +

If you live in an arid, hot climate like the desert southwest of the United States, you may find yourself working in the heat to perform activities of daily living. Given the circumstances, you may find yourself overheating. It will be important to consider preventative as well as curative methods to deal with hyperthermia.

The ill effects due to overheating are called heat exhaustion if mild to moderate, and heat stroke if severe. Heat exhaustion does not result in permanent damage, but heat stroke does; indeed, it can permanently disable its victim. Simply having muscle cramps or a fainting spell does not indicate a major heat-related medical event, unless there is a significant rise in the body's core temperature. You will see "heat cramps" often in children that have been running around on a hot day. Getting them out of the sun, massaging the affected muscles, and providing hydration will usually resolve the problem.

Heat exhaustion is characterized by:

- confusion
- mood swings
- rapid pulses
- nausea and vomiting
- diarrhea,
- headache and
- temperature elevations to as high as 105 degrees Fahrenheit

Heat stroke, in addition to all the possible signs and symptoms of heat exhaustion, will manifest with loss of consciousness, seizures, bleeding (seen in the urine or vomit), skin rashes, shock and a rise in temperature as high as 115 degrees! The patient also experiences dehydration; see the previous section on diarrheal disease to review this issue. Don't forget to replace electrolytes with oral rehydration solution. Needless to say, the patient may die from the condition if not treated.

You'll notice that the skin becomes red, not because it is burned, but because the blood vessels are dilating in an effort to dissipate some of the heat. The skin is also likely to be hot to the touch, but sweating is usually absent. This is due to the failure of the body's natural mechanism of sweating to release heat, which stops above 105 degrees Fahrenheit. In some circumstances, the patient's skin may actually seem cool; it is important to realize that it is the body CORE temperature that is elevated. A person in hyper thermic shock may feel "cold and clammy" to the touch, but taking a temperature with a thermometer will reveal the truth.

Using common sense, it is clear that the patient must be cooled off as soon as possible. The body makes efforts to cool down until it hits a temperature of 106 degrees or so. At that point, thermoregulation breaks down and the temperature can hit the roof. When the body can no longer cool itself, it will be up to you to take over.

The medic should remove the patient immediately from exposure to heat (e.g., the sun). The clothing should be removed and the patient should be drenched with cool water (and ice, if available). Elevate the legs above the level of the heart and head to allow blood flow to the brain. If you have only a small amount of ice, place packs in the armpits, neck and groin areas. Blood vessels run close to the skin in these places, and will transport cooler temperatures to the body core effectively. Immersion in a cold stream may be all you have in terms of a cooling strategy. If so, never leave the patient unattended.

Oral rehydration is useful, but only if the patient is awake and alert. If their mental status is impaired, they might aspirate the fluids into their lungs. If available, IV hydration would be used if a patient is unable to take in liquids. Fanning the patient will help with evaporation, which will dissipate the heat. Strangely, acetaminophen or ibuprofen is less helpful to lower temperature than you would think in this circumstance: they are meant to lower fevers caused by an infection, and they don't work as well if the fever was not caused by one.

If you can avoid dehydration, you will likely avoid heat exhaustion or heat stroke. Work or exercise in hot weather (especially by someone in poor physical condition) will easily lead to dehydration if the person does not take in at least 1 pint of water per hour. By the way, drinking water while exercising does not cause muscle cramps; in fact, drinking while exercising prevents heat-related illness as well as dehydration.

Wear clothing appropriate for the weather. Tightly swaddling an infant with blankets, simply because that is "what's done" with a baby, is a recipe for disaster in hot weather. The elderly are particularly prone to issues relating to overheating, and must be watched closely if exposed to the sun. Have everyone wear a head covering. A bandanna soaked in water would be effective. Much of the sweating we do comes from our face and head, so towel off frequently to aid in heat evaporation.

COLD-RELATED MEDICAL ISSUES: HYPOTHERMIA

✚ ✚ ✚

Hypothermia is a condition in which body core temperature drops below the temperature necessary for normal body function and metabolism. The normal body core temperature is defined as between 97.5-99.5 degrees Fahrenheit (36.0-37.5 degrees Celsius). Here are some common temperatures converted from Fahrenheit to Celsius:

Fahrenheit	Celsius
32	0
50	10
68	20
77	25
86	30
87.8	31
89.6	32
91.4	33
93.2	34
95	35
96.8	36
98.6	37
100.4	38
102.2	39
104	40
105.8	41
107.6	42
109.4	43

Once the body core cools down below 95 degrees Fahrenheit (35 degrees Celsius), the body kicks into action to make heat. The main mechanism for this is shivering. Muscles shiver to produce heat, and this will be the first symptom you're likely to see. As hypothermia worsens, more symptoms will become apparent if the patient is not warmed.

Aside from shivering, the most noticeable initial symptoms of hypothermia will be decreased mental status. The person may appear confused, uncoordinated, and lethargic. As the process worsens, speech may become slurred; the patient will appear apathetic or uninterested in helping themselves or may fall asleep. This occurs due to the effect of cooling temperatures on the brain; the colder the body gets, the slower the brain works. Brain function is supposed to cease at about 68 degrees Fahrenheit, although I have read of exceptional cases in which even lower temperatures resulted in full recovery.

The body loses heat in several ways. Heat radiates out of the body from unprotected surfaces. Most heat is lost from the head area, due to its large surface area and tendency to be uncovered. Direct contact with anything cold, especially over a large area of your body, will cause rapid cooling of your body core temperature. The classic example of this would be falling into cold water. In the Titanic sinking of 1912, hundreds of people fell into near-freezing water. Within 15 minutes, they were probably beyond medical help.

Wind removes body heat by carrying away the thin layer of warm air that exists at the surface of your skin. Wind chill is an important factor in causing heat loss. For example, if the outside temperature is 32 degrees F (0 C) and the wind chill factor is at 5 degrees F, your body loses heat as quickly as if the actual temperature outside was at five degrees F.

As with many other situations, the very young and the elderly are most at risk for hypothermia. Diabetics and those who suffer from low thyroid levels are also more at risk. One factor that most people don't take into account is the use of alcohol. Alcohol may give you a "warm" feeling, but it actually causes your blood vessels to expand, resulting in more rapid heat loss from the surface of your body. The body normally reacts to cold by constricting the blood vessels, so expansion would negate the body's efforts to stay warm. Alcohol also causes impaired judgment, which might cause those under the influence to choose clothing that would not protect them in cold weather. This also goes for various "recreational" drugs.

The diagnosis of hypothermia cannot be made with a standard rectal thermometer, which doesn't register below 94 degrees Fahrenheit (there are specific low temperature thermometers available, but will be scarce in a collapse). However, if you encounter a person in a cold environment who is confused and lethargic, and whose temperature does not register, you should assume the patient is hypothermic until proven otherwise.

If left untreated, hypothermia leads to complete failure of various organ systems and to death. People who develop hypothermia due to exposure to cold are also vulnerable to other cold-related injuries, such as frostbite and immersion foot.

Frostbite, or freezing of body tissues, usually occurs in the extremities and sometimes the ears and nose. Symptoms include a "pins and needles" sensation and numbness. Skin color changes from red to white to blue. If the color then changes to black, a condition known as "gangrene" has set in. Gangrene is the death of tissue resulting from loss of circulation. This usually results in the loss of the body part affected.

Immersion foot (formerly known as Trench Foot) causes damage to nerves and small blood vessels due to prolonged immersion in water. When seen in areas other than the feet, this condition is referred to as chilblains. Immersion foot appears similar to frostbite, but might have a more generally swollen appearance.

Rapid measures must be taken to reverse the ill effects of hypothermia. They are:

- Get the person out of the cold and into a warm, dry location. If you're unable to move the person out of the cold, shield him or her from the cold and wind as much as possible.
- Take off wet clothing. If the person is wearing wet clothing, remove them gently. Cover them with layers of dry blankets, including the head (leave the face clear). If you are outside, cover the ground to eliminate exposure to the cold surface.
- Monitor breathing. A person with severe hypothermia may be unconscious. Verify that the patient is breathing and check for a pulse. Begin CPR if necessary.
- Share body heat. To warm the person's body, remove your clothing and lie next to the person, making skin-to-skin contact. Then cover both of your bodies with blankets. Some people may cringe at this notion, but it's important to remember that you are trying to save a life. Gentle massage or rubbing may be helpful, but vigorous movements may traumatize the patient
- Give warm oral fluids. If the affected person is alert and able to swallow, provide a warm, nonalcoholic, non-caffeinated beverage to help warm the body. Remember, alcohol does not warm you up!
- Use warm, dry compresses. Use a first-aid warm compress (a fluid-filled bag that warms up when squeezed), or a makeshift compress of warm (not hot) water in a plastic bottle. Apply a compress only to the neck, chest wall or groin. These areas will spread the heat much better than putting warm compresses on the extremities, which sometimes worsens the condition.
- Don't apply direct heat. Don't use hot water, a heating pad or a heating lamp to warm the person. The extreme

heat can damage the skin or cause strain on the heart and even lead to cardiac arrest!

Frostbite or Immersion Foot is treated with a warm water (no more than 104 degrees F) soak of the affected extremity. Follow these tips when treating these conditions:

1. Don't allow thawed tissue to freeze again. The more often tissue freezes and thaws, the deeper the damage (think about what happens to a steak that goes from the freezer to outside and back again). If you can't prevent your patient from being exposed to freezing temperatures again, you should wait before treating, but not more than a day.

2. Don't rub or massage frostbitten tissue. Rubbing frostbitten tissue will result in damage to already injured tissues.

3. Don't use heat lamps or fires to treat frostbite. Your patient is numb and cannot feel the frostbitten tissue. Significant burns can ensue.

4. You can use body heat to thaw mild frostbite. You can put mildly frostbitten fingers under your arm, for example, to warm them up.

Prevention of Hypothermia

Remember the simple acronym C.O.L.D. This stands for: Cover, Overexertion, Layering, and Dry:

- Cover. Protect your head by wearing a hat. This will prevent body heat from escaping from your head. Instead of using gloves to cover your hands, use mittens. Mittens are more helpful than gloves because they keep your fingers in contact with one another. This conserves heat.
- Overexertion. Avoid activities that cause you to sweat a lot. Cold weather causes you to lose body heat quickly, and wet, sweaty clothing accelerates the process.
- Layering. Loose-fitting, lightweight clothing in layers insulate you well. Use clothing made of tightly woven,

water-repellent material for protection against the wind. Wool or silk inner layers hold body heat better than cotton does. Some synthetic materials work well, also.
- Dry. Keep as dry as you can. Get out of wet clothing as soon as possible. It's very easy for snow to get into gloves and boots, so pay particular attention to your hands and feet.

Cold-water Safety

Water doesn't have to be cold to cause hypothermia. Any water that's cooler than normal body temperature will cause heat loss. You could die of hypothermia off a tropical coast! To increase your chances of survival in cold water, do the following:

- Wear a life jacket. Whenever you're on a boat, wear a life jacket (did I really have to tell you?). A life jacket can help you stay alive longer by enabling you to float without using a lot of energy and by providing some insulation. The life jackets with built-in whistles are best.
- Keep your clothes on. While you're in the water, don't remove your clothing. Button or zip up. Cover your head if at all possible. The layer of water between your clothing and your body will help insulate you from the cold. Remove your clothing only after you're safely out of the water and do whatever you can to get dry and warm.
- Get out of the water, even if only partially. Get out of the water as much as possible, such as climbing onto a capsized boat or grabbing onto a floating object. However, don't use up energy swimming unless you have a dry place to swim to.
- Position your body to lessen heat loss. Use a body position known as the Heat Escape Lessening Position (think H.E.L.P.) to reduce heat loss while you wait for help to arrive. Hold your knees to your chest to protect your torso

- Huddle together. If you've fallen into cold water with others, keep warm by facing each other in a tight circle and holding on to each other.

Falling Through the Ice

How about if you're hiking in the wilderness and that snow field turns out to be the icy surface of a lake? Whenever you're in the wilderness, take a change of clothes in a waterproof container so that you'll have something dry to wear if the clothes you're wearing get wet. Also have a fire starter that will work even when wet.

You might be able to identify weak areas in the ice. If a thin area of ice on a lake is covered with snow, it tends to look darker than the surrounding area. Interestingly, bare ice without snow appears lighter! Beware of areas of contrasting color as you're walking.

Your body will react to a sudden immersion in cold water by increased pulse rate, blood pressure, and respirations. Keep calm. You have a few minutes to get out before you succumb to the effects of the cold.

Get your head out of the water by bending backward. Tread water and quickly get rid of any heavy objects that are weighing you down. Turn your body in the direction of where you came from; you know the ice was strong enough to hold you there.

Now, try to lift up out of the ice using your hands and arms. Kick with your feet to give you some forward momentum and to get more of your body out of the water. Lift a leg onto the ice and then lift and roll out onto the firmer surface. Do not stand up! Keep rolling in the direction that you were walking before you feel through. This will spread your weight out, instead of concentrating it on your feet. Then crawl until you're sure you're safe. Start working to get warm immediately.

ALTITUDE SICKNESS

✚ ✚ ✚

In a collapse situation, we might find ourselves having to move from a home at sea level to a retreat or "bug-out" location in the mountains. When this becomes necessary, it's likely that you will be moving fast. The rapid change in elevation will, for some, cause a condition known as Altitude Sickness or Acute Mountain Sickness (AMS). This occurs as a result of entering an area with lower oxygen availability without first acclimating oneself.

Although Altitude Sickness is usually a temporary condition, some patients may develop accumulation of fluid in the lungs (pulmonary edema) or brain (cerebral edema) which can be life-threatening. Altitude Sickness occurs most commonly at elevations approaching 8,000 feet above sea level, and is aggravated by exerting oneself.

You will usually see patients present to you with symptoms similar to a hangover or influenza. If mild, there will commonly be:

- Fatigue
- Insomnia
- Dizziness
- Headaches
- Nausea and Vomiting
- Lack of appetite
- Tachycardia (fast heart rate)
- Parethesia (pins and needles sensation)
- Shortness of breath

Those who will have major complications of Altitude Sickness will present with the following:

- Severe shortness of breath
- Confused and apathetic behavior
- Cough and chest congestion (not nasal)
- Cyanosis (blue or gray appearance of the skin, especially the fingertips and lips)
- Loss of coordination
- Dehydration
- Hemoptysis (coughing up blood)
- Loss of consciousness
- Fever (sometimes)

Like many illness, the best strategy against Altitude Sickness is prevention. Choose your route to your retreat so that the ascent is as gradual as possible. Do not attempt more than 2,000 feet of ascent per day. Ensure that your personnel do not over-exert themselves as they ascend, and provide lots of fresh water. Avoid the consumption of alcohol.

Treating Altitude Sickness first requires rest, if only to stop further ascent and allow more time to acclimate. If available, a portable oxygen tank will be useful upon onset of symptoms. A diet high in carbohydrates is thought to reduce ill effects.

A medication commonly used for both prevention and treatment is acetazolamide (Diamox). It helps the elimination of excess fluid from the body, and, thus, prevents the accumulation of fluid in the lungs or brain. This drug is superior to many other diuretics in that it also forces the kidneys to excrete bicarbonate. By increasing the amount of bicarbonate excreted, it makes the blood more acidic. Acidifying the blood stimulates ventilation, which increases the amount of oxygen in the blood. Usual dosages are 125 to 1,000 mg/day, usually starting a couple of days before the planned ascent.

Other medicines known to have a beneficial effect include the blood pressure medication Nifedipine and the steroid Decadron, especially in those with edema in the lungs and brain.

When you visit your physician, notify him that you are planning a trip into high elevations and would like to avoid altitude sickness. Usually, you will be given an acetazolamide prescription. The other medications mentioned will be more difficult to obtain, however.

There is some evidence that Gingko Biloba may be helpful in the natural prevention of altitude sickness. A small amount of an extract of this substance has been shown to allow the brain to tolerate lower oxygen levels. Native Americans have used Gingko for centuries with beneficial effect.

WILDFIRES AND SMOKE INHALATION

✚ ✚ ✚

Wildfire Preparedness

Many in the preparedness community either already have or are planning to have a rural retreat for when things go south. These fires mean that, if you're going to live or at least spend time in a remote location, you're going to have the responsibility to not only defend it from hordes of marauding zombies, but also acts of nature such as the occasional wildfire. Luckily, most of this involves something we Preppers have in abundance, and that is common sense.

One thing that's important is what we call "vegetation management". You'll want to direct fires away from your shelter. There are a few ways to do this: you'll want to clean up dead wood lying on the ground close to your buildings and off the roofs. Keep woodpiles and other flammables away from structures. Also, you'll have to remove some of the living vegetation from around your home. This is counter to some advice you'll get regarding keeping your home invisible, and it means that you'd have to remove those thorny bushes you've planted under your windows for defense. This can be a tough decision, but you just might have to make a choice between fire protection and privacy.

Another factor to consider is the material that your retreat is made of. How much fire resistance does your structure have? A wood frame home with wooden shingles will go up like a match in a wildfire. You should try to build as much flame resistance into your home as possible.

So, let's create a defensible space. A defensible space is an area around a structure where wood and vegetation are treated, cleared or reduced to slow the spread of wildfire towards a structure. Having a defensible space will also provide room to work for those fighting the fire.

The amount of defensible space you'll need depends on whether you're on flat land or on a steep slope. Flatland fires spread more slowly than a fire on a slope (hot air and flames rise). A fire on a steep slope with wind blowing uphill spreads fast and produces "spot fires". These are small fires that ignite vegetation ahead of the main burn, due to small bits of burning debris in the air.

You'll want to thin out those thick canopied trees near your house. Any nearby tree within 50 feet on flatland, or 200 feet if downhill from your retreat on top of the mountain, needs to be thinned, so that you're pruning branches off below 10-12 feet high, and separating them by 10-20 feet. Also, eliminate all shrubs at the base of the trunks.

Other things you should do:

1. Clean up all dead wood in the area.
2. Stack firewood at least 20 feet from any building.
3. Keep gardening tools and other items stored away.

Of course, once you have a defensible space, the natural inclination is to want to defend it, even against a forest fire. Unfortunately, you have to remember that you'll be in the middle of a lot of heat and smoke. Unless you're a 20 year old Navy Seal in full fire gear and mask, you're probably not going to be able to function effectively. The safest recommendation would be to hit the road if there's a safe way out. It's a personal decision, but it should also be a realistic decision.

If you're leaving, have your supplies already in the car, as well as any important papers you might need to keep and some cash. Make sure you shut off any air conditioning system that draws air into the house from outside. Turn off all your appliances, close all your windows and lock all your doors. Like any other emergency, you should have some form of communication open with your loved ones so that you can contact each other. Don't forget to bring some eye wash; smoke will irritate your eyes.

If there is any possibility that you might find yourself in the middle of a fire, make sure you're dressed in long pants and sleeves and heavy boots. A wool blanket is very helpful as an additional outside layer because wool is relatively fire-resistant. If you don't have wool blankets, this is a good time to add some to your storage, or keep some in your car. If you're in a building, stay on the side of the building farthest from the fire outside. Choose a room with the least number of windows (windows transfer heat to the inside).

Stay there unless you have to leave due to smoke or the building catching fire. If that's the case and you have to leave, wrap yourself in that blanket, leaving only your eyes uncovered. Some people think it's a good idea to wet it first. Don't! Wet materials transfer heat much faster than dry materials and will cause more severe burns. If you're having trouble breathing because of the smoke, stay low, and crawl out of the building if you have to. There's less smoke and heat the lower you go. Keep your face down towards the floor. This will protect your airway.

If you encounter a person that is actually on fire, you have to act quickly. In circumstances where a person's clothes are on fire, remember the old adage "Stop, Drop, and Roll".

- **Stop:** Your patient will be panicked and likely running around trying to put out the flames. This generates wind which will fan the flames. Stop the patient from running away.
- **Drop:** Knock the patient to the ground and wrap tightly with a wool blanket. Heavy fabrics are best.
- **Roll:** Roll the patient on the floor under the flames are extinguished. Immediately cool any burned areas of skin with copious amounts of water.

Smoke Inhalation

Other than burns, which are discussed in another part of this handbook, you can become seriously ill or even die from simple smoke inhalation. Remember, you can heal from burns on your skin, but you can't heal from burns in your lungs. The scars from the burns will damage the lungs' ability to absorb Oxygen. Common causes include:

- Simple Combustion: Combustion uses up Oxygen near a fire and can kill a person simply from Oxygen deficit. The larger the fire, the more oxygen it removes from the area. This is particularly troublesome in a building fire.
- Carbon Dioxide: Some by-products of smoke may not directly kill a person, but could take up the space in the lungs that Oxygen would ordinarily use. Even the expulsion of a large bubble of Carbon Dioxide can kill wildlife near it, such as in the example of "swamp gas".
- Chemical irritants: Many chemicals founds in smoke can cause irritation injury when they come in contact with

the lung membrane. This amounts to a burn inside the lung tissue, which causes swelling and airway obstruction. Chlorine gas used in World War I is an example of a deadly chemical irritant.

- Other asphyxiants: Carbon Monoxide, Cyanide, and some Sulfides may interfere with the body ability to utilize oxygen. Carbon monoxide is the most common of these.

Symptoms may include:

- Cough
- Shortness of breath
- Hoarseness
- Upper airway spasm
- Eye irritation
- Headaches
- Pale, bluish or even bright red skin
- Loss of consciousness leading to coma or death

Your evaluation of the patient with smoke inhalation may show soot in the throat and nasal passages. Both of these areas may be swollen and irritated. They will likely to be short of breath and have a hoarse voice.

Of course, you will want to get your patient out of the smoky area and into an environment where there is clean air. This may not be as easy as it seems. You must be very careful not to put yourself in a situation where you are likely to succumb to smoke inhalation yourself. Always consider a surgical mask or even a gas mask before entering a conflagration to rescue a victim. Be prepared to use CPR if necessary. It is important to have some way to deliver oxygen to your patient if needed. There are many portable commercially-available canisters which would be useful to get oxygen quickly into the lungs.

Don't expect a rapid recovery from significant smoke inhalation. Your patient will be short of breath with the slightest activity and will be very hoarse. These symptoms may go away with time, or may be permanent disabilities.

Prevention by planning escape routes and having regular drills will allow your people to get out of dangerous situations quickly. Know what to do before things happen.

STORM PREPAREDNESS

✚ ✚ ✚

There are few people who haven't been in the path of a major storm at one point or another. If you fail to plan ways to protect yourself and your family, you may find yourself having to treat significant traumatic injuries in the immediate aftermath. Later, flooding may contaminate your water supplies and expose you to serious infectious disease. Preparing to weather the storm safely will avoid major medical problems for you, as medic, later on.

A tornado is a violently rotating column of air that is in contact with both the surface of the earth and the storm cloud that spawned it. From a distance tornadoes, (also called twisters) usually appear in the form of a visible dark funnel with all sorts of flying debris in and around it. Because of rainfall, they may be difficult to see when close up. A tornado may have winds of up to 300 miles per hour, and can travel for a number of kilometers or miles before petering out. They may be accompanied by hail and will emit a roaring sound that will remind you of a passing train.

If you see a twister funnel, take shelter immediately. If your domicile is a mobile home, leave; they are especially vulnerable to damage from the winds. Find a place where family members can gather if a tornado is headed your way. A basements, bathrooms, closets or inside rooms without windows are the best options. Windows can easily shatter from impact due to flying debris. For added protection, get under a heavy object such as a table. Covering up your body with a sleeping bag or mattress will provide an additional shield.

If you are caught outside when the tornado hits, stay away from wooded areas. Although you may be hesitant to leave your vehicle, remember that they can be easily tossed around by the winds. Lying down flat in a low spot in the ground will give you some protection. Make sure to protect your head if at all possible.

Unlike tornados, which can pop up with little or no notice, hurricanes are first identified when they are thousands of miles away. If our long distance weather warning system ever fails, even a moderate storm can cause major loss of life. Despite this, if your family has a plan of action for hurricanes, even a large storm can be just a bump in the road, not the end of the road.

A hurricane is defined as a tropical system of strong thunderstorms with circular surface circulation and maximum sustained winds of 74 mph or higher. Unlike some collapse scenarios, you can actually outrun one of these storms if you get enough of a head start. That's actually one of your most important decisions: Should you leave the area?

If you live on the coast or in an area that floods often, rising waters (the storm "surge") might be enough of an issue to do so. If you live in a mobile home, you will most likely be told to evacuate by the authorities. Oftentimes there will be hurricane-resistant public buildings in your community that will be designated official shelters.

Hurricanes are categorized according to the strength of their winds by the Saffir-Simpson Hurricane Wind Scale:

- Category 1: 74-95 mph sustained winds
- Category 2: 96-110 mph sustained winds
- Category 3: 111-130 mph sustained winds
- Category 4: 131-154 mph sustained winds
- Category 5: 155 mph sustained winds or greater

If you leave the area, plan to go as far inland as possible. Hurricanes get their strength from the warm water temperatures over the tropical ocean; they lose strength quickly as they travel over land. To paraphrase an old saying: If you live on the Florida peninsula, "Head North, Young Man"! The state is relatively thin and winds will still be strong, even inland.

Usually, you will not be told to leave your homes (except in the cases mentioned above). As such, your planning will determine how much damage you sustain and how much risk you place yourself in. You should have an idea of what your home's weak spots are. Do you know what amount of sustained wind your structure can withstand? New homes in South Florida must have the strength to withstand 125 mph winds. Most homes, however, are made to handle 90 mph. If the coming storm has sustained winds over that level, you might consider hitting the road.

If you decide to stay, make sure you designate a safe room somewhere in the interior of the house. It should be in the area most downwind from the direction the hurricane is hitting you. Figure out who's coming to ride out the storm with you, and plan for any special needs they may have. Follow the instructions listed above for tornadoes.

After the storm, inland flood water will usually be polluted. Do not walk around in, drink nor bathe in this water. Thorough sterilization is required. Do not eat fresh food that has come in contact with floodwater; if cans of food have been exposed to the water, wash them off with soap and clean hot water before opening.

Also, watch for downed power lines; they have been the cause of a number of electrocutions. In some cases, entire families have lost their lives jumping into electrified water to save a relative. You should never touch someone who has been electrocuted without first shutting off the power source; if you can't shut off the power, you will have to move the victim. Use a nonmetal object, such as a wooden broom handle or dry rope. If you don't, the current could pass through the individual's body and shock you.

RADIATION SICKNESS

✚ ✚ ✚

You have probably heard about the nuclear plant meltdowns in Chernobyl and Fukushima. Meltdowns can occur as a result of damage caused by natural disasters, such as earthquakes or tsunamis. They can also be caused by human error or terrorist attack. Regardless of the cause, the release of radiation into the atmosphere has significant implications for populations living both near and far from the event.

This radiation is known as "fallout". Fallout is the particulate matter (dust) that is thrown into the air by a nuclear explosion. This dust travels on the prevailing winds, and can travel hundreds (if not thousands) of miles downwind, coating fields, livestock, and people with radioactive material. The higher the fallout goes into the atmosphere, the farther it will travel downwind. This material contains substances that are hazardous if inhaled or ingested, like Radioiodine, Cesium and Strontium. Even worse, fallout is absorbed by the animals and plants that make up our food supply. In large enough amounts, it is hazardous to our health.

The good news is that radiation from a nuclear power plant meltdown usually doesn't make it as high up in the sky as, let's say, a mushroom cloud from an atomic bomb. The worst effects will be felt by those in the area of the reactors. Lighter particles, like radioactive iodine, will travel the farthest, and are the main concern for those far from the actual explosion or meltdown.

The level of radiation in an area depends on the distance that it has to travel from the meltdown, and the time it took for the radiation to arrive. As medical provider, you should spend some time planning how to protect your people from exposure.

Radiation exposure is measured in "RADs". A RAD measures the amount of radiation energy transferred to some mass of material, typically humans. The medical effects of exposure are collectively known as "radiation sickness" or "Acute Radiation Syndrome" . A certain amount of radiation exposure is tolerable over time, but your goal is to shelter your group as much as possible.

These are the effects on humans of different amounts of total radiation exposure:

30-70 RADS: Mild headache or nausea within several hours of exposure. Full recovery is expected.

70-150 RADS: Mild nausea and vomiting in a third of patients. Decreased wound healing and increased susceptibility to infection. Full recovery is expected.

150-300 RADS: Moderate nausea and vomiting in a majority of patients. Fatigue and weakness in half of patients. Infection and/or bleeding due to a decreased immune response. Medical care will be required for some, especially those with burns or wounds. Occasional deaths at 300 RADS exposure may occur.

300-500 RADS: Moderate nausea and vomiting, fatigue, and weakness in most patients. diarrheal stools, dehydration, loss of appetite, skin breakdown, infection will be common. Hair loss is visible in most over time. At high end of exposure, a 50% death rate is expected. Medical care is required for majority of patients.

Over 500 RADS: Spontaneous bleeding, fever, anorexia, stomach and intestinal ulcers, bloody diarrhea, dehydration, low blood pressure, infections, and hair loss is anticipated in almost all patients. Death rates approach 100%.

These effects are related to exposure over time, and symptoms are noted over the course of time. Hair loss, for example, will appear at 10-14 days. Deaths may occur weeks after the exposure.

Your goal is to prevent exposures of over 100 RADS in the early going. A radiation dosimeter will be useful to gauge radiation levels and is widely available for purchase. This item will give you an idea of your risks for radiation sickness.

There are three basic ways of decreasing the total dose of radiation:

1) Limit the time unprotected. Radiation absorbed is dependent on the time spent in the radiation. Leave areas where high levels are detected and you are without adequate shelter. The activity of radioactive particles decreases over time. After 24 hours, levels usually drop to 1/10 of their previous value or less.

2) Increase the distance from the radiation. Radiation disperses over distance and the effects will be decreased. To make an analogy, you have less chance of drowning the farther away you are from deep water.

3) Shield people to decrease radiation where they are. Shielding will decrease exposure exponentially, so it is important to know how to construct a shelter that will provide a barrier between your people and the source. A dense material will give better protection that a light material.

Barrier effectiveness is measured in "halving thickness". This is the thickness of a particular shield material that will reduce gamma radiation (the most dangerous kind) by one half. When you multiply the having thickness, you multiply your protection. For example, the halving thickness of concrete is 2.4 inches or 6 centimeters. A barrier of 2.4 inches of concrete will drop exposure to one half. Doubling the thickness of the barrier drops it to one fourth (1/2 x 1/2) and tripling it will drop it to one eighth (1/2 x 1/2 x 1/2) the exposure, etc. Ten halving thicknesses will drop the total to 1/1024.

Here are the halving thicknesses of some common materials:

- Lead: 0.4 inches or 1 centimeter
- Steel: 1 inch or 2.5 centimeters
- Concrete: 2.4 inches or 6 centimeters
- Soil (packed):   3.6 inches or 9 centimeters
- Water: 7.2 inches or 18 centimeters
- Wood: 11 inches or 30 centimeters

Emergency treatment of radiation sickness involves dealing with the symptoms. Antibiotics may be helpful to treat infections, fluids for dehydration, and anti-nausea agents like Zofran (Ondansetron). In severely ill patients, stem cell transplants and multiple transfusions are indicated but will not be options in a collapse situation. This underscores the importance of an adequate shelter.

There is protection against some of the long term effects of radiation, however. Potassium Iodide (known by the chemical symbol KI) is a 130 mg tablet that prevents radioactive Iodine from damaging the specific organ that it targets, the thyroid gland. Radioactive Iodine is the most common component in fallout that is not in the immediate area of the nuclear event.

Taking KI 1/2 hour to 24 hours prior to a radiation exposure will prevent the eventual epidemic of thyroid cancer that will result if no treatment is given. In the 1986 Chernobyl nuclear meltdown, excessive radiation caused more than 4,000 cases of thyroid cancer, mostly in children and adolescents, with more expected in the coming years.

Although there is a small amount of KI in ordinary iodized salt, not enough is present to confer any protection by ingesting it. It would take 250 teaspoons of household iodized salt to equal one Potassium Iodide tablet!

If radiation exposure is expected, take the KI tablet once a day for 7-10 days, or longer if prolonged or multiple exposures are expected. Children should take 1/2 doses. It is also recommended to consider 1/2 tablet for large dogs, and 1/4 tablet for small dogs and cats. The largest commercial retailer for KI tablets is KI4U.com.

Don't depend on supplies of the drug to be available after a nuclear event. Even the federal government will have little KI in reserve to give to the general population. In recent power plant meltdowns, there was little or no Potassium Iodide to be found anywhere for purchase.

If you find yourself without a supply, consider this alternative: 2% tincture of Iodine solution (brand name Betadine). "Paint" 8 ml of Betadine on the abdomen or forearm 2-12 hours prior to a radiation exposure and re-apply daily; this will allow it to be absorbed through the skin and should give protection against radioactive Iodine in fallout. Apply 4 ml. on children 3 and older (but under 150 lbs./70 kg.). Toddlers should have 2ml painted on, and infants 1 ml. This strategy should also work on animals. If you don't have a way to measure in ml, remember that a standard teaspoon is about 5 milliliters. Discontinue the daily treatment after 3 days or when RadioIodine levels have fallen to safer levels.

Every Prepper should have Betadine or other Iodine solution in their supplies; it serves as an excellent antiseptic for skin, in the event of an injury. Be aware that those who are allergic to seafood will probably be allergic to Iodine. Adverse reactions may occur with medications such as diuretics and Lithium, so consult your doctor before a disaster to see if it is safe for you and your loved ones. It is also important to note that you cannot drink Betadine, as it is poisonous if ingested

SECTION 6

✚ ✚ ✚

INJURIES AND REACTIONS

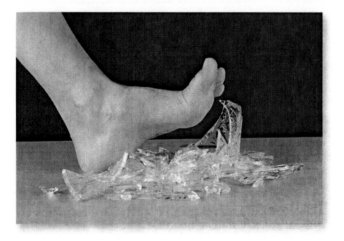

INJURIES TO SOFT TISSUES

✚ ✚ ✚

In a collapse situation, the performance of tasks like chopping wood, cooking food, etc. will likely lead to a number of soft tissue injuries (those that do not involve bony structures). From a simple cut to a severe burn, any damage to skin is akin to a chink in your body's protective armor. Skin is the largest organ in the body, and serves as a barrier against infection and loss of fluids. When this barrier is weakened by a laceration, your health is in jeopardy. Rapid and effective treatment of these injuries will prevent them from becoming life-threatening.

Being the rugged individualists that they are, Preppers may be likely to shrug off minor injuries as inconsequential. This couldn't be farther from the truth. Any minor injury has the potential to cause trouble down the road. As a healthcare provider, you must monitor the progress of healing of even the slightest cut or scrape. With close observation, your people will have the best chance of staying out of trouble when it comes to wounds.

MINOR WOUNDS

✚ ✚ ✚

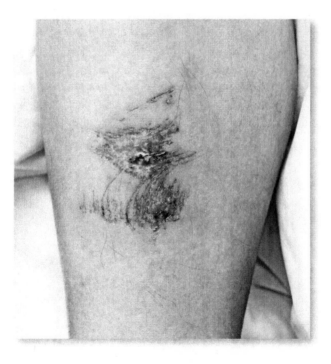

A soft tissue injury is considered minor when it fails to penetrate the deep layer of the skin, called the "Dermis". This would include cuts, scrapes and bruises.

- Cuts and Scratches: These tears in the skin only penetrate the epidermis (superficial skin layer) and become infected on an infrequent basis.
- Abrasions or Scrapes: A portion of the epidermis has been scraped off. You probably have experienced plenty of these as a child.
- Bruises or Contusions: These result from blunt trauma and do not penetrate the skin at all. However, there is bleeding into the skin from blood vessels that have been disrupted by the impact.

All of the above minor injuries can be treated by simply washing anywhere that the epidermis has been violated. The use of an antiseptic such as Betadine (Povidone-Iodine solution), honey, or triple antibiotic ointment such as Neosporin or Bactroban will be helpful to prevent infection. Applying pressure and ice wherever a bruise seems to be spreading will stop it from getting bigger. These injuries will heal over the next 7-10 days, dependent on the amount of skin area affected. Minor bleeding can be stopped with a wet styptic pencil. The wound, if it broke the skin, should have a protective adhesive bandage (Band-Aid) to prevent infection.

The Liquid Skin bandage is an excellent way to cover a minor injury with some advantages over a regular bandage. You apply it once to the cut or scrape; it dries within a minute or so and seals the wound. It also stops minor bleeding, and won't fall out during baths. There are various brands, such as Band-Aid Liquid Bandage, New Skin, Curad, and 3M No Sting liquid bandage. Many come as a convenient spray.

You don't always have to travel the traditional road to treat many medical problems. If you have one of the minor injuries mentioned, why not consider natural remedies? Here's an alternative process to deal with these issues:

1. Evaluate seriousness of wound; if minor, you may continue with herbal treatment.
2. Stop minor bleeding with herbal hemostatics and compress the area with gauze. Hemostatic agents help the blood to clot. Some natural substances that are reported to have this effect:

   - Essential oils- Geranium, Helichrysum, Lavender, Cypress, Myrrh, or Hyssop- Any oil applied to a gauze compress will help.
   - Medicinal Herbs- Cayenne pepper powder or cinnamon powder with direct application, Yarrow tincture soaked in a gauze compress.

3. After minor bleeding is stopped, Clean wound with an herbal antiseptic: Essential oils with this property include lavender, tea tree, rosemary, eucalyptus, and peppermint. Mix a few drops of oil with sterile water and wash out the wound thoroughly.
4. Apply Antiseptic to the wound using above essential oils; for example, use peppermint oil in a 50/50 mix with carrier oils such as olive or coconut oil. Other natural antiseptics include garlic, raw honey, Echinacea, witch hazel, and St. John's Wort.
5. If needed, use natural pain relievers: Essential oils of geranium, helichrysum, ginger, rosemary or oregano have these properties. Apply 2-4 drops of a 50/50 dilution around the wound's edges.
6. Dress the wound using clean gauze. Do not wrap too tightly.
7. Change dressing, reapply antiseptic, and observe for infection twice daily until healed

HEMORRHAGIC AND MAJOR WOUNDS

✚ ✚ ✚

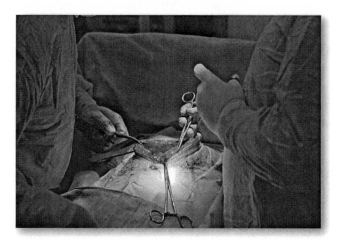

Cuts in the skin can be minor or catastrophic, superficial or deep, clean or infected. Most significant cuts (also called 'lacerations') penetrate both the dermis and epidermis and are associated with bleeding, sometimes major. Bleeding can be venous in origin, which manifests as dark red blood, draining steadily from the wound. Bleeding can also be arterial, which is bright red (due to higher oxygen content) and comes out in spurts that correspond to the pulse of the patient. As the vein and artery run together, a serious cut can have both.

The effect on the body caused by blood loss varies with the amount of blood loss incurred:

- 1.5 pints (0.75 liters) or less: little or no effect.
- 1.5-3.5 pints (0.75-1.5 liters): rapid heartbeat and respirations. The skin becomes cool and may appear pale. The patient is usually very agitated.
- 3.5-4 pints (1.5-2 liters): Blood pressure begins to drop; the patient may appear confused. Heartbeat is usually very rapid.
- Over 4 pints (more than 2 liters): Patient is now very pale, and may be unconscious. After a period of time with continued blood loss, the blood pressure drops further, the heart rate and respirations decrease, and the patient is close to death.

When you encounter a person with a bleeding wound, the first course of action is to stop the hemorrhage. Oftentimes, direct pressure on the bleeding area might stop bleeding all by itself. The medic should always have nitrile gloves in his or her pack; this will prevent the wound from contamination by a "dirty" hand. Try to avoid touching the palm or finger portions of the gloves as you put them on. If there are no gloves, grab a bandanna or other barrier and press it into the wound. Additionally, pressing on the "pressure point" for the area injured will help slow bleeding.

Pressure points are locations where major arteries come close enough to the skin to be compressed by pressure. Pressing on this area will slow down bleeding further down the track of the blood vessel. Therefore, we can make a "map" of specific areas to concentrate your efforts to decrease bleeding. For example, there is a large blood vessel behind each knee known as the Popliteal Artery. If you have a bleeding wound in the lower leg, say your calf, applying pressure on the back of the knee will help stop the hemorrhage. A diagram of the major pressure points is below:

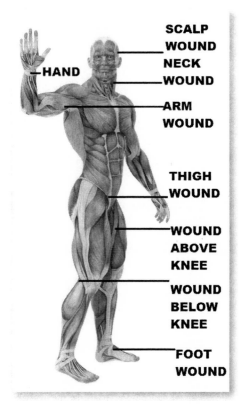

If this fails to stop the bleeding, it may be appropriate to use a tourniquet. The military uses a CAT tourniquet, which is simple to use and could be even be placed with one hand. It is important to note that the tourniquet, once placed, should be loosened every ten minutes or so, to allow blood flow to uninjured areas and to determine whether the bleeding has stopped. Tourniquets are painful if they are in place for too long, and prolonged use could actually cause your patient to lose a limb due to lack of circulation. As well, your body will build up toxins in the extremity; these become concentrated and rush into your body core when you release the tourniquet. It takes less than an hour or two with a tourniquet on to cause this problem.

Once you are comfortable that major bleeding has abated, remove the tourniquet. Irrigate the wound gently with sterile water or a 1:10 Betadine solution. Packing the wound with bandages is useful to apply pressure (they're not just for sopping up the blood). More than one bandage may be required to keep the wound from bleeding further. It's important to make sure that you put the most pressure where the bleeding was occurring in the wound. If the blood was coming from the top of the wound, start packing there. Again, keep compressing the wound.

Now, cover the whole area with a dry dressing for further protection. The Israeli army developed an excellent bandage which is easy to use and is found almost everywhere survival gear is sold. The advantage of the Israel battle dressing is that it applies pressure on the bleeding area for you. Don't forget that bandages get dirty and should be changed often. Twice a day is a minimum until it has healed.

The above process of stopping hemorrhage and dressing a wound will also work for traumatic injuries such as knife wounds and gunshot wounds. You have probably heard that you should not remove a knife because it can cause the hemorrhage to worsen. This will give you time to get the patient to the hospital, but what if there are no hospitals? You will have to transport your victim to your base camp and prepare to remove the knife. It can't stay in there for months while you're waiting for society to stabilize. Having substances that promote clotting will be useful here.

Bullet wounds are the opposite, in that the bullet is usually removed if at all possible when modern medical care is available. In a collapse situation, you will want to avoid digging for the bullet as it can cause further contamination and bleeding. For a historical example, take the case of President James Garfield. In 1881, President Garfield was shot by an assassin. In their rush to remove the bullet, 12 different physicians placed their (ungloved) hands in the wound. The wound, which would not have been mortal in all probability, became infected; the president died after a month in agony. Think twice before removing a projectile that isn't clearly visible and easily reached

In particularly heavy bleeding, the use of hemostatic powders such as Celox or Quik-Clot will help stop the hemorrhage. These products also come in "combat gauze", which is a bandage impregnated with the powder. Of course, if there is injury to bony structures, more intensive treatment will be necessary, and will be covered later. An alternative that might be helpful to control bleeding is Cayenne Pepper powder. I would recommend it for use in cases where the bleeding is not life-threatening. It should be noted that there is a risk of a minor burn using hemostatic agents in wounds.

Back to bandages: Wound dressings must be changed regularly (at least twice a day or whenever the bandage is saturated with blood, fluids, etc.) in order to give the best chance for quick healing. Whenever you change a dressing, it is important to clean the wound area with boiled water (cooled) or an antiseptic solution such as dilute Betadine (povidone-iodine). Use 1 part Betadine to 10 parts water. Remember the old saying, "The solution to pollution is dilution"! Using a bulb syringe will provide a little pressure to the flow of water (also called irrigation), and wash out old clots and dirt. Lightly scrub any wound that is open with diluted Betadine or even sterilized water. You may notice some bleeding restarting; apply pressure with a clean bandage until it stops.

It may also be a good idea to apply some triple antibiotic ointment around a healing wound to prevent infection from bacteria on the skin. Raw honey, lavender oil, and tea tree oil are some natural alternatives.

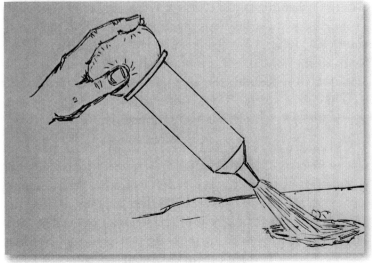

Irrigating the wound

As time goes on, you might see some blackish material on the wound edges. This is non-viable material and should be removed. It might just scrub out, or you might need to take your scissors and trim off the dead tissue. This is called debridement and removes material that is no longer part of the healing process.

There is always some controversy as to whether to close a wound. A laceration may be closed either by suture, tape, staples or a medical "superglue" such as Derma-Bond. When would you choose to close a wound, and what method should you use?

As Shakespeare might have said, "To stitch or not to stitch, that is the question"! After basic first aid is rendered, which includes removal of any foreign objects, hemostasis (stopping the bleeding), irrigation, and antiseptic application, you will need to assess a few things to determine the answer. The following section is a primer on wound closure....

A STITCH IN TIME...

✚ ✚ ✚

In a collapse situation, we will all be performing tasks that are not part of our daily routine. Few of us are required to chop wood for fuel at present, for example, but it might be standard operating procedure if things go south. Performing strenuous work that we're unaccustomed to could easily lead to injury. We're also going to expose ourselves to risk of injury in other ways, just by being out in the wild.

A sharp injury is known as a laceration. When we receive a cut, our body's natural armor (our skin) is breached and bacteria get a free ride to the rest of our body. Once there, our health is in real danger. Therefore, it only makes common sense that we want to close that breach.

I am asked to teach suturing more than any other first aid procedure, even though it really isn't FIRST aid at all. Suturing is best done by someone with experience, and you don't get that kind of experience in your typical first responder course. Survival medical training teaches you to stabilize and transfer the patient to modern facilities. But what about if there is no modern care available, as in a collapse? What if YOU are the end of the line when it comes to medical care? You'll need to obtain the knowledge to be able to function effectively, and that means knowing how to close a wound.

Human skin has probably been sutured ever since we learned to make needles from bone 30,000 years ago. If you can sew animal skins together, why not human skin? The first documentation of suturing was from the Egyptians 5,000 years ago, and actual stitches have been found in mummies more than 3,000 years old. The Greeks and Romans, as well as various native cultures, also worked with sutures. Using needles of bone, ivory and copper, they would use various natural materials such as hemp, flax, cotton, silk, hair and animal sinew to put wounds together. The classical era physician Galen, in the 2nd century A.D., was well known for stitching together the severed tendons and ligaments of gladiators, sometimes restoring function to a damaged extremity. He was one of the first to distinguish between a "clean" and a "dirty" wound.

In primitive cultures, ingenious ways were developed to close wounds. In some tropical rain forests, the natives would collect army ant soldiers whenever there was a wound to close. They would place the jaws of the ant on the skin, the ant would bite the skin closed, and then they would twist its body off! The head stayed on, with the jaws shut and the skin closed. Native Americans would pull off agave cactus needles along with a strip of the plant material attached, and use that as suture.

Suture technology didn't really advance much until the late 19th century, when the concept of sterilization of needles and suture material came into fashion. By this time, suture material was either "chromic catgut", actually made from the intestinal lining of sheep and cows, or silk. Both of these materials are still available today in one form or another.

Suture "string" is either absorbable or non-absorbable. "Catgut", for example, will dissolve in the body over the course of several weeks. Absorbable sutures are used for internal body work or areas such as the inside of the cheek or the vagina. Silk is non-absorbable, and is used on the skin (where it can be eventually removed) or anywhere internally that you are willing to have the suture material stay forever. Around 1930, synthetic materials made their debut in the form of Nylon and polypropylene (Prolene). These are non-absorbables that are also available to this day and are, essentially, like fishing line. Since that time, various different manufactured types of suture material have reached the market, both absorbable (the popular Vicryl) and non-absorbable.

Needles have progressed, also. Needles can be straight, curved, or various other shapes. Originally, needles were "eyed" and separate from the string. You threaded the needle and began your stitching, which caused two lengths of suture to go through the wound. This process caused some trauma to the tissues sutured, and so this type of needle is called a "traumatic" needle.

In 1920, a process called "swaging" was developed, which allowed the back end of the needle to be attached to the string. The diameter of the string was slightly thinner than the needle and only one single length of suture was passed through the tissue; this type of needle was named "atraumatic". Some swaged needles are built to "pop-off" with a quick tug after placing each stitch. This may be handy, but it is incredibly wasteful of suture material; therefore, I can only discourage its use in a collapse situation.

Needles are also categorized based on the point. The two most common needle points are "tapered" and "cutting", although there are various others. One is round and "tapers" smoothly to a point, like a sharpened pencil does. "Cutting" needles are triangular and have a sharp "cutting" edge on the inside curve of the needle. Cutting needles are used in dense tissue.

Now that we are acquainted with sutures, we must ask ourselves the following question: What am I trying to accomplish by stitching this wound closed? Your goals are simple. You close wounds to repair the defect in your body's armor, to eliminate "dead space" layers, and to promote healing. A well-approximated wound also has less scarring. However, here is where it gets complicated. Closing a wound that should be left open can do a lot more harm than good, and could possibly put your patient's life at risk! You will have to consider several factors before you proceed to suture a wound.

The most important consideration is whether you are dealing with a clean or a dirty wound. Most wounds you will encounter in a wilderness or collapse setting will be dirty. If you try to close a dirty wound, you have sequestered bacteria and dirt into your body. Within a short period of time, the wound will become red, swollen, and hot. An abscess may form, and pus will accumulate inside.

The infection may spread to your bloodstream and, when it does, you have caused a life-threatening situation. Leaving the wound open will allow you to clean the inside frequently and observe the healing process. It also allows inflammatory fluid to drain out of the body. Wounds that are left open heal by granulation; that is, from the inside out. The scar isn't as pretty, but it's the safest option in most cases.

Other considerations when deciding whether or not to close a wound are whether it is a simple laceration (straight thin cut on the skin) or whether it is an avulsion (areas of skin torn out, hanging flaps). If the edges of the skin are so far apart that they cannot be stitched together without tearing from the pressure, leave it open. If the wound has been open for more than 8 hours, it should be left open; bacteria have already had a good chance to colonize.

IF you're certain the wound is clean, you should close it if it is long, deep or gapes open loosely. Also, cuts over moving parts, such as the knee joint, will be more likely to require stitches. Remember that you should close deep wounds in layers, to prevent any un-approximated "dead space" from occurring. Dead spaces are pockets of air in a poorly sutured wound that may lead to a major infection.

Many injuries that require closure also should be treated with antibiotics to decrease the chance of infection. Natural remedies such as garlic or honey may be useful in a collapse situation. Nylon fishing line has also been improvised to serve as suture string. Deep layer sutures are never removed, so try to use absorbable material such as "catgut" or Vicryl. Silk, Nylon or Prolene sutures on the skin should be removed in 7 days; if over a joint, 10 – 14 days. Stitches placed over a joint, such as the knee, should be placed close together. In other areas, ½ inch between sutures is acceptable. Always be certain to keep the wound clean.

Don't forget that there is more than one way to stitch a cat! There are several methods available to close a laceration. The simplest and least invasive is to use Steri-Strips and butterfly closures. They are sterile strips which adhere on each side of the wound to pull it together. They don't require puncturing the skin and will fall off on their own, in time.

The second least invasive method is Cyanoacrylate, special "glue" sold as Derma-Bond or Liquiseal. This is medical- grade adhesive that is made specifically for use on the skin. Simply approximate the skin and run a thin line of glue down the laceration. It will naturally peel off as the skin heals. Some have recommended (the much less expensive) household "Super-Glue" for wound closure. This preparation is slightly different chemically, and is not made for use on the skin. It may cause skin irritation in some, and burn-like reactions have been reported. If it's all you have, you may choose to use it.

Another closure method is the use of skin staplers. They work by "pinching" the skin together (similar to the ancient army ant method) and should be removed in about 7 days. These are best removed with a specific instrument known as a staple remover.

These are widely available, but probably not as cost-effective as other methods.

Sutures are your most invasive method of wound or laceration closure, and the one that requires the most skill. Before you choose to close a wound by suturing, make sure you ask yourself why you can't use a less invasive method instead. I know, after watching Rambo do it on himself, you're ready to try it, too (maybe not on yourself). It's also important to remember, however, to keep it simple. Use the other methods first, and save your precious suture supplies for those special cases that really need them. In a collapse situation, it's unlikely you'll ever be able to replenish those items.

HOW TO SUTURE

✚ ✚ ✚

S uturing is best done by someone with experience, but you don't get that kind of experience in your typical first responder course. You'll need to obtain the know-how to be able to function effectively, and that means knowing how to close a wound. Here's a practice session that will give you an introduction to a brand new skill: Suturing.

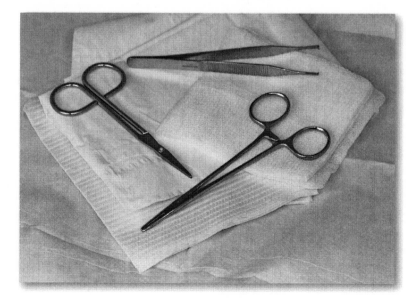

First, you need some supplies. Suture kits are available commercially at various online sites, and are comprised of the following items: A needle holder, a forceps (looks like tweezers), gauze pads, suture scissors, and a sterile drape to isolate the area being repaired. Some type of antiseptic solution such as Betadine or Hibiclens will be needed and, of course, don't forget gloves! Some people are allergic to latex, so consider nitrile products.

Of course, you'll need suture material. A good all-purpose suture material for skin would be silk, which is permanent and must be removed later. Other permanent materials include Prolene, Nylon, and Ethibond. There are other suture materials that are absorbable such as chromic ("catgut") which disappears after 2-3 weeks and Vicryl, which disappears after 6 weeks or so. These are best used on deeper layers.

Suture material comes in various thicknesses: 0, 2-0, 3-0, 4-0, 5-0 and 6-0 are most commonly used on humans. 0-Silk, for example, is thickest, with 6-0 Silk being very fine for use in delicate cosmetic work on, for example, the face. The heavier suture has more strength, but the finer suture leaves less of a scar. For purposes of practice, try 2-0 or 3-0..

Of course, you'll need something to stitch together. I have used pig's feet, chicken breast, orange peel, and even grape skin (for delicate work) as a medical student and none are exactly like living human skin. Pig's feet are probably the closest thing you'll find.

For the following, refer to the figures below and/or access my YouTube video called: HOW TO SUTURE WITH DR. BONES. This video goes through the entire process with narration.

Place your pig's foot on a level surface after defrosting it and washing it thoroughly. Put your gloves on. You will then paint the area to be sutured (this is called the "skin prep") with a Betadine 2% solution or other antiseptic. Alcohol may be used if no other antiseptic is available.

Next, you will isolate the "prepped" area by placing a sterile drape. The drape will usually have an opening in the middle for the area to be sutured, which is called the "surgical field". Although you are suturing a pig's foot, I'll describe the process as if you are working with living tissue.

Assuming your patient is conscious, you would want to numb the area with 1% or 2% Lidocaine solution (prescription). Use an alcohol wipe on the end of the bottle, then fill a small syringe with air. Inject the air into the bottle, and the local anesthetic will fill the syringe. Place an injection at a 45 degree angle to the skin, and then inject enough to form a raised area on each side of the laceration (see figure below). Within a few minutes, the area will be numb. Be careful not to inject into a blood vessel, as this could be dangerous. If you lack Lidocaine, you can apply an ice cube to the area to be sutured until sensation decreases.

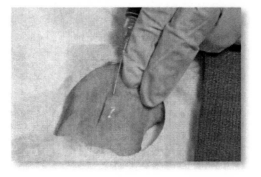

Now, open your suture package and use your needle holder to grasp the needle therein. Remove it and the attached "string" from the package. Now adjust the curved needle on the needle holder so that it is perpendicular to the line of the instrument. If you are holding the needle holder in your right hand, the sharp end of the needle should point to your left. For the best command of the suture, the needle should be held at the midpoint of the curve (see figure below).

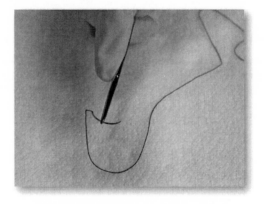

Now take your forceps (tweezers) and grasp the edge of the laceration near where you wish to place the stitch. Insert the suture needle at a 90 degree angle to the skin and drive it through that side of the laceration with a twist of the wrist (see figure below).

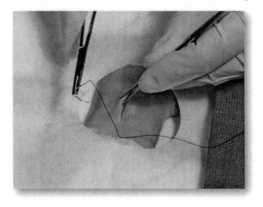

Release the needle and re-clamp it on the inside of the wound and pull it through. Replace the needle on the needle holder and, going from the inside of the wound, drive the needle with a twist of the wrist through the skin on the other side of the laceration.

Pull the string through, leaving a 2-3 inch length for knot-tying (see figure below).

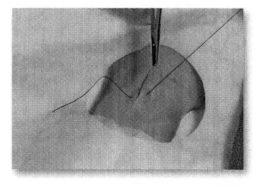

There are various ways to tie your knot, but the method that saves the most suture material (this is meant for collapse situations, after all), is the Instrument Tie. Placing the needle holder over the wound, wrap the long end of the string once or twice around the end of the needle holder (see figure below)

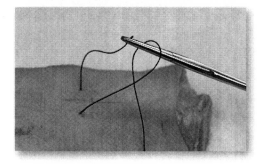

Open the needle holder end slightly and carefully grab the very end of the 2-3 inch length (see figure above), then clamp and pull it through the loops tightly to form a knot (see figure on next page). Repeat this knot 3 or 4 times per stitch.

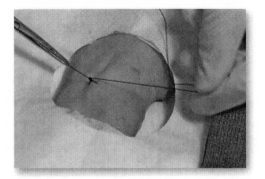

Finally, grasp the two ends and cut the remaining suture material ¼ inch from the knot with your suture scissors. Place each subsequent suture about ½ inch apart from the previous one (see figure below).

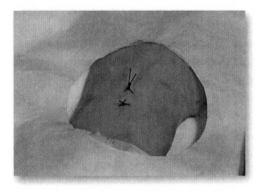

It's important to tighten your knots only enough to close the wound. Excessive pressure from a knot that is too tight will prevent healing in the area of the suture. You can identify sutures that are too tight easily. They will cause an indentation in the skin where the string is. To finish your suture job, paint it once again with Betadine solution and cover with gauze and tape. Monitor the progress of the wound closely.

To be successful in treating lacerations or other soft tissue injuries, you must be able to: 1) decide when it is better to close a wound than leave it open, 2) correctly place the sutures when they are indicated, and 3) provide close follow-up of the treated injury to assure complete healing. If you can absorb this knowledge and implement it, you will have learned an important skill.

BLISTERS, SPLINTERS, AND FISHHHOOKS

✚ ✚ ✚

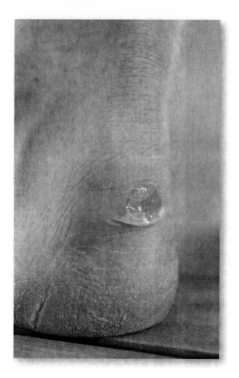

Blisters

Anyone who has done any hiking or has bought the wrong pair of shoes has experienced a friction blister. For a relatively small soft tissue injury, it can certainly cause more than its share of problems. More than one hike has come to a screeching halt because of blisters.

You can prevent blisters by wearing a light pair of socks under a thicker pair before heading out for your hike. Never underestimate the importance of a good pair of shoes. Spend some time walking around in the store in the shoes you are thinking of buying; several minutes of testing will help you determine if they're right for you.

If a blister is just starting, it will look like a tender red area where the friction is. Cover it with moleskin or Spenco Second Skin before it gets worse. These items are inexpensive and can be lifesavers. If you don't have any on hand, you can make use of gauze or a Band-Aid or even duct tape. The important thing here is to add padding to remove the friction from the blister. If possible, get off your feet.

Most people are just itching to pop their blisters, but this shouldn't be done with small ones, as this could lead to infection. Large blisters are different, however. First, clean the area with disinfectant. Alcohol or iodine is especially useful. Then, take a needle and sterilize with alcohol or heat it till it is red hot; then, pierce the side of the blister. This allows the fluid to drain. This will ease some discomfort and also will allow healing to begin. It is important not to rip the skin off but to place the loose skin back over the injury so that it offers some protection.

Apply antibiotic cream if you have it, or at least make sure the area is clean. Then take some moleskin or Spenco Second Skin and cut a hole in the middle a little bigger than the blister. Put it on so that the blister is in the middle of where the hole is. Then bandage it up with a gauze pad and a Band-Aid. Rest if you can. If you absolutely must keep walking, make sure that your bandage has stopped the friction to the area. Remember, bandages frequently come off, so check it from time to time to make sure it's still on. Change the bandage frequently to maintain cleanliness.

Home Remedies for Blisters:

- Apply a cold compress to the blister by soaking a cloth in salt water.
- Apply a 10 percent tannic acid solution to the blister two or three times a day.
- Apply a few drops of Listerine antiseptic to a broken blister to disinfect the wound.   Garlic oil is also very useful for this purpose.
- Place some aloe vera, vitamin E oil or zinc oxide
- ointment on the blister.
- Witch hazel on the blister three times a day helps with pain and is also a drying agent.
- Tea tree oil will help prevent infection.
- Apply lavender oil to help regenerate skin several times a day.

If you don't treat the blister and keep friction on it, there's a chance that it may turn into a foot ulcer. Diabetics need to be especially careful, because they're more susceptible to foot problems due to poor circulation and nerve issues. A foot ulcer is an open sore, and can become increasingly deep and even affect tendons, nerves, and bone. Infections are common. This is why prevention is so important when it comes to blisters.

Splinters

Being out in the woods or working with wood not uncommonly leaves a person with a splinter or two to deal with. You can remove a splinter by simply cutting the skin over it until the end can be grasped with a small forceps or tweezers. You'll need as fine an instrument as you can get to make this easy. Also consider a magnifying glass to make your job easier.

If you can see the entire length of the splinter, use a scalpel and cut the epidermis; you want to cut superficially and just enough to expose the tip of the wooden fragment. Then, take your tweezers and grasp the end of the splinter and pull it out along the angle that it entered the skin. Don't forget to wash the area thoroughly before and after the procedure.

It's unlikely that a major infection will come from simply having a splinter, with the exception of those that have been under the skin for more than 2-3 days. Redness or swelling in the area will become apparent if an infection is brewing. You might consider antibiotics in this circumstance to avoid having problems later.

Fishhooks

Even if you're an accomplished fisherman, you will eventually wind up with a fishhook embedded in you somewhere, probably your hand. Since the hook probably has worm guts on it, start off by cleaning the area thoroughly with an antiseptic.

Your hook probably has a barbed end. If you can't easily slide it out, the barb is probably the issue. Press down on the skin over where the barb is and then attempt to remove the hook along the curve of the shank.

If this doesn't work, you may have to advance the fishhook further along the skin until the end comes out again.

At this point, you can take a wire cutter and separate the barbed end from the shank. Then, pull the shank out from whence it came. Wash the area again and cover with a bandage. Observe carefully over time for signs of infection.

BURN INJURIES

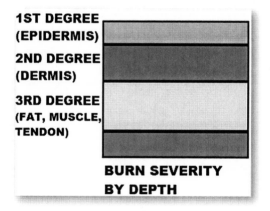

1ST DEGREE (EPIDERMIS)

2ND DEGREE (DERMIS)

3RD DEGREE (FAT, MUSCLE, TENDON)

BURN SEVERITY BY DEPTH

If we find ourselves off the power grid, we will be cooking out in the open more frequently. The potential for significant burn injuries will rise exponentially, especially if the survival group includes small children; naturally curious, they may get too close to our campfires. A working knowledge of burns and their treatment will be a standard skill for every group's medical provider.

The severity of the burn injury depends on the percentage of the total body surface that is burned, and on the degree (or intensity) of the burn injury. Although assessing the surface percentage is helpful to burn units in major hospitals, this practice will likely be of limited helpfulness in a collapse. Therefore, let's concentrate on learning to identify burns by their degree.

FIRST DEGREE BURNS: These burns will be very common, such as simple sunburn. The injury will appear red, warm and dry, and will be painful to the touch. Placing a cool moist cloth or Spenco Second Skin on the area will give some relief, as will common anti-inflammatory medicines such as Ibuprofen. Aloe Vera is also an effective treatment. Usually, the discomfort improves after 24 hours or so, as only the superficial skin layer, the epidermis, is affected.

SECOND-DEGREE BURNS: These burns are deeper, going partially through the skin, and will be seen to be moist, painful and have blisters with reddened bases. The area will have a tendency to weep clear or whitish fluid. Moist skin dressings such as Spenco Second skin may give some relief, as will lancing some of the larger, more tense blisters. Antibiotic ointment may also be useful, although burns are usually sterile for the first 2 days or so. Products that contain Silver Sulfadiazine (Silvadene) will prevent infection in healing wounds. Don't forget to remove rings and bracelets due to swelling that may occur.

THIRD-DEGREE BURNS: The worst type of burn injury; it involves the full thickness of skin and possibly deeper structures such as subcutaneous fat and muscle. It may appear charred, or be white in color. The burn may appear indented if significant tissue has been lost. Third-degree burns will cause dehydration, so giving fluid is essential to keep the patient stable. Spenco Second Skin is, again, useful, as a burn wound cover, for protection purposes. Also, Celox combat gauze, when wet, forms a reasonable dressing.

Silver Sulfadiazine (Silvadene) cream is helpful in preventing infections in third degree burns.

You might see fourth, fifth and sixth degree burns described in some other medical resource books. They are treated essentially the same as third degree burns.

Honey has been used as a coating for significant burns and this may be implemented by spreading it over the wound and covering it with plastic wrap. Any burn this severe that is larger than, say, an inch or so in diameter, will require a skin graft to heal completely. Unfortunately, this is unlikely to be available in a collapse situation. A person with third-degree burns over any significant percentage of the body could be in shock, and is in a life-threatening situation.

When a person gets burned, it's of paramount importance to remove the heat source immediately. Run cool water over any degree of burn for at least 10-15 minutes as soon as possible after the injury. Immersion in a cool bath is another option, especially for torso burns. Third degree burns receive somewhat less benefit from this. Cool water is preferable to ice as it is less traumatic to the injury. Be certain to remove rings or jewelry, as swelling is commonly seen in these kinds of injuries.

Application of topical burn ointments with Benzocaine will sooth first and second degree burns. Oral pain medications such as Ibuprofen or Acetaminophen may also be effective. Silvadene ointment is an excellent antibacterial agent (contains Silver Sulfadiazine) to prevent infection. Your patient will experience less discomfort if they wear fabrics that don't irritate the skin, such as light cottons or silks.

It's important to realize that our traditional medicine resources may not be available some day and a successful medic will ensure that everyone will have some knowledge regarding alternate burn treatments. Various plants will have properties that will allow you to improve burn healing, even if no modern medical supplies are available. Although of limited use for severe burns, many first and second degree burns will respond to their effects.

The first remedy is Aloe Vera; most people recognize this treatment as something they heard before and studies have shown that Aloe Vera helps new skin cells form and speeds healing. This would be an excellent option for first or second degree burns. If you have an aloe plant, cut off a leaf, open it up and either scoop out the gel or rub the open leaf directly on the burned area. Reapply 4-6 times daily, with or without a bandage covering. Simplicity and fast relief are the key benefits to using Aloe Vera on burns, especially in a collapse situation.

Most articles you can find on burn treatments also commonly include any type of vinegar as a treatment for burns. Vinegar works as an astringent and antiseptic and helps to prevent infections. First degree burns would be an epidemic in some of the hotter areas of the world, The best way to use vinegar on smaller sized burns is to make a compress with 1/2 vinegar and 1/2 cool water and cover the burn until the compress feels warm, then re-soak the compress and reapply. There is no limit to how many times you can apply the vinegar soaks. Another method is a cool bath with vinegar added. Start with tepid water and let the water cool off while the patient is soaking. if the burn is on the central body area use a cotton t-shirt soaked in vinegar and then wring it out. This method is especially useful as a treatment while sleeping.

Another "cooling off" treatment for burns is Witch Hazel compresses. Use the extract of the bark, which decreases inflammation and soothes a 1st degree burn. Soak a compress in full strength Witch Hazel and apply to the burned area. Reapply as frequently as desired. Elder flower and comfrey leaf decoctions are also an excellent remedy for burns.

For those unfamiliar with the term decoction, it is an extraction of the crushed herbs produced by boiling. Using lower water temperatures produces a tea instead. The Decoctions of these plants can also be used for compresses just like the Witch Hazel. However, they can also be freshly crushed and rehydrated and then applied directly to the burned area with a sterile gauze cover, this is called a poultice.

Black tea leaves have tannic acid that helps draw heat from a burn. There are several methods for the black tea treatment:

- Put 2-3 tea bags in cool water for a few minutes and use the water with compresses or just apply the liquid to the burned area.
- Make a concoction of 3 or 4 tea bags, 2 cups fresh mint leaves and 4 cups of boiling water. Then strain the liquid into a jar and allow it to cool. To use, dab the mixture on burned skin with a cotton ball or washcloth.
- If your patient has to be mobile, make a stay-in-place poultice out of 2 or 3 wet tea bags. Simply place cool wet tea bags directly on the burn and wrap them with a piece of gauze and some tape to hold them in place.

Both milk and yogurt have also been found to help cool and hydrate the skin after a burn. Wrap whole-milk, full-fat yogurt, inside gauze or cheesecloth and use as a compress. Replace the compress as the yogurt warms on the skin. Whole milk compresses can be used the same way.

Another method of application for large burn injuries is a yogurt "spa treatment" which involves spreading yogurt all over the burn then bathing with cool water after 15 minutes. Yet another home remedy is the baking soda bath. Add 1/4 cup baking soda to a warm bath and soak for at least 15 minutes or longer if needed until the water cools off.

There are two essential oils that can be used full strength on 1st or 2nd degree burns, Lavender and tea tree oils. They help with pain due to stinging and promote tissue healing. Mix tea tree oil with a small amount of water, or lavender can be used full strength; apply all over the burned area. A loose covering of gauze over the oil may be helpful when used for 2nd degree burns. It is important to know that butter or lard, commonly used for burns in the past, will hold in the heat and are not to be used in the treatment of your patient.

You can also make a poultice of Marigold (calendula) petals pounded with small amounts of olive or wheat germ oil; this can be spread lightly over the burned area and covered by loose gauze or a sterile covering. Marigold is a common ingredient in skin medication and it has been proven to have anti-inflammatory and antibacterial effects, which speed the healing of burns.

An oatmeal bath may be used to reduce itching related to healing, Crumble 1-2 cups of raw oats and add them to a luke-warm bath as the tub is filling and soak 15-20 minutes. Then, air dry so that a thin coating of oatmeal remains on your skin. You can do this as often as needed to reduce itching.

A time proven remedy related to Ancient Indian Yunani healing arts has been used for many centuries to treat even severe burns. Here are the steps to make cotton-ash paste:

- Take a large piece of cotton wool; or any kind of pure white cotton fabric and burn it into ashes in a Dutch oven.
- Use the ASH of the burned cotton and mix with olive oil or any kind of cooking oil available.
- Mix this into a thick paste and spread the black paste on the burned skin.
- Cover it with ordinary plastic cling wrap and perhaps some gauze to hold it all in place.
- Add new paste every day for a week or so, depending on the severity of the burn.

One of the best natural remedies that is useful in treating the burn patient is honey. Honey, in its raw unprocessed state, is the best to use, because of its antibacterial activity and hydrating properties. Honey has an acidic pH that is inhospitable to bacteria. Therefore, it will help prevent and even treat infections in many wounds. It can be used in 1st, 2nd and, if no other medical care is available, as a last resort for 3rd degree burns (along with a high protein diet, lots of water and a drink mixture of lemon juice, sugar and a pinch of salt in some water several times a day).

This is how to use the honey method:

- Immediately after the first 15 minute cooling-down treatment, apply a generous amount of honey in a thick layer all over the burned area.
- Cover the honey with cling wrap plastic or waterproof dressings. Use tape to hold the dressing in place.
- If the dressing begins to fill up with fluid oozing out of the wound, change the dressing. The worse the burn, the more frequently the dressing will need to be changed. Repeat for 7-10 days.
- Do not remove or wash off the honey for the first 20 days (or earlier if healing is complete). Add more honey often and fill up any deeper areas as needed. Always have a thick layer of honey extending over the edges of the burn. You do not want any air getting to the burned skin until healing is completed. This will cut down the infection rate.
- Change the dressing at least three times a day regardless of the amount of oozing fluid.

Treating burns without a medical system available will require intense care and close observation. Severe fluid losses lead to dangerous consequences for these patients, so always be certain that you do everything possible to keep them well hydrated. The damage to the skin caused by burns leaves those injured to the mercy of many pathogens, so watch for fevers or other signs of infection.

ANIMAL BITES

✚ ✚ ✚

Most people have, at some time of their life, run afoul of an ornery dog or cat. Most animal bites will be puncture wounds; these will be relatively small but have the potential to cause dangerous infections. Although many Preppers are wary of vaccines, it may be appropriate to make sure that everyone in your group has had a tetanus shot.

Besides the trauma associated with the actual bite, various animals carry disease which can be transmitted to humans. Here are just a few diseases and the animals involved:

- Rabies: Viral disease spread by raccoons, skunks, bats, opossums, and canines.
- Yersinia Pestis: Bacterial disease associated with rats and fleas; otherwise known as the "Plague".
- Tuberculosis: Bacterial disease associated with deer, elk, and bison.
- Brucella: Bacterial disease associated with bison, deer, and other animals.
- Hantavirus: Viral disease caused by mice.
- Baylisascaris (raccoon roundworm): Parasitic disease associated with raccoons.
- Histoplasma: Fungal disease associated with bat excrement (guano).
- Tularemia: Bacterial disease associated with wildlife especially rodents, rabbits, and hares.

Whenever a person has been bitten, the first and most important action is to clean the wound thoroughly after stopping any bleeding. Benzalkonium Chloride is the best antiseptic to use in treating animal bites, because it has some effect against the Rabies virus. Rabies is a dangerous but, luckily, uncommon disease that can be transmitted by an animal bite, especially those from wild animals such as raccoons, opossums, skunks, coyotes, etc. Any animal bite should be considered a "dirty" wound, and should not be taped or sutured.

In the United States, there has never been a rabies case transmitted by the following animals: domestic cattle, squirrels, rabbits, rats, sheep or horses. Although this is a good thing, the severity of the consequences of a rabies infection can't be underestimated. Once a person develops the disease, it is usually fatal. Vaccinations are available, and regardless of your opinion regarding them, it might be something to consider.

Frequent cleansing is the best treatment for an animal bite. Be sure to watch for signs of infection such as redness and swelling. Antibiotics may be appropriate in many cases. If the bite is on the hand, any rings or bracelets should be taken off; if swelling occurs, they may be very difficult to remove afterwards.

SNAKE BITES

✚ ✚ ✚

I n a collapse situation, you will find yourself out in the woods a lot more frequently, gathering firewood, hunting, and foraging for edible wild plants. As such, we will encounter all sorts of critters, including that slithery serpent, the snake. Most snakes aren't poisonous, but even non-venomous snake bites have potential for infection.

North America has two kinds of poisonous snakes: The pit vipers (rattlesnakes, cottonmouths and water moccasins) and Elapids (coral snakes). One or more of these snakes can be found almost everywhere in the continental U.S. Snakes are most active during the warmer months and, therefore, most bite injuries are seen then. Not every bite from a venomous snake transfers its poison to the victim; 30% of these bites will show no ill effects. This probably has to do with the duration of time the snake has its fangs in you.

An ounce of prevention, they say, is worth a pound of cure. Be sure to wear good solid high-top boots and long pants when hiking in the wilderness. Treading heavily creates ground vibrations and noise, which will often cause snakes to hit the road. Snakes have no outer ear, so they "hear" ground vibrations better than those in the air caused by, for instance, shouting.

Snake bites that cause a burning pain immediately are likely to have poison in them. Swelling at the site may begin as soon as five minutes afterwards, and may travel up the affected area. Pit viper bites tend to cause bruising and blisters at the site of the wound. Numbness may be noted in the area bitten, or perhaps on the lips or face. Some victims describe a metallic taste in their mouth.

With pit vipers, a serious bite might start to cause spontaneous bleeding from the nose or gums. Coral snake bites, however, will cause mental and nerve issues such as twitching, confusion and slurred speech. Later, nerve damage may cause difficulty with swallowing and breathing, followed by total paralysis. Coral snakes appear very similar to their look-alike, the non-venomous king snake. They both are red, yellow and black and are commonly confused with each other. The old saying goes: "red touches yellow, kill a fellow; red touches black, venom it lacks". I probably wouldn't bet my life on this, though.

The treatment for a poisonous snake bite is Anti-venin, but this will probably be unavailable in a collapse situation. The following strategy, therefore, will be useful: First, keep the victim calm. Stress increases blood flow and endangers the patient by speeding the venom into the system. Movement of the injured extremity will also move the venom into the circulation, so do your best to keep the limb still.

It is no longer recommended to make an incision and try to suck out the venom with your mouth. If done more than 3 minutes after the actual bite, it would remove perhaps 1/1000 of the venom and could cause damage or infection to the bitten area. A Sawyer Extractor (a syringe with a suction cup) is safer and can remove 1/3 of the venom from the wound if used very soon after the bite occurs.

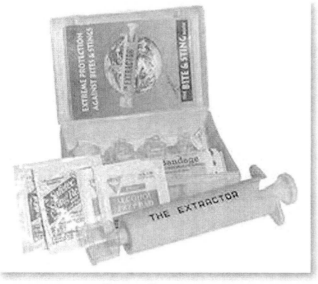

Sawyer Extractor

As with any bite, clean the wound thoroughly to remove any venom on the skin, and remove rings and bracelets from an affected extremity. If you can, position the extremity below the level of the heart; this also slows the transport of venom.

Wrap with compression bandages as you would an orthopedic injury, but continue it further up the limb than usual. Bandaging begins two to four inches above the bite (towards the heart), winding around and moving up, then back down over the bite and past it towards the hand or foot. The bandage should be about as tight as when strapping a sprained ankle. If it is too tight, the patient will reflexively move the limb, and move the venom around. The limb should then be rested, and perhaps immobilized with a splint or sling. This strategy also works for bites from venomous lizards, like Gila monsters.

INSECT STINGS

✚ ✚ ✚

Black Widow Spider

Insect bites usually cause pain with local redness and swelling, but are rarely life-threatening. The exceptions are black widow spiders, brown recluse spiders, and various caterpillars and scorpions. For most victims, the offender will be a bee, wasp, hornet or ant. Most stings heal with little or no treatment.

There are quite a few people, however, who are allergic to these stings; some are so allergic that they will have what is called an anaphylactic reaction. Instead of just local symptoms like rashes and itching, they will experience dizziness, difficulty breathing and/or faintness. Severe swelling is seen in some, which can be life-threatening if it closes the person's airways.

For those that experience only local reactions, the following actions will be sufficient: Clean the area thoroughly. Remove the stinger, if visible, as soon as possible. Cold packs and anesthetic ointments will relieve discomfort and local swelling. Itching and redness may be controlled by the use of oral antihistamines, like Benadryl or Claritin. Acetaminophen or ibuprofen may be helpful to reduce discomfort. Antibiotic ointments are useful to prevent infection.

Topical essential oils may be applied (after removing the stinger) with beneficial effect. Use Lavadin, helichrysum, tea tree or peppermint oil, applying 1 or 2 drops to the affected area, 3 times a day. A baking soda paste (baking soda mixed with a small amount of water) may be useful when applied to a sting wound.

Those experiencing an anaphylactic reaction will require treatment with epinephrine as well as antihistamines. People who are aware that they are highly allergic to stings should carry antihistamines and epinephrine on their person whenever they go outside. Epinephrine is available in a pre-measured dose cartridge known as the Epi-Pen (there is a pediatric version, as well). The Epi-pen is a prescription medication, but few doctors would begrudge a request for one. Make sure to make them aware that you will be outside and may be exposed to possible causes of anaphylaxis. See the section on allergic reactions for a more in-depth discussion.

Although antidotes known as "antivenins" exist for poisonous spider and scorpion stings, these will be scarce in a collapse. Use the above treatment strategy for local wounds and watch carefully for symptoms that are generalized, such as tingling, numbness, weakness, dizziness, difficulty breathing and mental changes. Many of these will subside over the course of a day or two, but some will be difficult to treat without the antivenin. It's important to be aware of your environment and look for dangerous insects and snakes whenever you are doing outside work.

Some insect bites are not dangerous due to toxins, but can cause infectious disease. Ticks can transfer Lyme disease and mosquitos can transfer Malaria, for example. The best way to prevent these is by wearing protective clothing whenever you go outside, and having insect repellant (DEET) in good amount in your storage. Citronella, commonly used as an insect repellant in candles, can be found naturally in some plants. If you find a tick has attached itself to you, you can use a tweezers (also known as a forceps) to remove it, being especially careful to remove the whole insect. Leaving parts in can lead to infection.

POISON IVY, OAK, AND SUMAC

✚ ✚ ✚

Poison Ivy

U nless you live in Alaska or Hawaii, a mountaintop, or the middle of the desert, the outdoors will have a population of poison ivy, poison oak, and/or poison sumac. Once you have been exposed to one or the other, you will develop antibodies against it that will generate an itchy rash of varying degrees of severity. Winter does not eliminate the possibility of a reaction, as you can react against even the dormant vines or shrubs.

The rash takes from several hours to several days to become apparent, and will appear as red itchy lumps that tend to be patchy. Sometimes the rash appears almost linear. Itching can be prolonged and severe.

The resin from the plant that causes the reaction will remain active even on your clothes, so thorough laundering will be required. Routine body washing with soap will not be useful after 30 minutes of exposure, as your system will already be producing antibodies. Some recommend an over-the-counter lotion called Ivy Block as a preventative. Apply it like you would a sunblock to likely areas of exposure. Cleansers that remove resin or oil such as Fels-Naptha or Tecnu Poison Oak and Ivy Cleanser are more effective than regular detergent and can be used even several hours after exposure.

The good news is that, even if you choose not to treat the rash, it will go away by itself over 2-3 weeks. Diphenhydramine (Benadryl) at 25-50 mg dosages 4 times a day will be helpful in relieving the itching, although the 50mg dosage will make you drowsy. Calamine lotion, an old standby, will probably not be very effective, however. Severe rashes has been treated with the prescription Medrol dose pack, a type of steroid known as Prednisone, and will be more effective in preventing the inflammatory reaction that your antibodies will cause. Some astringent solutions such as Domeboro have been reported to give relief from the itching.

There are several alternative treatment for poison ivy, oak and sumac. Cleansing the irritated area with apple cider vinegar is thought to be effective, as are oils such as tea tree, lemon, lavender, peppermint, geranium, and chamomile. These oils are best used for the condition when mixed with Aloe Vera gel.

Baking soda paste may also be helpful, as are Epsom salt baths. Chamomile tea bag compresses have also been used with some effect. For those who prefer drinking their tea, passion flower, skullcap, and chamomile are all thought to be beneficial.

ALLERGIC REACTIONS AND ANAPHYLAXIS

✚ ✚ ✚

If we find ourselves in a situation where we have to "get out of Dodge", we will exposing ourselves to insect stings, poison oak and ivy, and strange food items that we aren't accustomed to. Substances that cause allergies are called "allergens". When we develop an allergic reaction, it might be mild or severe. If severe enough, we refer to it as anaphylaxis or anaphylactic shock. Anaphylaxis is the word used for serious and rapid allergic reactions usually involving more than one part of the body which, if severe enough, can kill.

Mild allergic reactions usually involve itching and the development of a patchy, raised rash on the skin. These types of reactions can be transient and go away by themselves or medications such as Diphenhydramine (Benadryl). Chronic allergies may manifest as a condition known as "eczema". This will be a red patchy rash in different places which is itchy and flaky. This type of rash usually responds well to 1% hydrocortisone cream (non-prescription), although sometimes a stronger steroid cream such as Clobetasol (prescription) may be necessary. In the very worst cases, chronic dermatitis (inflammation of the skin) may require oral steroids such as Prednisone.

There are a plethora of essential oils you can apply to relieve itching. Cypress, peppermint, lavender, german and roman chamomile, helichrysum, calendula, myrrh, blue tansy, wintergreen, and eucalyptus. You would dilute 50/50 with a carrier oil and apply 2 drops to affected area. Other natural substances that you could apply to a rash include witch hazel, oatmeal baths or compresses, Aloe Vera, Shea butter and vitamin E oil. Apply to the affected area as needed.

Hay Fever, also known as "allergic rhinitis" or "seasonal allergy", is a collection of symptoms, mostly affecting the eyes and nose, which occur when you breathe in something you are allergic to. Examples of allergens would include dust, animal dander, insect venom, fungi, or pollens. Sufferers of allergic rhinitis would present with:

- Nasal congestion
- Sneezing
- Red eyes with tearing
- Itchy throat, eyes, and skin

Antihistamines such as Claritin and Benadryl are old standbys for this type of allergy. Alternative therapies for hay fever include essential oils for use on the skin: German chamomile, roman chamomile, lavender, eucalyptus, and ginger. Apply 2 drops to each temple, 2-4 times per day. Steam inhalation, 1 drop of the oil to a bowl of steaming water, involves covering the head with a towel and inhale slowly for 15 minutes. A number of teas to drink that may be useful are licorice root, stinging nettle, and St. John's Wort. Drink 1 cup daily 3 times a day.

A Neti Pot is a useful item to have to deal with allergic reactions affecting the nasal passages. It looks like a small teapot. You place the spout in your nostril and drain it into the nostril. Use with saline or salt water daily. A Neti Pot washes out pollen, clears congestion and mucus, and decreases nasal inflammation.

More severe allergic issues involve various organ systems and can be quite dangerous. Anaphylactic reactions were first identified when researchers tried to protect dogs against a certain poison by desensitizing them with small doses. Instead of being protected, many of the dogs died suddenly the second time they got the poison. They were killed by their own immune systems going out of control.

The word used for preventative protection is "PROphylaxis". Think of a condom, also known as a prophylactic. A condom protects you from and prevents sexually transmitted diseases. The word "anaphylaxis", therefore, means the opposite of protection. The dog experiment allowed scientists to understand that the same "anti-protective" (harmful) effect can occur in humans.

This allergic reaction can be caused by drug exposure or pollutants, but even ordinary foods such as peanuts can be culprits. Our immune system, which is there to protect us from infection, sometimes goes haywire and inflicts real damage. Anaphylaxis has become a timely issue because of the increased numbers of people who are experiencing the condition. Why the increase? When medicines are the cause, the explanation is likely that we are simply using a lot of drugs these days.

Why foods should be causing anaphylaxis more often, however, is more perplexing. Common allergies such as asthma, food allergies and hay fever are becoming epidemic all over the world. Pollutants in our air are certainly a factor. As well, it wouldn't surprise me if food allergies are being caused by the proliferation of so many genetically modified (GMO) foods in our diet.

Proven causes of anaphylaxis are:

- Drugs: dyes injected during x-rays, antibiotics like Penicillin, anesthetics, aspirin and ibuprofen, and even some heart and blood pressure medicine
- Foods: Nuts, fruit, seafood

- Insects stings: Bees and Yellow Jacket Wasps, especially
- Latex: rubber gloves mad of latex, especially in health-care workers
- Exercise: often after eating
- Idiopathic: This word means "of unknown cause"; a substantial percentage of cases

It's important to recognize the signs and symptoms of anaphylaxis because the faster you treat it, the less likely it will be life-threatening. You will see:

- Rashes: often at places not associated with the actual exposure, such as a bee sting
- Swelling: can be generalized, but sometimes isolated to the airways or throat
- Breathing difficulty: wheezing is common as in asthmatics
- GI symptoms: diarrhea, nausea and vomiting, or abdominal pain
- Loss of consciousness: The patient may appear to have fainted
- Strange sensations on the lips or oral cavity: especially with food allergies
- Shock: Blood pressure drops, respiratory failure leading to coma and death

Fainting is not the same thing as anaphylactic shock. You can tell the difference in several ways. Someone who has fainted is usually pale in color, but anaphylactic shock will often present with the patient somewhat flushed. The pulse in anaphylaxis is fast, but a person who has fainted will have a slow heart rate. Most people who have just fainted will rarely have breathing problems and rashes, but these will be very common signs and symptoms in an anaphylactic reaction.

In food allergies, victims may notice the effects occur very rapidly; their life may be in danger within a few minutes.

Sometimes, the reaction occurs somewhat later. People who have had a serious anaphylactic reaction should be observed overnight, as there is, on occasion, a second set of symptoms. This can happen several hours after the exposure. Some reactions are mild and probably not anaphylactic, but a history of mild symptoms is not a guarantee that every reaction will be that way.

Why does our immune system go awry in anaphylactic situations? Anaphylaxis happens when the body makes an antibody called immunoglobulin E (IgE for short) in response to exposure to an allergen, like food or a medication. IgE sticks to cells which then release substances that affect blood vessels and air passages. The second time you are exposed to that allergen, these substances drop your blood pressure and cause swelling. The airways, however, tighten and cause respiratory difficulty.

Histamine is a substance released in this situation. Medications which counteract these ill effects are known, therefore, as antihistamines. These drugs may be helpful in mild allergic reactions, but tablets, like Benadryl, take about an hour to get into the bloodstream properly; this isn't fast enough to save lives in serious reactions. If it's all you have, chew the pill to get it into your system more quickly. Other antihistamines like Claritin come in wafers that melt on your tongue, and get into your system more quickly; it is an option, but probably too weak for a severe reaction. The same cells with IgE antibodies release other substances which may cause ill effects, and antihistamines do not protect you against these.

As such, we look to another medicine that is more effective: Adrenaline, known in the U.S. as Epinephrine.

Adrenaline (Epinephrine) is a hormone. Your body produces it from the adrenal glands. This medicine activates the "flight or fight" response you've probably heard about. It makes your heart pump faster, widens the air passages so you can breathe, and raises your blood pressure. Adrenaline (Epinephrine) works successfully against all of the effects of anaphylaxis. It should be part of your medical supplies if you are going to responsible for the medical well-being of your family or group in a collapse situation.

Unfortunately, Adrenaline (Epinephrine) comes as an injectable. Inhalers have been tried in the past, but have disadvantages. Anaphylactic reactions cause difficulty breathing. If you can't inhale, you won't get much benefit from an inhaler.

The Epi-pen is the most popular of the various commercially available kits to combat anaphylaxis. It's important to learn how to use the Epi-Pen properly. You can cause more harm than good if you fail to follow the instructions. Adrenaline (Epinephrine) can constrict the blood vessels if injected into a finger by mistake, and prevent adequate circulation to the digit. In rare cases, gangrene can set in. Also, remember that the Epi-Pen won't help you if you don't carry it with you or don't have it readily accessible.

Since it's a liquid, Adrenaline (Epinephrine) will not stay effective forever, like some pills or capsules might. Be sure to follow the storage instructions. Although you don't want to store it someplace that's hot, the Epi-pen shouldn't be kept in any situation where it could freeze, which will damage its effectiveness significantly. If the solution changes color, it is losing potency. It can do that without changing color also, so use with caution if expired. Adrenaline (Epinephrine) must be protected from light and usually comes in a brown container. Make sure you know exactly where it is in your medical kit.

You will have limited quantities of this drug in collapse situations, so when do you break into those precious supplies? An easily remembered formula is the Rule of D's:

- Definite reaction: Your patient is obviously having a major reaction, such as a large rash or difficult breathing.
- Deterioration: Use the Epi-pen before the condition becomes life-threatening.
- Danger: Any worsening of a reaction after a few minutes.

Having said that, an imminent danger is probably likely only if your patient has difficulty breathing or has lost consciousness. Inhalation of stomach acid into the lungs or respiratory failure is a major cause of death in these cases. Know your CPR.

If you are ever in doubt, go ahead and give the injection. The earlier you use it, the faster a person will resolve the anaphylaxis. One injection is enough to save a life, but have more than one handy, just in case. This is especially pertinent when you are away from your retreat or base camp.

Some people may not be able to take Adrenaline (Epinephrine) due to chronic heart conditions or high blood pressure. Make sure that you consult with your doctor now, to determine that it wouldn't be dangerous to receive the drug. In a collapse, you'll be exposed to a lot of strange stuff and you never know when you might be allergic. Get the medicine, learn the signs and symptoms of anaphylaxis, and you'll stay out of trouble.

DERMATITIS

✚ ✚ ✚

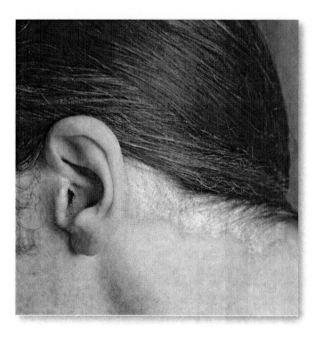

Seborrheic Dermatitis

Dermatitis simply means an inflammation of the skin. This condition may have many causes and may vary in appearance from case to case. Most types of dermatitis usually present with swollen, reddened and/or itchy skin. Continuous scratching traumatizes the irritated area and may lead to cellulitis once the skin is broken.

Some of the more common types are:

- Contact dermatitis: Caused by allergens and chemical irritants. A good example would be poison ivy.
- Seborrheic dermatitis: A commonly seen condition that affects the face and scalp (common cause of dandruff).
- Atopic Dermatitis or Eczema: A chronic itchy rash that can be found in various areas at once and tends to be intermittent in nature. This may be accompanied by hay fever or asthma.
- Neurodermatitis: A chronic itchy skin condition localized to certain areas of the skin (as seen in a herpes virus called Shingles).
- Stasis dermatitis: An inflamed area caused by fluid under the skin, commonly seen on the lower legs of older individuals. Poor circulation is a major factor here.

You will most likely see contact dermatitis in a collapse situation, as your people will be exposed to substances while scavenging that may cause reactions. Some of these include:

Soaps. laundry soap and detergents.

- Cleaning products.
- Rubber or Latex.
- Metals, such as nickel.
- Weeds, such as poison ivy, oak or sumac.

Once you're sensitized to an allergen, future exposures will cause skin reactions. Your patient will probably experience these reactions for the rest of his or her life.

Corticosteroid creams, moist compresses and avoiding irritants will be the cornerstones of treatment. Use these only until the rash is improved. Antihistamines such as Benadryl or Claritin will help relieve itching. Of course, if the dermatitis was caused by contact with an irritant, avoid it if at all possible.

Scalp irritations caused by Seborrhea may be treated by shampoos that contain tar, pyrithione zinc, or ketoconazole. Neurodermatitis caused by Shingles may be treated with antiviral agents, such as Acyclovir, Valtrex, or Famvir.

Natural supplements that improve dermatitis often involve Omega-3 fatty acids, which have an anti-inflammatory effect. Used with evening primrose oil, it is especially effective. Chamomile cream is thought to be as potent as a mild hydrocortisone. Calendula has skin-soothing properties and may protect against contact dermatitis. Be aware that it may trigger an allergic reaction on broken skin.

HEAD INJURIES

✚ ✚ ✚

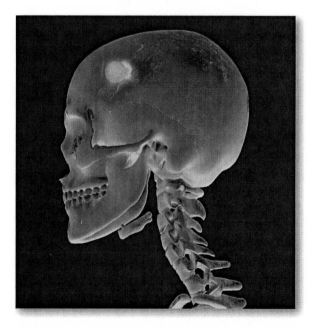

H ead injuries can be soft tissue injuries (brain, scalp, blood vessels) or bony injuries (skull, facial bones), so I've placed this section between soft tissue and orthopedic problems. Damage can be caused by direct impact, such as a laceration in the scalp or a fracture of the part of the skull that contains the brain (also called the "cranium"). It can also be caused by the rebound of the brain against the inside walls of the skull; this may cause tearing of the blood vessels in the brain, which can result in a hemorrhage. Accumulation of blood in the cranium increases the pressure inside the brain (the "intracranial pressure"), which can be life-threatening. Anyone with a traumatic injury to the head must always be observed closely.

The brain requires blood and oxygen to function normally. An injury which causes bleeding or swelling inside the skull will increase the intracranial pressure. This causes the heart to work harder to get blood and oxygen into the brain. Without adequate circulation, brain function ceases. Pressure that is high enough could actually cause a portion of the brain to push downward through the base of the skull. In a collapse situation, this will almost invariably lead to death.

Most head injuries result in only a laceration to the scalp and a swelling at the site of impact. Cuts on the scalp or face will tend to bleed, as there are many small blood vessels that travel through this area. This bleeding, although significant, is rarely a sign of internal damage. There are a number of signs and symptoms, however, which might identify those patients that are more seriously affected. They are:

1. Loss of Consciousness
2. Convulsions (Seizures)
3. Worsening Headache
4. Nausea and Vomiting
5. Bruising (around eyes and ears)
6. Bleeding from Ears and Nose
7. Confusion/Apathy/Drowsiness
8. One Pupil More Dilated than the Other
9. Indentation of the Skull

A person with trauma to the head may be knocked unconsciousness for a period of time or may remain completely alert. If consciousness is not lost, the patient may experience a headache and could require treatment to superficial injuries. After a period of observation, a head injury without loss of consciousness is most likely not serious unless one of the other signs and symptoms from the above list are noted.

Loss of consciousness for a very brief time (say, 2 minutes or so) will merit close observation for the next 48 hours. A head injury of this type is called a "concussion". This patient will usually awaken somewhat "foggy", and may be unclear as to how the injury occurred or the events shortly before. It will be important to be certain that the patient has regained normal motor function. Even so, rest is prescribed for the remainder of the day, so they may be closely watched.

When your patient is asleep, it will be appropriate to awaken them every 2-3 hours, to make sure that they are easily aroused and have developed none of the danger signals listed above. In most cases, a concussion causes no permanent damage unless there are multiple episodes of head trauma over time, as in the case of boxers or other athletes.

If the period of unconsciousness is over 10 minutes in length, you must suspect the possibility of significant injury. Vital signs such as pulse, respiration rate, and blood pressure should be monitored closely. The patient's head should be immobilized, and attention should be given to the neck and spine, in case they are also damaged. Verify that the airway is clear, and remove any possible obstructions. In a collapse, this person is in a life-threatening situation that will have few curative options if consciousness is not regained.

Other signs of a significant injury to this area are the appearance of bruising behind the ears or around the eyes (the "raccoon" sign) despite the impact not occurring in that area. This could indicate a fracture with internal bleeding. Bleeding from the

ear itself or nose without trauma to those areas is another indication. The fluid may also be clear, and may represent spinal fluid
leakage. Again, these signs are indicative of a skull fracture and
could be life-threatening. In addition, pressure from intracranial
bleeding may compress nerves that lead to the pupils. In this
case, you will notice that your unconscious patient has one pupil
more dilated than the other.

SPRAINS AND STRAINS

✚ ✚ ✚

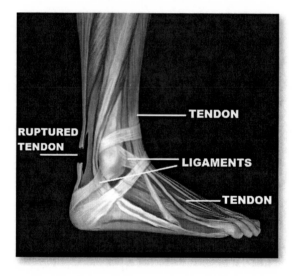

RUPTURED TENDON · **TENDON** · **LIGAMENTS** · **TENDON**

B ones, joints, muscles and tendons give the body support and locomotion, and there is no substitute for having all your parts in good working order. The amount of work these structures will be called upon to do after a disaster will be greatly increased, when modern work-saving devices are no longer available. The additional strain put on the body will cause more injuries, and it is important to know how to identify and treat these problems.

Prior to a collapse, it is recommended to have whatever surgical repairs of any orthopedic faults you happen to have. Knees, shoulders, ankles and other joints are commonly damaged due to long-term abuse, and it pays to "tune" these up while modern surgical care is still available. Many surgeries these days are done through very small incisions, and most can be done as an outpatient.

A ligament is the fibrous tissue that connects one bone to another, oftentimes across a joint. A "sprain" is caused by the excessive stretching of a ligament when a joint is forced beyond its normal range of motion. When the muscle or its connection to the bone (called a tendon) in the area is partially torn as a result of the injury, it is referred to as a "strain". When the tear of the ligament or muscle is complete, it is called a rupture.

These injuries may be associated with some bleeding into the tissues, and bruises may be seen at the site of injury. Swelling is commonly seen as well. The most common areas affected for sprains are the wrist, ankle, foot, knee, and the fingers and toes. Strains often involve the back muscles.

There is a simple way to remember how to treat these types of injuries: R.I.C.E.S. This stands for Rest, Ice, Compression, Elevation, and Stabilization.

- REST: It is important to avoid further injury by not further testing the injured joint. Stop whatever activity that led to the injury.
- ICE: Cold therapy decreases both swelling and pain. The earlier it is applied, the better effect it will have in speeding up the healing process. This should be performed several times a day for 30 minutes or so each time.
- COMPRESSION: A compression bandage is useful to decrease swelling and should be placed after each cold therapy. This will also help provide support to the joint. After applying some padding to the area, wrap an elastic

"ACE" bandage, starting below the joint and working your way up beyond it. The wrap should be tight, but not uncomfortably so. Any tingling, increased pain or numbness tells you that the wrap is too tight, and should be loosened somewhat. Loss of color from the fingers or toes is another sign that the bandage should be relaxed.

- ELEVATION: Elevate the sprain above the level of heart. This will prevent swelling from worsening at the site of the injury.

- STABILIZATION: Immobilizing the injury will prevent further damage. This may be accomplished by the compression bandage alone, or may best be treated with a splint if the patient is unable to place any weight on, for instance, the ankle. Splints may be commercially produced, such as the SAM splint, or may be improvised with sticks and cloth or duct tape. Another popular improvisation is the "Pillow Splint", which wraps a pillow around the joint and secures it with duct tape. Make sure the injured joint is immobile after placement of the splint.

Strains, especially back strains, involve injury to the muscle and their tendons (which connects them to the bone). As the lower part of the back holds the majority of the body's weight, you can expect the most trouble here. Some of these injuries are preventable with some simple precautions.

Every morning, you should perform some stretching, to increase blood flow to cold, stiff muscles and joints. When you lift a heavy object, such as a backpack, keep your back straight and let your legs perform the work. The object should be close to your body as you lift it (don't reach for it). For packs, keep the weight on the hips rather than the shoulders. If you are on rocky or unstable terrain, consider using a walking stick for balance. Remember, any weight-lifting action that you perform while being off-balance is likely to result in a strained muscle.

Ibuprofen is an excellent anti-inflammatory and pain reliever for these types of injury. For muscle injuries, prescription relaxants such as Valium or Flexeril will also provide relief. If these are not available, the patient will benefit from mild massage. Normally, an X-ray or MRI of the affected part would be recommended to identify any hairline fractures. In a disaster scenario, however, this may not be possible. Some sprains and strains, (such as wrist and ankle sprains or back strains) commonly heal well over time with the above therapy. Others, however, such as severe knee sprains, may heal completely only with the aid of surgical intervention.

A number of alternative remedies exist for the treatment of sprains and strains. Essential oils are considered helpful to clear up bruising. Apply 2-3 drops of oil of Helichrysum, cypress, clove, or geranium, mixed half and half with a carrier oil such as coconut or olive, 3-5 times a day on the area of bruising.

To decrease swelling, apply Helichrysum oil, undiluted, to the affected area. Willow under bark or ginger tea has anti-inflammatory properties; drink with warm raw honey, several times a day.

Common herbal pain relievers for orthopedic injuries include direct application of Oil of wintergreen, helichrysum, peppermint, clove, or diluted arnica to the affected area. Blends of the above may also be used. Herbal teas that may give relief are valerian root, willow under bark, ginger, passion flower, feverfew, and turmeric. As always, drink warm with raw honey several times a day.

DISLOCATIONS

✚ ✚ ✚

A dislocation is an injury in which a bone is pulled out of its joint, usually in an extremity. Shoulders, fingers, and elbows are common victims but knees, ankles and hips may also be affected. If the dislocation is momentary and the bone slips back into its joint on its own, it is called a subluxation. Subluxations can be treated the same way that sprains are, using the R.I.C.E.S. method. It should be noted that the traditional medical definition of subluxation is somewhat different from the chiropractic one.

Of course, if there is medical care readily available, the patient should go directly to the local emergency room. In a collapse, however, you are on your own and will probably have to correct the dislocation yourself. This is known as "reducing" the injury. Reduction is easiest to perform soon after the dislocation, before muscles spasm and the inevitable swelling occurs. Not only does reducing the dislocation decrease the pain experienced by the victim, but it will lessen the damage to all the blood vessels and nerves that run along the line of the injury. Expect some pain on the part of the patient during the actual procedure, however.

Attempts to reduce the dislocation should be performed as soon as possible. Some pain relievers like ibuprofen might be useful to decrease discomfort from the reduction. Muscle relaxers are also helpful, but these are "by prescription only". The use of traction will greatly aid your attempt to fix the problem. Traction is the act of pulling the dislocated bone away from the joint to give the bone room to slip back into place.

The procedure is as follows:

- Stabilize the joint that the bone was dislocated from (the shoulder, for example) by holding it firmly.
- Using a firm but slow pulling action, pull the bone away from the joint. This will make space for the bone to realign.
- Use your other hand (or preferably a helper's hands) to push the dislocated portion of the bone so that it will be in line again with the joint socket. The bone will naturally want to revert to its normal position in the joint.
- After the reduction is complete and judged successful, splint the bone as if it were a fracture (see next section).

FRACTURES

✚ ✚ ✚

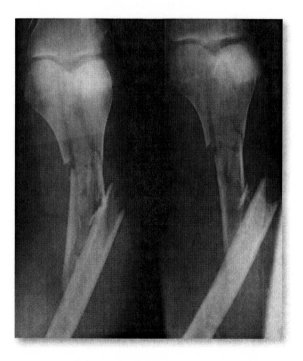

When a bone is broken, it is termed a fracture. There are several types of fractures, but they are all either "closed" or "open". A closed fracture is when there is a break in the bone, but the skin is intact. An open fracture is when the skin is broken. Sometimes the sharp end of a broken bone protrudes through the opening. Needless to say, there is usually more blood loss and infection associated with an open wound. The infection may be in the skin (cellulitis), the blood (sepsis), or the bone itself (osteomyelitis) and could be life threatening if not treated. If poorly managed, a closed fracture can become an open fracture.

The diagnosis of a broken bone can be simple, as when the bone is obviously deformed, or difficult, as in a minimal, "hairline" fracture. X-rays can be helpful to differentiate a small fracture from a severe sprain, but that technology won't be available in a power-down situation. There are some ways to tell, however:

- A fracture will manifest with severe pain and inability to use the bone (for example. The patient cannot put any weight whatsoever on a broken ankle). Someone with a sprain can probably put some weight, albeit painfully, on the area.
- More pronounced swelling and bruising will likely be present on a fracture than a sprain.
- A grinding sensation may be felt when rubbing a fractured limb.
- A deep cut in the area of the injury may be a sign of an open fracture.
- Motion of the bone in an area where there is no joint is another dead giveaway that there is a fracture. If you notice that your injured finger appears to have 5 knuckles, you're probably dealing with a fracture!

Dealing with a fractured bone involves first evaluating the injured area for the above signs and symptoms. Use your bandage or EMT scissors to cut away the clothing over the injury. This will prevent further injury that may occur if the patient was made to remove their own clothing. Check the site for bleeding and the presence of an open wound; if present, stop the bleeding before proceeding further.

Fractures may cause damage to the patient's circulation in the limb affected, so it is important to check the area beyond the level of the injury for changes in coloration (white or blue instead of normal skin color) and for strong and steady pulses. To see what a strong pulse feels like, place two fingers on the side of your neck until you feel your neck arteries pulsing. You will do this same action on, say, the wrist, if the patient has broken their arm. Lightly prick the patient in the same area with a safety pin to make sure they have normal sensation. If not, the nerve has been injured.

If the bone has not deformed the extremity, a simple splint will immobilize the fracture, prevent further injury to soft tissues and promote appropriate healing. Oftentimes, however, the bone will be obviously bent or otherwise deformed, and the fracture must be "reduced" as we discussed with dislocations. Although this will be painful, normal healing and complete recovery will not occur until the two ends of the broken bone are realigned to their original position.

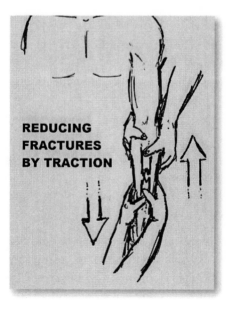

Reducing A Fracture

Reducing a deformity is best performed with 2 persons. One supports and provides traction on the side closest to the torso, and the other exerts steady traction on the area beyond the fracture. There are risks to this procedure and nerves and blood vessels can be damaged, but normal healing will not occur in a deformed limb.

Splint the extremity immediately after performing the reduction. In an open fracture, thorough washing of the wound is absolutely necessary to prevent internal infection. Infection will invariably occur in a dirty wound, even if the reduction is successful. Antibiotics are important to prevent osteomyelitis. Always check for pulses after the reduction is performed, to assure adequate circulation beyond the level of the injury.

The cornerstone of fracture management is an adequate splint. It is very important to immobilize the fractured bone in such a fashion that it is allowed to heal. When you are responsible for the complete healing of the broken bone, remember that the splint should immobilize it in a position that it normally would assume in routine function.

- For legs: The leg should be straight, with a slight bend at the knee.
- For arms: The elbow should be flexed at a 90 degree angle to the upper arm.
- For ankles: The ankle should be at a 90 degree angle to the leg.
- For wrist: The wrist should be straight or slightly extended upward.
- For fingers: The fingers should be slightly flexed, as if holding a glass of water.

As previously mentioned, splints can be commercially produced (SAM splints), or may be improvised, using straight sticks and bandannas or T-shirts to immobilize the area. Another option, as mentioned earlier, is to fold a pillow around the injury and duct tape it in place. In any case, your goal is to immobilize the fracture in a position of function. Use as much padding under the splint as possible to keep the injured area stable. Most fractures require 6-8 weeks to form a "callous"; this is newly formed tissue that will reunite the broken ends of the bone. Larger bones or more complicated injuries take longer. If not well-realigned, the function of the affected extremity will be permanently compromised.

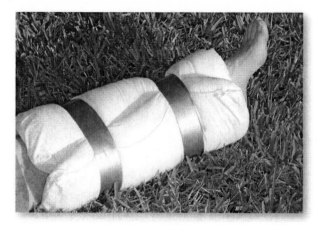

Pillow Splint

Fingers and toes may be splinted by taping them to an adjoining digit. This is called the "buddy method". There are small manufactured splints that will also do the job. Neck injuries may be particularly serious, and an investment should be made in purchasing a good neck "collar".

Rib Fractures and Pneumothorax

Rib fractures are commonly treated by firmly taping the affected area, as it is the motion of breathing that causes the pain associated with the injury. Although reduction is usually not necessary, taping the area may help provide pain relief. Rib fractures become more serious if the fracture punctures a lung, causing a condition known as a "pneumothorax". Air from the puncture enters the chest cavity, which compresses the lung and collapses the organ.

Although a person with a rib fracture will complain of pain with breathing, a person with a pneumothorax will have signs of bluish skin coloration (this is called cyanosis), distended neck veins, and signs of shock. If you use a stethoscope, you will hear the sounds familiarly associated with Rice Krispies when you listen to the lungs, or perhaps no breath sounds at all from the affected area.

If, and only if, the pneumothorax has become life-threatening (known as a "tension pneumothorax"), should you act. Lung decompression can't be taken lightly, and should only be attempted if it's clear the patient will die without action taken on their behalf.

This is what you do: Clean the area of the chest above the third rib midway between the top of the shoulder and the nipple. Using a sharp object no wider than a pencil, poke a hole ABOVE the rib (the blood vessels travel below the rib) until you hear air pass through. A large gauge (14g or larger) spinal needle will be large and long enough to do the job, so consider purchasing this from a medical supply store.

You goal is to provide a way for the air to continue to escape from the incision you made, but not to go back in. Take a square of saran wrap or a plastic bag and firmly tape it above the skin incision on three sides only. This will serve as a valve, and allow air to escape, while allowing the lung to re-inflate. It should be noted that there are lung decompression kits that are available commercially.

Inflammatory or bloody fluid is likely to accumulate in many lung wounds. You will have to rig a drainage system to prevent too much fluid from preventing adequate air passage. Using a rubber tube connected to a jar placed below the patient may perform this duty, but will not be as efficient as the electric suction systems available at your local hospital. It's important to realize that this type of wound will be difficult to recover from. If modern medical care is not available, expect the worst.

SECTION 7

✚ ✚ ✚

CHRONIC MEDICAL PROBLEMS

One of the issues most problematic in a collapse situation is that of the chronic medical problem. Thyroid malfunction, Diabetes (caused by failure of the pancreas to produce sufficient insulin to control blood sugar) and heart disease are just some of the issues; these illnesses require medications that will not be manufactured in times of trouble. We must, sometimes, think "outside the box" to formulate a medical strategy for these patients. The lack of modern technology will be a challenge for the medical provider to effectively treat these conditions.

Its goes without saying that medical conditions that are poorly controlled now will be completely out of control in a collapse situation. The most important way to preserve your health will be to have any chronic condition appropriately treated and monitored now. While you have the benefit of modern medical care, take full advantage of any option that will put you in the best condition. In hard times, you'll need to function at 100% efficiency. If you ignore your medical issues now, how can you expect to keep it together if things fall apart?

This section will discuss some of the most common diseases that people have to deal with today. Develop a plan of action that will allow you to keep them under control if we ever find ourselves on our own.

THYROID DISEASE

✚ ✚ ✚

The thyroid gland is positioned just in front of the Adam's apple and produces hormones that help regulate your metabolism. The organ produces substances that regulate growth, energy and the body's utilization of other hormones and vitamins. Thyroid disease usually involves the production of either too little or too much of these hormones. These malfunctions are most commonly seen in women.

A thyroid problem that we can expect in a collapse situation is the development of a lump on the thyroid known as a goiter. This is the result of a deficiency of iodine in the body, and is one of the reasons why common table salt is "iodized". A person may have a lump on the thyroid without symptoms or even disturbed Thyroid hormone levels. This may present as a cyst (a mass filled with fluid) or a nodule (a solid mass), and usually has no major ill effect.

These are considered to be "cold" tumors. Some thyroid tumors, however, are "hot" and produce excessive hormone levels. Thyroid cancer is relatively rare, even in the elderly, unless there has been exposure to radiation.

Hyperthyroidism

The excessive production of thyroid hormone is known as Hyperthyroidism. Determination of thyroid malfunction depends on certain blood tests and sometimes a scan of the gland. These modalities will be gone in a collapse, so it's important to learn what a person with elevated thyroid levels looks like. Some common signs and symptoms of this condition in adults are:

- Insomnia
- Hand tremors
- Nervousness
- Feeling excessively hot in normal or cold temperatures
- Eyes appear to be bulging out or "staring"
- Frequent bowel movements
- Losing weight despite normal or increased appetite
- Excessive sweating
- Weight loss
- Menstrual period becomes scant, or ceases altogether
- Growth and Puberty issues (children)
- Muscle Weakness, Chest Pain and Shortness of Breath (elderly)

Severely out of control hyperthyroidism leads to a condition known as Thyroid Storm, which causes major effects on the heart and brain. Without treatment, this person is in danger of losing his or her life.

Treatment of hyperthyroidism involves medications such as Propylthiouracil and Methimazole, which block thyroid function. These medications should be stockpiled if you're aware of a member of your group with hyperthyroidism, as they will be hard to find if modern medical care is no longer available. Radiative substances such as I-131 has been used to actually destroy the thyroid, which unfortunately often results in the patient producing no thyroid hormone. This is useful in severe hyperhyroidism, but is also unlikely to be available in a collapse. Iodide is also useful in blocking the excessive production of thyroid hormone, and can be found in Kelp at high levels. The anti-radiation medication KI (Potassium Iodide) might be helpful in this situation. Unfortunately, the use of Iodides, while a known treatment, occasionally actually worsens the condition.

Dietary restriction of nicotine, caffeine, alcohol and other substances that alter metabolism will be useful as well. Vitamins C and B12 are thought to have a beneficial effect on those with this condition, as is L-Carnitine. L-Carnitine is beneficial in that it may lower thyroid hormone levels without damaging the gland. Foods that are thought to depress production of thyroid hormone include cabbage, cauliflower, broccoli, Brussels sprouts, and spinach. Foods high in antioxidants are thought to reduce free radicals that might be involved in hyperthyroidism. These include blueberries, cherries, tomatoes, squash and bell peppers, among others.

Hypothyroidism

More commonly seen than hyperthyroidism, hypothyroidism is the failure to produce enough thyroid hormone. The most commonly seen signs and symptoms of hypothyroidism in adults are:

- Fatigue
- Intolerance to cold
- Constipation
- Poor appetite
- Weight gain
- Dry skin
- Hair loss
- Hoarseness
- Depression
- Menstrual irregularity
- Poor Growth (Children)

The treatment of hypothyroidism is based on the oral replacement of the missing hormone. These come in a variety of dosages, and it is important to determine the appropriate dose for your patient while modern medical care is still available. Once you have determined this, you may consider asking a physician for additional supplies or perhaps a prescription for a higher dose, which would allow you to use, say, half of the pill in the present and stockpile the other half for the uncertain future. Only do this if you intend to follow your physician's advice as to your dose. There is no benefit and significant risk to taking more thyroid replacement medicine that you should.

Besides standard thyroid medications such as Synthroid and Levothyroid, there are a number of other remedies that may have effect in improving hypothyroidism. A number of thyroid extracts are available which consist of desiccated and powdered pig or cow thyroid gland. The amount of thyroid hormone in these extracts may be variable; therefore, the medical establishment recommends against the use of these supplements. Having said this, in the absence of modern medications, it is better than nothing.

One strategy that may help you decide what natural supplement may be right for you is to ask your physician to monitor your thyroid levels for 2 weeks or more while you try it out. If you thyroid levels drop precipitously, it may have little or no effect, and you should research other options.

From a dietary standpoint, you should avoid foods that depress thyroid functions, such as cabbage, cauliflower, broccoli, Brussels sprouts, and spinach. A number of natural supplements, such as Thyromine, are commercially available. They are combinations of various herbs that are touted as beneficial for both low and high thyroid conditions. Your experience may vary.

DIABETES

✚ ✚ ✚

Diabetes in its mild (type 2) or severe (type 1) forms is in epidemic proportions in many developed countries. The medications used to treat the condition are unlikely to be produced in mass quantities if a collapse situation occurs, so we will have to formulate a strategy to keep diabetics from losing control of their blood sugar.

Type 1 Diabetes (also known as juvenile Diabetes or Insulin-dependent Diabetes) results from the failure of the pancreas to produce insulin. Insulin is a hormone that controls the level of sugar in your system. The destruction of the cells in the pancreas that produce Insulin is thought to be caused by an autoimmune response. This means that the body's own immune system attacks parts of itself.

Type 2 Diabetes (also known as adult-onset Diabetes) is more commonly the result of the resistance of the cells in your body to the Insulin produced by the pancreas. Diabetes (mild or severe) may also be present in some pregnancies.

The three classic symptoms of diabetes are:

1. Excessive thirst
2. Excessive hunger
3. Frequent urination.

Uncontrolled diabetes causes eye and kidney problems, leading to blindness and renal failure. It worsens coronary artery disease, increasing the chances for heart attacks and other cardiac issues. Cuts and scrapes, especially in the extremities, are slow to heal. Over time, nerve damage occurs, again frequently in the extremities, causing numbness, pins and needles sensation and, in the worst cases, gangrene. Many diabetics, later on, may require amputation.

Type 2 Diabetes is often seen in older, heavier, and less active individuals. Weight control and close attention to controlling the amounts of carbohydrates (which the body turns into sugars) in the diet is the cornerstone of controlling this condition. In some cases, decreasing excess weight and frequent small meals may reverse Type 2 diabetes in its entirety. Regular exercise will also decrease blood sugar levels, and improve glucose control. The most popular medication used for treatment is called Metformin.

Type 1 Diabetes is more problematic, as many with this medical problem have large swings in their sugar (glucose) levels. Insulin has been used since its formulation in 1921 to control severe diabetes. Regular monitoring of blood glucose levels and appropriate treatment with the right amount of Insulin is necessary to remain healthy.

There are two common diabetic emergencies. These are related either to very low or very high glucose levels. If a diabetic, especially Type 1, fails to eat regularly or in accordance with his Insulin therapy, he or she may develop hypoglycemia. Hypoglycemia can occur very rapidly, and symptoms commonly seen are sweating, loss of coordination, confusion, and loss of consciousness.

In this case, a drink containing sugar will rapidly resolve the condition. Never give liquids to someone who is unconscious, however; the fluids could go down the respiratory passages and suffocation could occur. If the patient is not mentally alert, place some sugar granules under the tongue. This will absorb rapidly without causing the tendency to choke.

Very high glucose levels lead to a condition called Diabetic Ketoacidosis. This occurs as a result of missed Insulin doses and/ or chronically under dosed Insulin. The patient will have a characteristic "fruity" odor to his or her breath. In addition to the usual symptoms, there will be nausea, vomiting, and abdominal pain as well. This is a major emergency which could lead to coma and even death. Small amounts of clear liquids are acceptable in someone with this condition, but without Insulin, the prognosis is grave.

Needless to say, Insulin, like most liquid medications, will lose potency relatively soon after its expiration date. Due to the complexity of the manufacturing process, it is unlikely to be available in a collapse situation. What, then, can be done to maximize glucose control?

Prevention is the best way to avoid hypoglycemia and/or Diabetic Ketoacidosis. In a collapse situation, alternatives will be needed to provide a modicum of diabetic control. In hard times, the goal will be to prevent ketoacidosis. Diabetics will be unlikely to have perfect control, especially Type 1 diabetics, but it may be possible to keep their sugars low enough to prevent a major complication.

Even a few months of less than optimal control will be survivable and will allow society a chance to re-stabilize.

One therapeutic option is to stockpile the highest dose of Metformin (oral diabetes medicine) in the hope that it will have some benefit to the Insulin-deprived Diabetic. Metformin is not as strong a drug as Insulin, but it may prevent the diabetes from going completely out of control, at least temporarily. Another option is to regulate diet severely and decrease caloric intake. This will be harmful in the long run, but frequent very small meals may give some time for a short-term societal destabilization to resolve.

HIGH BLOOD PRESSURE

✚ ✚ ✚

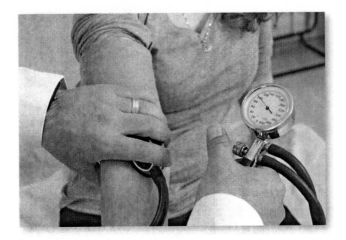

O ne of the most common chronic medical conditions that we will see in a collapse situation is high blood pressure. The blood pressure is the measure of the blood flow pushing against the walls of the arteries in your body. If this pressure is elevated over time, it can cause long-term damage. Many millions of adults in the U.S. have this condition, which is often asymptomatic (no signs or symptoms). Because of this, it has been referred to as a "silent killer". Blood pressure tends to rise with increasing age and weight.

The group medic should have, as part of his equipment, a stethoscope for listening and a pressure monitor called a sphygmomanometer (blood pressure cuff). This is relatively inexpensive and will allow evaluation of the blood pressures of the members of the community. To use, place the cuff around the upper arm and fill it up with air, using the attached bulb. Place your stethoscope over an area with a pulse (commonly the inside of the crook of the arm – see figure above) and listen while looking on the gauge on the cuff. Some new compact blood pressure units are shaped like wristbands and are one piece.

When you take a blood pressure, you are listening for the pulse to register on your stethoscope. A Blood pressure is measured as systolic and diastolic pressures. "Systolic" refers to blood pressure when the heart beats and "Diastolic" refers to blood pressure when the heart is at rest. Therefore, blood pressure is written down as systolic over diastolic: for example: (systolic pressure) 120 over 80 (diastolic pressure).

Wherever the gauge is when you first hear the pulse is the "systolic" pressure. As the air deflates from the sphygmomanometer, the pulse will fade away. When it first appears to fade is the "diastolic" pressure. You should be concerned with numbers that are above 140/90 in the supine or sitting position. As blood pressures tend to vary at different times of the day and under different circumstances, you would be looking for at least 3 elevated pressures in a row before making the diagnosis of high blood pressure (hypertension). Readings above 160/100 are associated with higher frequency of complications. Persistent hypertension can lead to stroke, heart attack, heart failure and chronic kidney failure. Commonly seen symptoms include headaches, blurred vision, or nausea and vomiting.

Sometimes, elevated pressures can cause a blood vessel in the brain to have an "accident". Strokes (also known as "cerebrovascular accidents" or CVAs) are bleeding episodes or clots in the brain that occur as a high pressure event, and can cause paralysis. Suspect this condition if your patient has suddenly found themselves unable to control the extremities on one side of their body, or is unable to speak and cannot move one side of their face. They will usually complain of a severe headache as well.

Pregnancy-induced hypertension ("Pre-Eclampsia") is a serious late pregnancy condition that may lead to seizures ("Eclampsia") and blood clotting abnormalities.

The first step to controlling elevated blood pressures is to return to a normal weight for your height and age. Most people who are obese find that their pressures decrease (often back to normal) when they lose weight. Physical exercise and dietary control are the best way to get there. Dietary restriction of Sodium is paramount in importance when it comes to decreasing pressures. Alcohol, Nicotine, and perhaps Caffeine are also known to raise blood pressures, so abstention from these substances is an additional strategy.

The National Institute of Health recommends the DASH (Dietary Approaches to Stop Hypertension) diet. A major feature of the plan is limiting intake of sodium and it generally encourages the consumption of nuts, whole grains, fish, poultry, fruits and vegetables while lowering the consumption of red meats, sweets, and sugar. It is also rich in protein, potassium, calcium, and magnesium. Studies have found that the DASH diet can reduce high blood pressure within two weeks in certain cases. These are the daily guidelines of the DASH diet:

- 7 to 8 servings of grains
- 4 to 5 servings of vegetables
- 4 to 5 servings of fruit
- 2 to 3 servings of low-fat or non-fat dairy
- 2r less servings of meat, fish, or poultry
- 2 to 3 servings of fats and oils

- 4 to 5 servings per week of nuts, seeds, and dry beans
- Less than 5 servings a week of sweets

Serving Sizes

-1/2 cup cooked rice or pasta
-1 slice bread
-1 cup raw vegetables or fruit
-1/2 cup cooked vegetables or fruit
-8 oz. of milk
-1 teaspoon olive oil

Optimize your results on this diet by implementing the following tips:

- Choose foods that are low in saturated fat, cholesterol, and total fat, such as lean meat, poultry, and fish.
- Eat plenty of fruits and vegetables; aim for eight to ten servings each day.
- Include two to three servings of low-fat or fat-free dairy foods each day.
- Choose whole-grain foods, such as 100 percent whole-wheat or whole-grain bread, cereal, and pasta.
- Eat nuts, seeds, and dried beans – four to five servings per week (one serving equals 1/3 cup or 1.5 ounces nuts, 2 tablespoons or 1/2 ounce seeds, or 1/2 cup cooked dried beans or peas).
- Go easy on added fats. Choose soft margarine, low-fat mayonnaise, light salad dressing, and unsaturated vegetable oils (such as olive, corn, canola, or safflower).
- Cut back on sweets and sugary beverages.

A number of medications with impressive names are available for the control of high blood pressure: ACE inhibitors, alpha blockers, angiotensin II receptor antagonists, beta blockers, calcium channel blockers, diuretics, and others. Those with hypertension will be placed on one or more of these medications until their readings are back to normal.

All of these commercially prepared products will be scarce in a collapse, so consider asking for higher doses of your specific medication than what you need, so that you can break them in half and store some of it. Again, always take your medication in the dosage prescribed by your physician.

Natural supplements have been used to help lower blood pressure, as well. Any herb that has a sedative effect will likely also lower pressures. Valerian, Passion Flower, and Lemon Balm are some examples. Garlic and Cayenne Pepper is also well-known to have a modest lowering effect. Coenzyme Q10 has shown some promise in this field. Antioxidants like Vitamin C and fish oil may prevent free radicals from damaging artery walls. Foods rich in Potassium, like bananas, are also recommended.

Don't forget natural relaxation techniques. Meditation, Yoga, and mild massage therapy will relax your patient. Take their blood pressure after a session and see what effect it has had. You will probably be quite surprised! Hypertension related to stress will be most likely to respond to this approach.

HEART DISEASE
AND CHEST PAIN

✚ ✚ ✚

U nlike most medical books, I will not be spending a great deal of time discussing coronary artery disease, even though it is one of the leading causes of death in today's society. Why? It will difficult in a collapse situation to do very much about heart attacks, due to the loss of all the advances that have been made to deal with coronary disease. There will not be a cardiac intensive care unit or a cardiac bypass surgeon at your disposal. We will have to accept that some folks with heart problems will do better than others in hard times.

Heart attacks, also called "myocardial infarctions" involve the blockage of an artery that gives oxygen to a part of the heart muscle. That portion of the muscle subsequently dies, either killing the patient or leaving them so incapacitated as to be unable to function in a post-collapse scenario. This decrease in function is most likely permanent.

Does that mean that you can't or shouldn't do anything if you suspect that your patient is having a heart attack? No, there are low tech approaches; they just won't do much if there has been a lot of damage caused. You would suspect a heart event if you see the following:

- "Crushing" sensation in the chest area
- Pain down the left arm
- Pain in the jaw area
- Weakness
- Fatigue
- Sweating
- Pale coloring

The main approach is to immediately give your patient a chewable adult aspirin (325 mg). This will aid in preventing further damage to the coronary artery and preserve oxygen flow. A natural alternative is Salicin, which is found in the under bark of willow, poplar, and aspen trees. You will want them to directly chew the bark, which would be the fastest way to get the substance into their system. A tea will also deliver the Salicin, but will take some time to brew. The only problem here is that you won't know exactly how much of the substance you've actually given your patient.

A person suffering a heart attack will feel most comfortable lying down at a 45 degree angle. Complete rest will cause the least oxygen demand on the damaged heart. Don't forget to loosen constrictive clothing; tight clothes make a cardiac patient feel anxious and cause their heart to beat faster.

Aspirin, in small doses, is also reasonable as a preventative strategy. One baby aspirin (81 mg) daily is thought to prevent the deposition of plaque inside the blood vessels. You might consider having all of your adults 40 and over on this treatment. Men are most likely to have coronary artery disease, as female hormones seem to protect women, at least before menopause. If your patient takes heart medications, administer them immediately.

Those in your survival community with coronary artery issues should stockpile whatever medications they take to deal with their symptoms. Angina (cardiac-related chest pain) can be treated with nitroglycerine tablets. Placed under the tongue, they will give rapid relief in most cases.

There are various other causes of chest pain. Injury to muscles and joints in the torso may mimic cardiac pain. In this type of pain, you will notice that the pain gets worse with movement of the affected area, or that you can elicit pain from pressing on it. Rest the patient and give them Ibuprofen or Acetaminophen for pain.

Chest pain is also seen in some patients with anxiety issues. This is usually accompanied by tremors, a rapid heart rate and hyperventilation. Sedative herbs like Valerian Root, Passion Flower, and Chamomile may be helpful in this situation, as are some prescription medications such as diazepam (Valium). Relaxation techniques will also help.

Another common cause of chest pain relates to heartburn. See the next chapter for a discussion of this and other acid reflux conditions.

ULCER AND ACID REFLUX DISEASE

✚ ✚ ✚

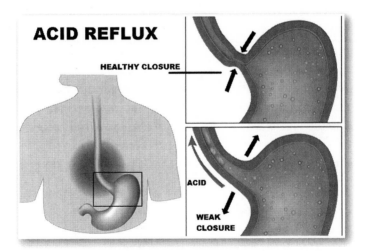

Acid Reflux Disease

Ulcers

Chronic stress issues will be epidemic in a collapse. They can manifest in ways that are both emotional and physical. One of the physical effects is increased stomach acid levels.

THE DOOM AND BLOOM™ HANDBOOK

Excessive acid can cause an inflammation of the esophagus (the tube that goes from the throat to the stomach), the stomach itself and/or the next part of the bowel, called the duodenum. The irritated lining becomes weak and forms an erosion. This erosion is called an "ulcer" and can cause bleeding or even perforate the lining.

The major symptom of an ulcer is a burning or gnawing discomfort in the stomach area. This pain is often described as heartburn, indigestion or hunger pangs. It usually occurs in the left or mid-upper abdomen or may travel up to the breastbone. The discomfort that goes along with this problem is hard to ignore and will decrease work efficiency. Therefore, diagnosis and treatment are important to get your group member back to normal.

There are many causes of pain in the chest and stomach areas. Chest pain caused by coronary heart disease ("angina") is just one of the possibilities. To make the diagnosis of ulcer or acid reflux disease, the timing of the discomfort is important. Ulcer and acid reflux discomfort occurs after eating but is sometimes seen several hours afterward. It can be differentiated from other causes of chest pain in another way: it gets better by drinking milk or taking antacids. As you can imagine, this wouldn't do much for angina.

Many ulcers and lining inflammation are caused by a bacterium known as Helicobacter pylori. H. pylori may be transmitted from person to person through contaminated food and water, so proper water filtration and sterilization will decrease the likelihood of this infection. Antibiotics such as Amoxicillin and Metronidazole in combination are the most effective treatment for Helicobacter pylori ulcers. Other causes include the use of Ibuprofen and Aspirin, which can be an irritant to the stomach in some people. Avoidance of these drugs will prevent these ulcers. Smoking and alcohol abuse are also known causes.

Acid Reflux Disease

Acid reflux disease is caused by acid traveling up the esophagus. This is sometimes caused by a relaxation at the stomach-esophagus border, or by an out pouching of the area called a Hiatal Hernia. The primary symptom is heartburn, but severe disease can cause chest pain. It is usually relieved by antacids or by sleeping with the upper body raised.

Your patient may benefit from avoiding certain foods. These commonly include acidic fruit such as oranges, fatty foods, coffee, tea, onions, peppermint, and chocolate. Eating smaller meals and avoiding acidic foods before bedtime is a good strategy to prevent reflux. Obese individuals seem to suffer more from this problem, so weight loss might be helpful.

Medications that commonly relieve acid reflux include antacids such as Maalox, Mylanta or Pepto-Bismol, as well as Ranitidine (Zantac), Cimetidine (Tagamet), and Omeprazole (Prilosec). These medications are available in non-prescription strength and are easy to accumulate in quantity.

Home remedies abound for acid reflux:

Organic apple cider vinegar: Mix one tablespoon in four ounces of water, drink before each meal.

Aloe Vera Juice: Mix one ounce in two ounces of water before a meal.

Baking soda: Mix one tablespoon in a glass of water and drink right away when you begin to feel heartburn

Glutamine: An amino acid that has an anti-inflammatory effect and reduces acid reflux. It can be found in milk and eggs.

It's important to remember to communicate with your patients. Many Preppers are rugged individualists and are unlikely to tell the medic about something they consider trivial, like heartburn. Someone that is clearly in pain, losing efficiency, or unable to sleep should always be questioned about their symptoms. It could be something you just might be able to help them with.

SEIZURE DISORDERS

✦ ✦ ✦

S eizures occur when the brain's electrical system misfires. Instead of sending out signals in a controlled manner, a surge of energy goes through the brain. This can cause involuntary muscle contractions, loss of organ control, and loss of consciousness. A person with chronic problems with convulsions is called an "epileptic". There are several types of seizures:

Generalized Seizures:

These are also known as Grand Mal seizures. Loss of consciousness, bladder control, and spastic shaking are commonly seen. These last several minutes and are followed by a period of extreme drowsiness. A much lesser form is the Petit Mal seizure. The patient stops whatever they were doing and just stares out into space, apparently unaware of their surroundings. These seizures are caused by electrical disturbances throughout the brain.

Partial Seizures:

Once known as Jacksonian seizures, these are caused by issues in one part of the brain and may involve involuntary shaking of just one limb, or specific twitching behavior. The patient may notice strange tastes in the mouth or strange smells. Vision may be temporarily impaired. There may or may not be changes in mental status.

There are various causes of convulsive disorders, such as:

- High fever (in children, mostly)
- Head injury
- Meningitis (Infection of the central nervous system)
- Stroke
- Brain tumors
- Genetic predisposition
- Idiopathic (unknown – about 50% of cases)

In a collapse situation, there won't be the sophisticated equipment such as EEGs (electroencephalograms) and Brain Scans to make the diagnosis, so we will have to watch for symptoms to identify the problem. One seizure does not make someone an epileptic. Multiple episodes are required to be certain.

Epileptic seizures are sometimes preceded by an "aura", a strange feeling that gives some warning that an attack may be imminent. There are also triggers that sometimes cause a convulsion: a good example is a bright flashing light. Avoidance of these triggers will decrease the number of episodes.

The most important aspect of treatment when intravenous medication is no longer available will be to prevent the patient from injuring themselves during an attack. A tongue depressor with gauze taped around it and placed in the mouth will prevent the patient from obstructing their airway by "swallowing" their tongue. You shouldn't restrain the person physically, but remove nearby objects that could cause injury.

Do not give oral fluids or medications to an epileptic until they are fully awake and alert. If the convulsion is caused by a fever, as in children, cool them down with wet compresses. Anyone in your survival group with a convulsive disorder should work towards stockpiling their medicine. Popular drugs are Dilantin, Tegretol, Valproic Acid, and Diazepam (Valium).

Natural alternatives have long been espoused to decrease the frequency and severity of convulsions. Many herbal supplements have a sedative effect, which calms the brain's electrical energy. They may be taken as a tea (1 teaspoon of the herb in a cup of water) or as a tincture (an extract with grain alcohol). Here are some that have been reported as beneficial for prevention:

- Bacopa (*Bacopa monnieri*
- Chamomile *(Matricaria recutita)*
- Kava (*Piper methysticum*) – (too much may damage your liver)
- Valerian (*Valeriana officinalis*,
- Lemon balm (*Melissa officinalis*),
- Passionflower (*Passiflora incarnata*)

Supplements of Vitamin B12 and E may also be helpful.

JOINT DISEASE

✚ ✚ ✚

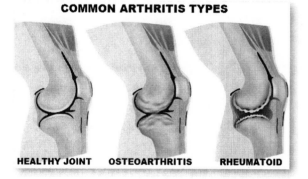

COMMON ARTHRITIS TYPES

HEALTHY JOINT   OSTEOARTHRITIS   RHEUMATOID

Over the course of time, joints suffer wear and tear just like the moving parts of any other machine. Damage to ankles, knees, hips, and even the spine occurs chronically over the course of years. This degenerative damage is called osteoarthritis, and will be accelerated in a collapse situation due to the increase in repetitive work to be done.

Arthritis can also be caused by auto-immune conditions; antibodies are formed that attack tissues in the joints and sometimes cause striking deformities. Bacterial infections, some of which are sexually transmitted, also damage joint tissue significantly and must be identified and treated quickly.

Regardless of the cause of the arthritis in the joint, the symptoms are generally the same. You will see:

- Pain (mild or severe)
- Swelling
- Joint stiffness and decreased range of motion
- Muscle weakness (with chronic arthritis)
- Fever (septic arthritis)
- Reluctance to use the affected joint

As you can imagine, Osteoarthritis is the most common form of arthritis, especially in older individuals. It can affect both the larger and the smaller joints of the body. Hands, feet, back, hip, and knee are most commonly affected. The disease is acquired by daily wear and tear on the joints, although it can also be a long term effect of a previous injury.

Rheumatoid arthritis is a disorder in which the body's own immune system starts to attack body tissues. The attack is not only directed at the joint but to other parts of the body. Rheumatoid arthritis affects joints in the fingers, wrists, knees and elbows. The disease is symmetrical and can lead to severe deformity in a few years if not treated. Rheumatoid arthritis occurs in younger populations than Osteoarthritis, even striking children on occasion. Treatments concentrate on easing the symptoms, but no cure exists. Treatments focus around strong anti-inflammatory medications such as oral steroids.

Another auto-immune disorder is known as Systemic Lupus; it can be differentiated from rheumatoid arthritis due to the presence of body rashes and hair loss. It is seen primarily in women.

Osteoarthritis, like rheumatoid arthritis, cannot be cured but you can prevent the condition from worsening. Weight loss is the key to improving symptoms and preventing progression. Physical therapy to strengthen muscles and joints is very helpful. Pain medications are widely required by individuals with osteoarthritis, such as Acetaminophen or Ibuprofen.

Gout is another condition that destroys joints over time. It is caused by deposition of uric acid crystals in the joint, causing inflammation. In the early stages, the gouty arthritis usually occurs in one joint, often the big toe. With time, it can occur in many joints and be quite crippling. Eventually, the joint is destroyed, eliminating any movement in it for the life of the patient. This illness occurs primarily in men.

From an alternative standpoint, there are several treatments for joint pain caused by Arthritis. Two teaspoons of lemon juice or apple cider vinegar mixed with a teaspoon of honey twice a day is a time-honored treatment. Turmeric powder, bathua leaf juice, and alfalfa tea have also been reported as effective against joint pain.

For external use, warm vinegar applied to aching joints may give some relief. Sandalwood powder, mixed into a paste, has a cooling effect when rubbed on a joint. An ointment made of 2 parts olive oil and 1 part Kerosene may be helpful when used as a salve (caution: Kerosene is flammable!).

KIDNEY STONES/GALL BLADDER DISEASE

✚ ✚ ✚

The kidney and gall bladder are two organs that have the propensity in some people to develop certain crystals; these crystals form masses known as "stones". Some are large and some are as small as grains of sand, but any size can cause pain (sometimes excruciating) that will put a person out of commission.

Kidney Stones

Kidney stones are commonly seen in those persons who fail to keep themselves well hydrated. Even small stones can lead to significant pain (known as "renal colic"), and the larger ones can cause blockages that can disrupt the function of the organ. If you have had a kidney stone before, it is likely that you will get one again in the future.

Once formed in the kidney, stones usually do not cause symptoms until they begin to move down the tubes which connect the kidneys to the bladder (the "ureter"). When this happens, the stones can block the flow of urine out of the kidneys. This causes swelling of the kidney affected as well as significant pain. Kidney stones as small as grains of sand may reach the bladder without incident and then cause pain as they attempt to pass through the tube that goes from the bladder to the outside (the "urethra").

There are several different types of kidney stones:

- Calcium stones are most common. They occur more often in men than in women, usually in adults 20 to 40 years old. Calcium can combine with other substances, such as oxalate, phosphate, or carbonate to form a stone.
- Cysteine stones can form in people who have cysteinuria, a condition that tends to run in families.
- Struvite stones are mostly found in women and can grow quite large; they can cause blockages at any point in the urinary tract. Frequent and chronic infections are a risk factor for this variety of stone.
- Uric acid stones are more common in men than in women, and are associated with conditions such as gout.

To diagnose a kidney stone, look for pain that starts suddenly and comes and goes. Pain is commonly felt on the side of the back. Lightly pound on the right and left side of the back at the level of the lowest rib. This will cause significant pain in patients with kidney stones or kidney infections. The pain will move down the abdomen and could settle in the groin area or even the urethral area.

Other symptoms of renal stones can include:

- Bloody urine.
- Fever and chills.
- Nausea and vomiting.

Your goal as medical provider is to assist the stone to pass as quickly as possible through the system. Have your patient drink at least 8 glasses of water per day to produce a large amount of urine. . If the stones are Calcium in nature, avoid foods such as spinach, rhubarb, beets, parsley, sorrel, and chocolate. Also, decreasing dairy intake will restrict the amount of Calcium available for stone formation. This will keep the them as small as possible and easier to pass.

Pain relievers can help control the pain of passing the stones (renal colic). For severe pain, Ibuprofen is a treatment of choice, but stronger pain medications, if you can get them, may be necessary for severe cases.

Some of the larger stones will be chronic issues, as the high technology and surgical options used for these will not be available in a collapse scenario. Medications specific to the type of stone may be helpful:

- Allopurinol (prescription medicine for uric acid stones).
- Antibiotics (for struvite stones).
- Diuretics to increase urination.
- Sodium bicarbonate or sodium citrate (which increases the alkalinity of the urine) will decrease the likelihood of formation of some stones.

A good home remedy to relieve discomfort and aid passage of the stone is lemon juice, olive oil, and apple cider vinegar. With the first twinge of pain, drink a mixture of 2 ounces of lemon juice and 2 ounces of olive oil. Then, drink a large glass of water. After 1 hour, drink a mixture of 1 tablespoon of raw apple cider vinegar with 2 ounces of lemon juice in a large glass of water. Repeat this process every 1 to 2 hours until improved.

Other natural substances that may help are:

- Horsetail tea (a natural diuretic)
- Pomegranate juice
- Dandelion root tea
- Celery tea
- Basil tea

Gall Bladder Stones

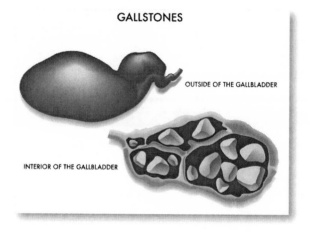

GALLSTONES

OUTSIDE OF THE GALLBLADDER

INTERIOR OF THE GALLBLADDER

The gall bladder is a sac that is attached to the liver and stores the bile that the liver secretes. Gallstones are firm deposits that form inside the gallbladder and could block the passage of bile; this can cause a great deal of pain and inflammation (known as "cholecystitis").

There are two main types of gallstones:

4. Cholesterol stones: The grand majority, these are not related to the actual cholesterol levels in the bloodstream.
5. Bilirubin stones: These occur in those people who have illnesses that destroy their red blood cells. This releases a substance called bilirubin into the bile and forms a stone.

Risk factors for this condition can be described as the 4 "F's":

- FAT: The majority of those with gallstones are overweight.
- FEMALE: The majority of sufferers are women.
- FORTY: Most people with gallstone issues are over 40 years old.
- FERTILE Most women with gallstones have had children.

Additional risk factors include Diabetes, Liver Cirrhosis, and certain types of anemia.

Luckily, most people with this problem don't have any symptoms. If a large stone causes a blockage, however, you may experience what is called "biliary colic". Symptoms of biliary colic include:

- Cramping right upper abdomen pain (constant, spreading to the back).
- Fever.
- Jaundice (yellowing of the skin and whites of the eyes).
- Discolored bowel movements (gray or grayish-white).
- Nausea and vomiting.

Unfortunately, the main treatment for gallstones is to surgically remove the gall bladder. As surgical suites are unlikely to be available in a collapse situation, you might consider some alternative remedies. These are mostly preventative measures:

- Apple cider vinegar (mixed with apple juice)
- Peppermint
- Turmeric
- Alfalfa
- Ginger root
- Dandelion root
- Artichoke leaves
- Beet, Carrot, Grape, Lemon juices

VARICOSE VEINS

✚ ✚ ✚

Varicose veins are dilated blood vessels, usually in the legs, which have lost tone in the valves that control blood flow. This swelling of the vascular structures occurs in about 15% of the population, and becomes more common with age (50%). In addition, women are several times more likely to have this problem than men. Varicose veins are gravity dependent; they may be more common in people whose occupation requires constant standing.

Varicose veins are similar to but not the same as "spider veins". Spider veins are tiny vessels called capillaries and exist everywhere in your body. When they become varicose, they appear like little red or blue spider webs; you may find them on your legs, face, or just about anywhere. Standard varicose veins are blue, swollen, and stick out from the skin. They tend to look "twisted".

Varicosities cause the circulation to become less efficient. This causes pain and fatigue in the legs, and could lead to an inflammation known as "phlebitis".

You're more likely to get varicose veins if you:

- Are 50 years of age or older. The valves in your veins weaken as you age.

- Have a family history. If your mother had varicose veins, you are likely to get them as well.
- Are a woman. High levels of estrogen as seen in puberty, pregnancy, and while taking birth control pills increase your risk.
- Are obese. Extra weight put pressure on the veins and causes them to dilate.
- Work in a profession that requires long periods of standing, lifting weights or sitting with your legs bent.
- Spend longs hours in the sun, especially if your complexion is fair. You may notice them first on your cheeks or nose.

Besides the discomfort and an unpleasing cosmetic appearance, varicose veins are usually not dangerous. Occasionally, however, you might see:

Thrombophlebitis: a varicose vein on the surface of the skin can become inflamed; this is due to a blood clot which formed due to the poor circulation in the area. Symptoms include swelling, redness, heat, and pain. A hemorrhoid is a type of superficial thrombophlebitis: See the section describing it later in this book.

Deep vein thrombosis (DVT): A blood clot that forms in a deep vein. The patient will experience a "full" feeling, usually in the calf area. This will be accompanied by pain, heat, swelling, and redness as in superficial thrombophlebitis. This can be dangerous if the blood clot dislodges and makes it way to the lungs or other vital organs.

If your patient has varicose veins, have them stock up on compression stockings or support pantyhose while times are good. These will be unavailable in a collapse setting and neither will curative treatments like surgery, lasers, or chemical injections. Encourage your patients at risk to:

- Exercise their legs to improve tone; this will provide support to the blood vessels.
- Avoid standing for long periods of time. Shift their weight from foot to foot often and take a short walk if they sit all day.
- Keep their weight down to avoid putting strain on their legs.
- Elevate their legs above the level of the heart for a half hour daily, and perhaps during sleep.
- Wear support stockings.
- Avoid wearing high heels for long periods.
- Eat a low-salt diet. Less salt consumption can help with the swelling that you see with varicose veins.
- Wear sunscreen; this will limit spider veins in people with fair complexions.

The herbal remedy most quoted to treat varicose veins is the horse chestnut (Aesculus hippocastanum. Horse chestnuts contain a substance called aescin, which appears to block enzymes that damage capillary walls. Make a tincture (grain alcohol-based mixture) with the herb and take 1 tablespoonful up to 3 times a day. For external use only, rub a mixture of 4 parts witch hazel with 1 part tincture of horse chesnut and rub on affected varicosities.

SECTION 8

✚ ✚ ✚

OTHER IMPORTANT
MEDICAL ISSUES

CPR IN A
COLLAPSE SITUATION

✚ ✚ ✚

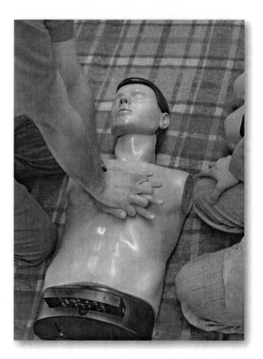

Most medical books start off with a chapter on CPR (Cardio-Pulmonary Resuscitation), so you might wonder why this subject has not been given coverage so far in this volume. Although an important skill that everyone should know, there are fewer situations in a collapse scenario where CPR will return a victim to normal function.

Resuscitation is best used as a stabilization strategy. You want to get the heart pumping and breathing supported so that you can get your patient as quickly as possible to a facility where there are ventilators, defibrillators, and other high technology. But what about a situation where this technology is no longer available?

There won't be cardiac bypasses or catheterizations for your patient who has had a heart attack. There won't be surgical suites for your patient with a shotgun blast to the abdomen or chest. The sobering truth is that many of these injuries will be what was once called a "mortal" wound. This means that death is the likely end result, no matter what you try to do. The poor prognosis for these people in hard times makes you truly appreciate the benefits of modern medicine.

There are still circumstances, however, where CPR may actually restore a gravely ill person to normal function. Airway obstruction with a foreign object can be dealt with by using the Heimlich maneuver. Environmental conditions such as hypothermia, heat stroke or smoke inhalation will oftentimes respond to resuscitative efforts. Severe anaphylactic reactions may require CPR until the patient responds to Epinephrine and resolves the attack. Rarer events such as lightning strikes or drowning may require resuscitation to revive the victim.

I chose not to put a large number of illustrations or write an entire course on how to do CPR in this book simply because There is no substitution to learning it in person by taking a hands-on course. I don't want you to think that you don't have to do this just because you read this book.

Airway Obstruction

One situation where you can save a life by knowing how to perform a simple maneuver is in the case of an airway obstruction. This most commonly occurs as a result of a bite of food lodging in the back of the throat, cutting off respiration.

If you see a conscious adult in sudden respiratory distress, ask quickly: Are you choking on something? If they can answer you, there is still air passing into their lungs. If it's a complete blockage, they will be unable to speak. They will probably be agitated and holding their throat, but they will hear you and (frantically) nod their head "yes". This is your signal to jump into action.

So what should you do for an adult in this situation? Tell the victim that you're there to help them and immediately get into position for the Heimlich maneuver, otherwise known as an "abdominal thrust" (see figure above). Go behind the victim and make a fist with your right hand. Place your first above the belly button and wrap your other arm around the patient to grasp the fist. Make sure your arms are positioned below the ribcage. With a forceful upward motion, press your fist abruptly into the abdomen. You might have to do this multiple times before you dislodge the foreign body.

If your patient loses consciousness and you are unable to dislodge the obstructive item, place the patient in a supine position and straddle them across the thighs or hips. Open their mouth and make sure that the object can't be removed manually. Give several abdominal thrusts with the heels of your palms (one above the other) and check again; you might have partially dislodged it.

In old movies, you might see someone slap the victim hard on the back; this is unlikely to dislodge a foreign object and will waste precious time. An exception to this is in an infant: place the baby over your forearm (facing down) and apply several blows with the heel of your hand to the upper back.

CPR in the Unconscious Patient

If you come across someone who is apparently unconscious, be certain to verify their mental status. Simply ask them loudly: "Are you OK?" No answer? Grasp the person's shoulders and move them gently while continuing to ask them questions. If they are still unresponsive (which you should be able to determine in a few seconds), it's time to check their pulse and respirations. If they aren't breathing, it's time to start resuscitative efforts.

You'll want to open the airway first. Check inside the mouth for a foreign object. If there is none, place the patient head in a position that will allow the clearest passage for air to enter the body. This is called the "Chin-Lift". Tilt the head back (unless there is evidence of a neck injury) and grasp the underside of the chin and lower jaw with one hand and lift. The tongue and other throat structures will then occupy a position that will allow you to help the patient take in oxygen. A useful medical item to achieve this goal is a plastic "airway".

Check for signs of breathing. If breathing is absent, give 2 long breaths mouth-to-mouth (3-5 seconds between each one). You can determine the effectiveness of your efforts by watching the patient's chest rise as you give the breaths. If you are concerned about infection, take a nitrile glove and cut the ends off of the two middle fingers. Place over the victim's mouth (cut fingers down) as you breathe for them. This provides a barrier that still allows air flow.

A useful item for your medical supplies is a bag valve mask, otherwise known by the brand name "Ambu-Bag". This can be placed on the patient's mouth to form a seal through which you can ventilate them by pressing on an air-filled "bag". This provides pressure to force air inside the respiratory passages.

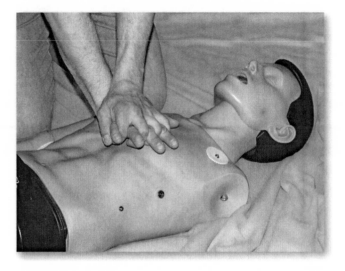

If there is a pulse, breathe about 12-14 times per minute for the patient. If there is no pulse, perform chest compressions by placing the heels of your palms 2 finger-breadths above the lowest part of the breastbone (one hand above the other). Keeping yourself positioned directly above your hands (arms straight), press downward in such a fashion that the breastbone (also called the "sternum") goes in about 2 inches. This works well for adults but you would want less pressure in a child. Be certain to avoid the rib cage, as broken ribs are a common complication of the procedure.

If you are the lone resuscitator, perform 15 compressions and then deliver 2 more breaths as before. If you have a helper, perform 5 compressions for every 2 breaths. Try for a compression rate of 80-100 beats per minute. Perform several cycles of the above; then re-evaluate the patient's pulse and respirations. Once you have started CPR, don't stop until the patient has responded or it is clear that they will not.

After 30 minutes of CPR without result, the pupils of the patient's eyes will likely be dilated and will not respond to light.

At this point, your patient has expired and you can cease your efforts. Some may feel this is not long enough resuscitation; in truth, just a few minutes without oxygen in enough to cause irreversible brain damage. You will not be equipped to provide long term chronic care to someone who no longer has brain activity.

There are units known as defibrillators available that, though quite expensive, may be useful in a cardiac arrest. These machines produce an electric shock to the heart and sometimes can restart a pulse that has stopped. If caused by a heart attack, a cardiac arrest without defibrillation will have a very low survival rate. It would be wise for your survival group to chip in and purchase a unit. "Home" defibrillators can be found online and are surprisingly easy to use:

Turn the unit on and connect the electrodes per the instructions. Place one electrode pad on the right chest about the nipple and below the collarbone. Place the other on the left chest outside the nipple and several inches below the armpit. The unit will analyze the heart rate (or lack of one) and tell you (believe it or not) whether a shock is necessary or not. If one is indicated, clear everyone away from the patient and press the button to activate the electric shock. Recheck vital signs.

If you are successful in establishing a pulse and breathing in your unconscious patient, but for some reason must leave them to get help, do this: Position them so that they will not vomit and possibly aspirate stomach acid into the lungs. Gently roll them so that they are on their side, with one hand cradling their cheek and the uppermost leg bent at a right angle. Make sure their head is in a position that keeps the airways open. This is known as "the recovery position" (see figure on the following page).

Recovery position for an unconscious patient

Although CPR will have limited effectiveness for some conditions in a collapse situation, it is still important to know. A survival community medic should not only be skilled in performing CPR, but should also teach it to every group member.

HEADACHE

✚ ✚ ✚

Headache may be a sign of head trauma, but is much more likely to be related to other causes. One of the most common symptoms a human can get, most of us have had to deal with headaches at one point or another. There are almost more causes for headaches than you can reasonably write down; in a collapse, however, common causes will be dehydration, stress, infections, fever, high blood pressure, and withdrawal from substances such as caffeine and alcohol.

By far, the most frequently-seen type of headache is the tension headache. This is caused by spasms of the muscles of the neck and head. This headache is bilateral (on both sides) and the back of the head. Discontinuing any stressful activities is recommended here, but pain can persist for hours and even days. This type of headache may be improved by massaging the back of the neck and temples. Ibuprofen and Acetaminophen are old standbys as treatment.

Headache caused by dehydration will be rampant in a collapse. This variety is also bilateral and is commonly made worse by standing up from a lying position. These patients need fluids, which will gradually improve their symptoms.

The other common cause of headache is the migraine. A specific pattern will emerge here: Your patient will often notice the pain only on one side. There may be eye signs, such as discomfort when looking into a bright light or pain behind one eye. Those with severe migraines frequently have nausea and vomiting. In the worst cases, vision changes known as "auras" manifest as blurred vision, lights and colors. Bed rest in the dark will be helpful here, as well as Ibuprofen and/or Acetaminophen. Some migraine medications use caffeine, and sometimes are effective. Teas and Coffee might be alternatives in a collapse. If you are a chronic migraine sufferer, ask you physician for Imitrex, a strong anti-migraine medication, to stockpile.

If you would like a strategy to deal with a headache without drugs, try the following:

- Place an ice pack where the headache is.
- Have someone massage the back of your neck.
- Using two fingers, apply rotating pressure where the headache is.
- Lie down in a dark, quiet room. Get some sleep if at all possible.
- Track what you were doing or perhaps what you ate before the headache started, and avoid that activity or food if possible.

A number of herbal remedies are available that might help headache. Feverfew is an herb that stops blood vessel constriction and is anti-inflammatory. This can be taken on a daily basis (1-2 leaves) for those with chronic problems (warning: Feverfew should not be ingested during pregnancy or nursing). Gingko Biloba has a similar action.

The pain of tension headaches can be relieved if you utilize herbs that have sedative and antispasmodic properties. Teas made from Valerian, skullcap, lemon balm, and passion flower have both. Herbal muscle relaxants may also help: rosemary, chamomile, and mint teas are popular options.

For external use, consider lavender or rosemary oil. Massage each temple with 1-2 drops every few hours.

Less common causes of headache would include an infection of the central nervous system called "meningitis". Along with headaches, meningitis presents with a stiff neck, fever, and possibly a rash. This condition may be caused by bacteria or viruses. Without modern medical facilities and labs, you could treat this condition with antibiotics and antivirals in the hope of improvement. Expect variable results.

Uncontrolled high blood pressure or a burst blood vessel in the brain may cause a stroke (medical name: cerebrovascular accident or CVA). Besides the sudden onset of a severe headache, you will notice that your patient has lost strength in the arm and leg on one side; you will also note decreased motion on one side of the face and absent or slurred speech. Loss of vision in one eye is sometimes seen. This condition, in a collapse, will be treated only with bed rest. There is often some improvement over the first 48 hours or so. Beyond this point, further recovery may be limited. This is one of the main reasons why it is so important for you as medic to treat all cases of high blood pressure.

EYE CARE

+ + +

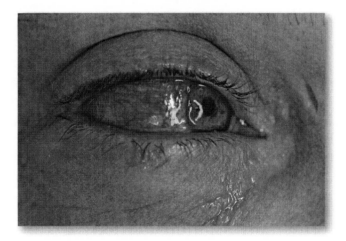

Ask anyone on the street which of the five senses they would least be willing to sacrifice. They probably will tell you that their vision is the sense they would most want to preserve. Human beings aren't perfect, and one of our most common imperfections is that of being nearsighted (also known as myopia) or farsighted (also known as hyperopia).

Most of us correct our eye issues with eyeglasses or contact lenses. In a collapse setting, these vision aids become more precious than gold, but most people haven't made provision for multiple replacement pairs of contact lenses or spare eyeglasses. Having a few pairs of reading glasses would be useful as well, as everyone reaches an age when eyesight naturally changes.

Also, many of us with perfect vision will be negligent about wearing eye protection when they chop wood or other chores likely to be part of normal off-grid living. Without eye protection, the risk of injury when performing strenuous tasks will be much higher.

It is of paramount importance to stockpile multiple pairs of eyeglasses even if you currently only use contact lenses at present. Let's face it, there will be a limited supply of contacts in a collapse situation, and one day you will have to throw away your last pair. Your current eyeglasses will eventually fall apart or become scratched beyond repair, and the last thing you will want is to not be able to see.

Early in this book, I mentioned that you should deal with your medical issues BEFORE a societal collapse occurs. Bad eyesight might be one of those issues. One option you may not have considered is having your eyesight corrected to 20/20 with LASIK surgery. Lasik surgery uses pinpoint lasers to change the shape of your retina so that you are less nearsighted or farsighted. It has been routinely available for years now, and is one of the safest surgical procedures in existence.

The LASIK procedure for both eyes takes less than ten minutes from beginning to end, and the actual laser surgery usually takes less than 20 seconds for each eye. You will be able to see immediately, and there is usually no downtime.

At most, you might feel the sensation of a grain of sand in your eye for a few days. The procedure isn't cheap, but where else can you get such a tangible benefit (perfect vision) from your investment? I, myself, have had this procedure and recommend it highly to those with vision problems.

If you have perfect vision already, you should have a stockpile of eye protection glasses which you should use regularly when you perform any chore that has a remote possibility of injuring your eyes. Even if you are just taking a hike outdoors, sunglasses should also be a standard item. Ultraviolet (UV) light causes, over time, damage to the retinal cells which can lead to a clouding over of your eye's lenses (also called "cataracts"). This condition can only be repaired by surgery that will not be available in a collapse. Protection from ultraviolet (UV) light will help prevent long-term damage.

In cold weather conditions, failure to use sunglasses can cause a type of vision loss known as snow blindness. Snow blindness is painful and dangerous in the wilderness, but usually will go away on its own with eye patching. The truth of the matter is that, whenever you are doing chores or are outdoors, you should ask yourself why you SHOULDN'T have on your eye protection!

There are various eye conditions that will be more common in a grid-down situation. The most common will be conjunctivitis. Conjunctivitis is an inflammation which causes the affected eye to become red and itchy, and many times will cause a milky discharge (see photo at the beginning of this section). It can be caused by chemical irritation (soap in your eyes, for example), a foreign body, an allergy, or an infection.

This infection is also called "Pinkeye" and is highly contagious among children due to their rubbing their eyes and then touching other people or items. Irritated red eyes with tears may also be seen in allergic reactions, which can be treated with antihistamines orally or anti-histamine eye drops. Eye allergies can be differentiated from eye infections; they are less likely to have a milky discharge associated with them.

To avoid spreading the germs that can cause eye infections:

- Don't share eye drops with others.
- Don't touch the tip of a bottle of eye drops with your hands or your eyes because that can contaminate it with germs. Keep the bottle 3 inches above your eye.
- Don't share eye makeup with others.
- Never put contact lenses in your mouth to wet them. Many bacteria and viruses — maybe even the virus that causes cold sores — are present in your mouth and could easily spread to your eyes.
- Change your contacts often, the longer they stay in your eyes, the more chance you eye can get infected or even develop corneal ulcers.
- Wash your hands regularly.
- Any time you have an eye examination, ask the doctor if he/she has any samples of medicated eye drops to give you, in case of emergency.

Antibiotics like Doxycycline 100mg twice a day for a week (or less if improved) will relieve infectious conjunctivitis. Herbal treatment may also be of benefit. To treat pinkeye using natural products, pick one or more of the following methods:

- Apply a wet Chamomile or Goldenseal tea bag to the closed, affected eye, for 10 minutes, every two hours.
- Make a strong chamomile or Eyebright (*Euphrasia officinalis*) tea, let cool and use the liquid as an eyewash (using an eyecup) three to four times daily. Alternatively,
- Use 1 teaspoon of baking soda in 2 cups of cool water as an eyewash solution
- Dissolve1 tablespoon of honey dissolved in 1 cup hot water; let cool and use as an eyewash.

Using the above tea, baking soda liquid or honey solution, on gauze or cloth, apply a compress to affected eye for 10 minutes, every two hours. . For relief from the discomfort of conjunctivitis, a slice of cucumber over the eyes will be effective due to its cooling action.

The other common issue we can expect in a survival situation would be injuries to the eye from an embedded object. This risk is minimized with eye protection, but it is likely you will come upon this kind of injury at one point or another. The most important thing to do when anyone presents to you with eye pain is a careful examination. A foreign object is the most likely cause of the problem, and it's up to you to find it.

Use a moist cotton swab (Q-tip) to lift and evert the eyelid. This will allow you to effectively examine the area. Use a large amount of water as irrigation to flush out the foreign object, or touch it lightly with the Q-tip to dislodge it. After assuring that there is no foreign object still present, look at the cornea (the area covering the colored portion of the eye). You may see what appears to be a scratched area. This is called an abrasion. The patient will probably relate to you that they feel as if there's a grain of sand in their eye. After cleaning the eye out with water and using antibiotic eye drops (if available), cover the closed eye with an eye pad and tape. Ibuprofen is useful for pain relief. Over the next few days, the eye should heal.

Another common eye issue is called a "sty". A sty is essentially a pimple which has formed on the eyelid. It causes redness and some swelling and is generally uncomfortable. Warm moist compresses are helpful in allowing the sty to drain. Using antibiotic eye drops (brand name Tobradex) will prevent worsening of this infection, which will usually resolve over the next few days. Oral antibiotics will also work. Use Doxycycline 100mg twice a day for several days. For natural alternatives, use any of the treatments used for "pinkeye".

Occasionally, blunt trauma to the eye or even simple actions like coughing or sneezing may cause a patch of blood to appear in the white of the eye. This is called a subconjunctival hemorrhage or "hyphema", and certainly can be alarming to the patient. Luckily, this type of hemorrhage is not dangerous, and will go away on its own without any treatment. However, loss of vision with areas of bleeding after blunt trauma IS cause for concern, and should be evaluated as described above. Additionally, the patient should be kept with the head elevated, to allow any blood to drain to the lower part of the eye chamber. This may help preserve vision.

NOSEBLEEDS
AND NASAL TRAUMA

✚ ✚ ✚

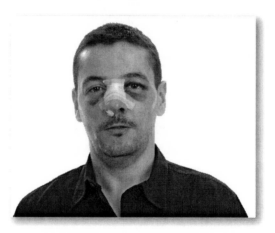

Nosebleeds due to trauma can be treated by simply exerting
pressure by pinching the nose at about the midpoint
between the tip of the nose and its connection to the rest
of the face. This should be done for several minutes. Whether the
bleeding is due to trauma or not, "Blowing" the nose to eject blood
and clots should be avoided, as it may restart the bleeding. If there
is a fracture, the patient will find that any pressure on the nose is
very painful. Although it may be painful, an obvious deformity of
the nose due to trauma may be adjusted back into place.

In extreme circumstances, the bleeding nostril can be flushed with water and a thin strip of cloth drenched in epinephrine (from an Epi-pen or other anaphylactic shock kit) can then be gently introduced into the nostril with a tweezers or Kelly clamp. Hold the nose at the level of the bleed and apply pressure for several minutes. Keep the gauze packing in place for at least several hours.

Hemostatic agents like Celox also produce powder-impregnated gauze that is effective in controlling the bleeding. The gauze is too wide to go into a nostril, so you'll have to cut a thin long strip to use. Again, keep the cloth in place until a period of time with no bleeding has passed. Primatene Mist, a milder delivery system for epinephrine, may also be helpful with gauze and pressure. Stock up now, as Primatene Mist is going off the market in the near future. Neosynephrine nose drops may also be helpful.

A natural hemostatic agent is geranium oil. A few drops on a strip of gauze could be placed in the bleeding nostril with good results in many cases.

Traumatic injury to the nose can result in damage to the cartilage. This may cause deformity and difficulty breathing due to swelling. Few major medical problems will result from this type of injury, but it is important to understand the best way to treat it.

First, you may choose to reduce the deformity by using both hands to straighten the cartilage. This may be appropriate as the broken nose, if deformed, will not straighten out by itself. Be aware that this may cause further damage. You might consider taping the nose in its normal position. Then, place some ice wrapped in a cloth over the nose, for periods of 20 minutes throughout the day. This will be useful for the first 48 hours only. This treatment will help reduce swelling and discomfort. Acetaminophen and Ibuprofen will also be helpful in this circumstance. Swollen nasal passages may be improved by a nasal decongestant such as Neosynephrine.

EARACHE

✚ ✚ ✚

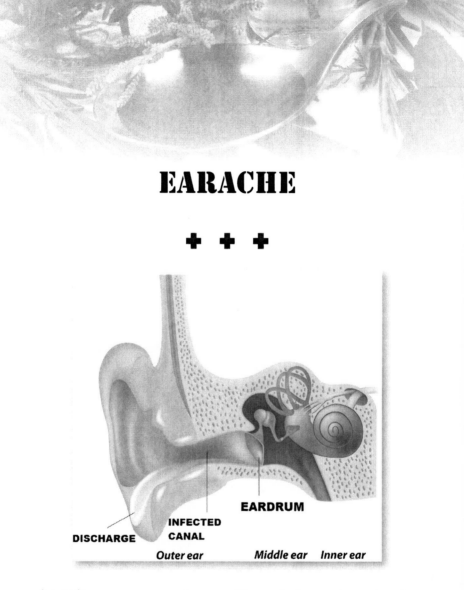

DISCHARGE **INFECTED CANAL** **EARDRUM**

Outer ear   *Middle ear*   *Inner ear*

The most common issue you'll see relating to the ear is pain, especially in children. The ear is divided into 3 chambers, the outer, middle and inner ear. Inflammation and/or infection of the ear is called Otitis. Evaluation of the ear canal is performed with a special instrument known as an otoscope. The most common ear infections will be in the external and middle ear chambers.

Infection of the outer ear canal is called Otitis Externa (see image on the preceding page). This commonly occurs as a result of retained water in the ear canal, which then becomes colonized with bacteria (and, rarely, fungus). Some redness or swelling may be apparent and discharge may be noted coming out of the ear.

The easiest way to prevent this is to carefully use cotton swabs moistened with rubbing alcohol to dry the ear canal after swimming or excessive sweating. The other cause of the problem will be due to some type of trauma to the canal, which could, coincidentally, be caused by injuring the ear with forceful use of a cotton swab! Symptoms of Otitis Externa include:

- Gradual development of an earache or, possibly, itching
- Pain worsened by pulling on the ear
- Ringing in the ears (tinnitus) or decreased hearing
- A "full" sensation in the ear canal with swelling
- Thick drainage from the ear canal

Home remedies may include a warm compress to the ear to help with pain control. An antibiotic/steroidal ear drop will be useful, and should be applied for 7 days. In order to get the most effect from the medicine, place the drops in the ear with the patient lying on their side. They should stay in that position for 5 minutes to completely coat the ear canal. Severe cases may be treated with oral antibiotics (such as Amoxicillin) and ibuprofen.

The most common cause of earache is an infection of the middle ear, called Otitis Media. Normally, the eardrum is shiny when viewed with an otoscope. When there is an infection in the middle ear canal, the eardrum will appear dull. This is because there is pus or inflammatory fluid behind it. Besides pain, the patient may feel somewhat off-balance and may run a fever. The ear canal itself may have less redness than in Otitis Externa. In severe cases, the eardrum may actually rupture and milky drainage may be noted. Otitis Media is common in infants and toddlers, and one way to prevent this problem is to make sure to never breast-feed or bottle-feed a baby in a supine (laying down flat) position. Treatment often includes oral antibiotics and ibuprofen, especially in adults with the infection.

A number of natural remedies are available for earache. Follow this procedure:

- Mix rubbing alcohol and vinegar in equal quantities, or alternatively, hydrogen peroxide.
- Place 3-4 drops in the affected ear.
- Wait 5 minutes; then, tilt head to drain out the mixture.
- Next, use either plain warm olive oil, or add 1 drop of any one of these essential oils to 2 ounces of the olive oil: tea tree, eucalyptus, peppermint, thyme, lavender, garlic, or Mullein.
- Warm the olive oil slightly and place 2-3 drops into the ear canal. This does not have to be drained or removed.
- A cotton ball with 2 drops of eucalyptus oil may be secured to the ear opening during sleep.

Some patients find a heat source soothing to a painful ear. If you are in a collapse situation, dip a sock or other absorbent material into heated water. Wring it out and place it on the outside of the affected ear.

HEMORRHOIDS

✚ ✚ ✚

Hemorrhoids are painful, swollen veins in the lower portion of the rectum and often protrude from the anus. They are thought to be caused from pressure due to the human trait of standing on two legs; animals that walk on four legs rarely get them. Another likely cause is straining during bowel movements. They are extremely common during pregnancy and are usually asymptomatic unless they develop a clot and become inflamed.

Hemorrhoids may be internal or external. Symptoms of hemorrhoids include:

- Anal itching.
- Bleeding, usually seen on toilet tissue.
- Pain, worse in the sitting position.
- Pain during bowel movements
- Painful bumps near the anus.

Diagnosis is easily made simply by looking at the area. They will appear as a bluish lump at the edge of the anal opening.

Hemorrhoids only require treatment when symptomatic. Treatments for hemorrhoids include:

- Mild corticosteroid creams such as Anusol-HC or wipes such as Tucks pads to help reduce pain and swelling
- Stool softeners to decrease further trauma to the inflamed tissue.
- Witch Hazel compresses to reduce itching.
- Warm water baths (known as "Sitz baths" to reduce general discomfort.

Even painful hemorrhoids will usually go away by themselves over a few weeks, but sometimes the discomfort is so severe that you may be required to remove the clot from the swollen vein. A scalpel may be used (preferably under local anesthesia) to incise the hemorrhoid after cleaning the area thoroughly with Betadine. After evacuating the clot, the patient will experience relief. Gauze pads should be placed at the site to absorb any bleeding. Be prepared to suture the incision site if there is heavy bleeding.

It should be noted that this procedure is not the best way to remove a hemorrhoid, as simple incision does not remove it in its entirety. It may come back at a later time. Modern procedures such as banding are less traumatic and more permanent in their results, but will not be available in a collapse situation.

BIRTH CONTROL, PREGNANCY, AND DELIVERY

✚ ✚ ✚

I t's a rare individual that doesn't have a wife, girlfriend, mother, daughter or granddaughter that isn't of childbearing age (say 13 to 50 year old). Even if they aren't related to you personally, they could be in your survival group. Remember that, even if you have a little girl that's 5 years old now, one day she will come of reproductive age.

In a collapse situation, society will be unstable and organized medical care will be spotty at best and nonexistent at worst. When we reach the point that we are scrambling to survive, one of the least welcome events is one that, for many families, is ordinarily considered a blessing: A pregnancy. Further down the road, when and if society re-establishes itself, we will have the responsibility to repopulate the world. Until that time, however, a pregnancy and the possible complications that accompany it will be a burden.

So why is it important to prevent pregnancies in the early going of a societal collapse? Well, we know that the death rate among pregnant women (also known as the Maternal Mortality Rate) at the time of the American Revolution was about 2-4% per pregnancy. Given that the average woman in the year 1800 could expect 6-10 pregnancies over the course of her reproductive life, the cumulative Maternal Mortality Rate easily approached 25 per cent. That means that 1 out of 4 women died due to complications of being pregnant, either early, during the childbirth, or even soon after a successful delivery.

If the collapse comes, we might be faced with unacceptable levels of risk to our women because we won't have either medicine or medical supplies in which treat pregnancy and childbirth complications. There could be deaths simply because there are no IV fluids or medications to stop bleeding or treat infection. This would happen at a time that we will need every member of our survival group to be productive individuals. Growing food, managing livestock, perimeter defense, and caring for children will take the energy of all involved. When a pregnancy goes wrong, it takes away a valuable contributor from the survival family (sometimes permanently) and places an additional strain on resources and manpower.

Let's discuss some of the reasons that women could cease to become productive group members (or even die) during pregnancy or childbirth:

Hyperemesis Gravidarum:

Simply put, this is medical-speak for excessive vomiting during pregnancy. Almost every woman will experience nausea and vomiting in the early stages. A small percentage of them, however, have an exaggerated response to the hormones of pregnancy that causes them to vomit so much that they become dehydrated. Since they can't maintain a reasonable fluid intake, intravenous hydration is required. As a practicing obstetrician for 25 years, it seemed to me that I always had someone in the hospital with this condition.

How many survival groups will have access to IV equipment and the know-how to institute IV fluid therapy? One of my hobbies is collecting old medical books, most of them from at least 100 years ago (in other words, where we will be medically if a collapse occurs). When these books discuss Hyperemesis Gravidarum, they relate death rates in 10% to 40% in severe cases!

Miscarriage:

The human race is not perfect, and we don't always produce perfect pregnancies. Approximately 10% of all pregnancies end in miscarriage. When a woman miscarries, many times she will not pass all of the dead tissue relating to the pregnancy. On occasion, this tissue will become infected or cause excessive bleeding.

The treatment in this case would be something called a dilatation and curettage (D & C), which is a procedure that use scrapers called curettes to remove the retained tissue. This will stop the bleeding and prevent infection. Again, how may survival groups have the ability and knowledge to perform this procedure or have access to the antibiotics necessary to treat possible infection?

Hypertension:

There is a condition known as Pregnancy-Induced Hypertension. When a woman reaches the last month of a pregnancy (usually her first baby), she might begin to have elevated blood pressures that cause extreme swelling (called edema). Normal pregnancy causes swollen ankles, but pregnancy-induced hypertension swells up the entire body, including the face. Left untreated, this condition leads to seizures and can be life-threatening. If a collapse situation happens, the only treatment available would be bed rest, which at best takes away a productive member of your group, and at worst will fail to prevent a worsening of the condition.

Childbirth Itself:

Let's say the pregnancy itself was uncomplicated. The birth process, while usually perfectly natural and routine, could also present some dangers. Every childbirth, for example, involves some bleeding. It could be a little; it could be a lot. It could be caused by lacerations from the passage of the infant through the vaginal canal or from a stubborn placenta (afterbirth) that does not expel itself spontaneously.

When childbirth is associated with excessive bleeding, certain procedures and maneuvers are performed by trained midwives or obstetricians to stop the hemorrhage. When hemorrhage occurs and no trained individuals are present at the birth, the bleeding may not stop before major damage has been done to the mother. Sometimes it's necessary to actually reach into a woman's uterus, grab the placenta and remove it, especially when part of the placenta is "retained". If a portion of the placenta is "stuck", this tissue will prevent the uterus from contracting (which is the natural way that bleeding stops). Of course, retained tissue could become infected, also. Does your group have the knowledge, equipment and medications that might be needed to safely get your women through childbirth?

After Childbirth:

Conditions in the delivery room after a societal collapse could be conducive to the development of infections, even if the delivery goes without a hitch. This was a major cause of maternal mortality before modern medical care and antibiotics became available. As well, a woman who has a hemorrhage during childbirth could be so weakened by anemia that she is unable to return to normal activities for a very long time.

Now, I don't want everyone to think that I'm saying all women will die during their pregnancy. What I am saying is that not all survival groups have prepared to obtain the knowledge, resources, and ability to deal with the complications that could occur. Every Prepper should stop and think about the danger to which you could be exposing Mrs. Prepper, if you aren't ready for every possibility. Also, if people are rioting in the streets and your garden isn't doing so well yet, do you really need to add a newborn baby to your list of responsibilities?

So, what's your plan? Even long-time Preppers haven't spent much time figuring out what birth control method they will use in a collapse situation. Have you included condoms in your bug-out bag? The majority have not, so congratulations if you did. That means you've thought about more than just beans and bullets.

It's important to have condoms in your storage, but condoms can break; even if they don't, they won't last forever. With spermicide, condoms expire after 2 years; without spermicide, perhaps at most 5 years. Some women use IUDs (intrauterine devices) to prevent pregnancy. Some of these use hormones that wear off over time. They must be inserted into the body of the uterus, something best done by someone with experience to prevent injury.

Birth control pills are useful, but are difficult to get more than a few months' supply at any one time. Insurance companies tightly control when women can get their next pack of pills. Some offer 3 month's supply at a time, but you still have to wait until the end of those 3 months to get more. Even if you could get them, they cost a bundle if purchased outside of insurance plans. The cost of stockpiling several years' worth these can be difficult for the average person.

As such, we will have to go back to a natural form of birth control: The Rhythm Method. Although not as effective in preventing pregnancy as the Pill, it is 80% effective if implemented correctly. There is no need to put hormones into your system and no side effects. The Rhythm Method is a time-honored strategy to prevent pregnancy that fits in well with any collapse strategy.

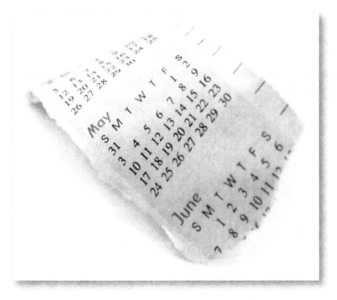

This method involves trying to figure out your fertile period and avoiding unprotected intercourse during that time. This method works best on women who have relatively regular cycles. Cycles are predictable if a woman releases an egg for fertilization (this is called ovulation) on a regular basis. If you or your partner has 28 day menstrual cycles, you can bet that ovulation is occurring. A pregnancy is likely in any couple having regular sexual relations. The egg will disintegrate in 48 hours or so, however, if not fertilized.

You can tell the day that you or your partner is ovulating by doing a little research. This involves taking your temperature with a thermometer daily for a cycle or two. There are actually special thermometers that are used for this purpose called Basal Body Temperature Thermometers, although I would think that any thermometer that goes up by 1/10 degree increments would do (e.g., 98.1, 98.2, 98.3).

When you ovulate, your basal body temperature goes up about half a degree and stays up until the next period. Make a graph or chart of the daily temperatures and you'll see a pattern develop. Always count Day #1 as the first day of menstrual bleeding to start with. Once you've done this for a few cycles, you will have a good idea about when you or your partner is at risk for getting pregnant. A common physical symptom that goes along with this: Many women will notice some one-sided discomfort in the lower abdomen when they ovulate.

Let's say that you or your partner has 28 day cycles and that the temperature rise occurs around day 14. You should avoid having unprotected sexual intercourse from about day 10 - day 18 (a few days prior and a few days after the likely day of ovulation). If ovulation occurs later, say day 16, just move the "danger" period over to day 12 - day 20. Ovulation may occur a couple of days earlier or later in any one cycle, so you want to have a margin of error in determining the time period eligible for fertilization.

Performed correctly, the Rhythm Method is an effective and completely natural way to prevent pregnancy. In a collapse, it will help you decide when things are stable enough to bring a newborn into the world.

Pregnancy Basics

Sometimes, the best laid plans of mice and men go awry. Accidentally or on purpose, you may find yourself responsible for the care of a pregnant woman. It will be important to know how to support that pregnancy and, eventually, deliver that baby. In a collapse situation, you won't have access to ultrasound technology to take a look at the fetus; whether it's a boy or a girl will once again become a mystery. Even twins might be a surprise. Without prenatal mega-vitamins, babies will be smaller at birth. This may also not be so bad, since Caesarean Section will no longer available. It's less traumatic for the mother to deliver a 6 or 7 pound baby than a 10 pounder.

Despite all the possible complications that I mentioned in the previous section, pregnancy is still a natural process. It usually proceeds without major complications and ends in the delivery of a normal baby. Although your pregnant patient will not be as productive for the survival group as she would ordinarily be, she will probably still be able to contribute to help make your efforts a success. To make a pregnancy a success, the medic will need to have a little knowledge of the subject and an idea of how to deliver the fetus.

We are, of course, fortunate to have simple tests that can identify pregnancy almost before your miss a period. What if these tests are no longer available? You will have to rely on the following tried and true symptoms to identify the condition:

- Absent menstruation
- Tender Breasts
- Nausea and Vomiting
- Darkening of the Nipples/Areola
- Fatigue
- Frequent Urination
- Backache

These symptoms in combination are indicative of pregnancy, although some will be noticed earlier than others. It should be noted that this investigation will likely be necessary only in those women experiencing their first pregnancy. Once you have been pregnant, you will most likely know when it happens again. Of course, as time goes on, the abdominal swelling associated with uterine and fetal growth will be undeniable. Stretch marks come later, as do hemorrhoids, backache, and varicose veins (all very common but not universal). Most of these will improve after the pregnancy is over, but may not disappear completely.

So, what's the due date? This is the question everyone will want answered once a pregnancy is identified. A human pregnancy is 280 days or 40 weeks from the first day of the last menstrual period to the estimated date of delivery. This used to be called the "estimated date of confinement" because, yes, they confined women to their beds as they approached it. This date is simple to calculate if you have regular monthly periods. To get the due date, subtract 3 months and add 7 days to the first day of the last period. Example: If the first day of last menstrual period (LMP) is 9/7, then the due date is 6/14.

If the woman does not know when her last cycle started, you can still estimate the age of the pregnancy by physical signs. When you gently press on the woman's abdomen, you will notice a firm area (the uterus) and a soft area (the intestines). Identify the uppermost level of firmness, and you will able to estimate the approximate age of the pregnancy. If the "lump" is peaking just over the pubic bone, you're at 12 weeks. Halfway between the pubic bone and the belly button is 16 weeks. At the belly button is 20 weeks. Each centimeter above the belly button adds a week, so have a measuring tape handy. A term pregnancy will measure 36-40 Centimeters from the pubic bone to the top of the uterus. Twins, as you might imagine, will throw all of these measurements out the window.

Once you have identified the pregnancy, you should make every effort to assure that your patient is getting proper nutrition. Deficiencies can affect the development of the fetus, so obtaining essential vitamins and iron through the diet will give the best chance to avoid complications. If you have stockpiled prenatal vitamins, use them.

Common early pregnancy issues will include hyperemesis, as described in the last section. Be sure to ask your physician for prescriptions for Zofran and/or other anti-nausea medications to add to your stockpile. Hyperemesis will disappear in almost all women as they advance in the pregnancy. Dry bland foods, like crackers, are helpful in getting a woman through this stage. Ginger tea is a time-honored home remedy to decrease "morning sickness".

Another early pregnancy issue is the threatened miscarriage. This will be characterized by bleeding or spotting from the vagina, along with pain that simulates menstrual cramps. As 10% of pregnancies end in miscarriage and a higher percentage threaten to, this will be an issue that you must know how to deal with.

Other than placing your patient on bed rest, there will not be much you'll be able to do in this circumstance. Some of these pregnancies don't continue because the fetus is abnormal, and no amount of rest will stop many of these pregnancies from ending very early. The good thing is that a single miscarriage generally does not mean that future pregnancies will be unsuccessful.

Keep a close eye out for evidence of infection, such as fever or a foul discharge from the vagina. Women with these symptoms would benefit from antibiotic therapy.

Pregnant women should be evaluated periodically to see how the fetus is progressing. Besides verifying progressive growth in the size of the uterus, the fetal heartbeat should be audible via stethoscope at around 16-18 weeks, or much earlier if you have a functioning battery-powered fetal heart monitor (also called a Doppler ultrasound). These are available for sale online. Your exams should be more frequent as the pregnancy advances.

Weight gain is desirable during pregnancy; you should shoot for 25 pounds or so, total. Blood pressure should be taken to rule out pregnancy-induced hypertension. Elevated blood pressures behoove you to place your patient on bed rest. Lying on the left side will keep her blood pressure at its lowest. Check for evidence of edema (swelling of the feet, legs and face) as well as excessive weight gain).

Delivery

As the woman approaches her due date, several things will happen. The fetus will begin to "drop", assuming a position in the pelvis. The patient's abdomen may look different, or the top of the uterus (the "fundus") may appear lower. As the neck of the uterus (the cervix) relaxes, the patient may notice a mucus-like discharge, sometimes with a bloody component. This is referred to as the "bloody show" and is usually a sign that things will be happening soon. If you examine your patient vaginally by gently inserting two fingers of a gloved hand, you'll notice the cervix is firm like your nose when it is not ripe and soft like your lips when the due date is approaching. This softening of the cervix is called "effacement".

Contractions will start becoming more frequent. To identify a contraction, feel the skin on the soft area of your cheek, and then touch your forehead. A contraction will feel like your forehead. False labor, or Braxton-Hicks contractions, will be irregular and will abate with bed rest, especially on the left side, and hydration. If contractions are coming faster and more furious even with bed rest and hydration, it may just be time to have a baby! A gush of watery fluid from the vagina will often signify "breaking the water", and is also a sign of impending labor and delivery. The timing will be highly variable.

The delivery of a baby is best accomplished with the help of an experienced midwife or obstetrician, but those professionals will be hard to find in a collapse situation. If there is no chance of accessing modern medical care, it will be up to you to perform the delivery.

To get ready for delivery, wash your hands and then put gloves on. Then set up clean sheets so that there will be the least contamination possible. Tuck a sheet under the mother's buttocks and spread it on your lap so that the baby, which comes out very slippery, will land onto the sheet instead of landing on the floor if you lose your grip on it. Place a towel on the mother's belly; this is where the baby will go once it is delivered. It will be very important to dry the baby and wrap it in the towel, as newborns lose heat very quickly. Newborns are also susceptible to infection, so avoid touching anything but mother and baby if you can.

As the labor progresses, the baby's head will move down the birth canal and the vagina will begin to bulge. When the baby's head begins to become visible, it is called "crowning". If the water has not yet broken (which can happen even at this late stage), it will appear as a slick gray surface. Some pressure on the membrane will rupture it, which is okay at this point. It will help the process along.

To make space, place two gloved fingers in the vagina by the perineum. This is the area between the vagina and anus. Using gentle pressure, move your fingers from side to side. This will stretch the area somewhat to give the baby a little more room to come out. With each contraction, the baby's head will come out a little more. Don't be concerned if it goes back in a little after the contraction. It will make steady progress and more and more of the head will become visible. Encourage the mother to help by taking a deep breath with each contraction and then pushing while slowly exhaling. On occasion, a small cut is made in the bottom of the vagina to make room for the baby to be delivered. I discourage this if at all possible, as the cut has to be sutured afterward. I always make this decision as the head is crowning.

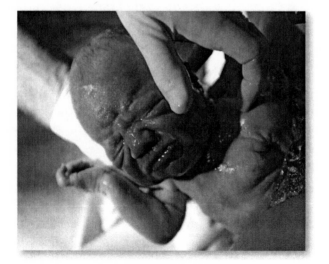

As the baby's head emerges, it will usually face straight down or up, and then turn to the side. The cord might appear to be wrapped around its neck. If this is the case, gently slip the cord over the baby's head. In cases where the cord is very tight and is preventing delivery, you may have to doubly clamp it and cut between. Gently holding each side of the baby's head and applying gentle traction straight down will help the top shoulder out of the birth canal. Occasionally, steady gentle pressure on the top of the uterus during a contraction may be required if the mother is exhausted. Once the shoulders are out, the baby will deliver one last push. The new mother can now rest.

Put the baby immediately on the mother's belly and clean out its nose and mouth with a bulb syringe. It will usually begin crying, which is a good sign that it is a vigorous infant. Spanking the baby's bottom to get it to cry is rarely needed, and is more of a cliché than anything else. A better way to stimulate a baby to cry is to rub the baby's back.

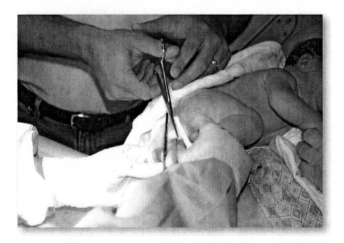

Dry the baby and wrap it up! Clamp the cord twice (2 inches apart) with Kelly or Umbilical clamps, and cut in between with a scissors. Delivery kits are available online with everything you need, including drapes, clamps, bulb syringes, etc.

Once the baby has delivered, it's the placenta's turn. Be patient, the placenta will deliver in a few minutes in most cases. Pulling on the umbilical cord to force the placenta out is usually a bad idea. You can ask the mother to give a push when it's clear the placenta is almost out. A moderate amount of bleeding is not unusual afterwards.

The uterus (the top of which is now around the level of the belly button) contracts to control bleeding naturally. In a long labor, the uterus may be as tired as the mother after delivery, and may be slow to contract. This may cause excessive bleeding. Gentle massage of the top of the uterus (known as the "fundus") will get it firm again and thus limit blood loss. You may have to do this from time to time.

Place the baby on the mother's breast soon after delivery. This will begin the secretion of "colostrum", a clear yellow liquid rich in substances that will increase the baby's resistance to infection. Suckling also causes the uterus to contract; this is also a factor in decreasing blood loss.

ANXIETY AND DEPRESSION

✚ ✚ ✚

If we ever find ourselves in the midst of a societal upheaval, it goes without saying that we will experience epidemics of both anxiety and depression. The stress of living off the grid will be (for most) a wrenching emotional roller-coaster. As such, an effective medic will have to be skilled in identifying those with the condition, and doing everything possible to treat it. The stability of your survival community is dependent on the stability of its members.

Anxiety

Anxiety is really a hodgepodge of related symptoms, so sufferers may present quite differently from one another. The symptoms may be mostly emotional, mostly physical or some combination of both. Here are the various things you may notice:

Emotional Symptoms:

- Irrational fear
- Difficulty concentrating
- Jumpiness
- Extreme pessimism

- Irritability
- Mental paralysis/Inability to act
- Inability to stand still

Physical Symptoms:

- Shortness of breath
- Palpitations (rapid pulse)
- Perspiration
- Upset stomach/diarrhea
- Tremors/tics/twitches
- Tense muscles
- Headache
- Insomnia

Acute anxiety attacks, also known as "panic attacks" may occur without warning and are characterized by intense feelings of fear and impending doom. Panic attacks are usually short-lived but severe enough that a person may feel they are having an actual heart attack! These patients, usually young adults, will appear to be hyperventilating and may complain of chest pain or feeling faint. Patients with panic attacks have some classic complaints:

- Chest pain
- Choking sensation
- Feeling they are in a unreal or surreal environment
- Nausea or strange "pit of the stomach" feelings
- Hot flashes (sensations of heat and flushing)

Panic attacks may sometimes last an hour or more, but a single episode will usually resolve without medication. Despite this, the most success in treatment of frequent attacks appears to come from a combination of medications and/or supplements (both anti-anxiety and anti-depressant) and behavioral therapy.

Unless your patient had a history of anxiety problems pre-collapse, you won't have stockpiled many anti-anxiety medications like Xanax. As such, you should look to your medicinal herb garden for plants that may have an effect. Alternative therapies include massage therapy combined with herbs such as Valerian, Kava, Chamomile, and Passionflower.

Essential oils used as aromatherapy may also be helpful: bergamot, cypress, geranium, jasmine, lavender, rose and sandalwood have been used.

Essential oils of lavender, frankincense, geranium, and chamomile are versatile and can be used as direct inhalation therapy or for topical use. Just rub the oil between your hands and bring them up to your nose and slowly inhale. For topical use, a 50/50 mixture of essential oil with a carrier oil (such as olive) will be beneficial when applied on temples, neck and shoulders twice a day.

A multitude of teas are known to be especially helpful in people with anxiety disorders. Catnip, valerian root, fennel, passionflower, ginseng, lemon balm, mullein, peppermint, lavender, and verbena are all reported to have a calming effect and help with sleep. Drink the tea warm with honey, 1 cup three times daily, as needed.

Perhaps most importantly, you will have to treat your anxious patient with good counseling technique. When you have an honest conversation with your anxious group member, listen calmly and attentively. Ask them to tell you exactly what they're worrying about, and then have them write those concerns down on paper. Sometimes just the act of acknowledging their fears and seeing them in black and white will result in an improvement of the condition.

There will things on the list that relate to the uncertainty of their current situation. Inform them that there is always some uncertainty in life, both in good times and bad times. Try to convince them that dwelling on those issues will not make them any less uncertain, but WILL prevent them from functioning normally. Convince your patient to set aside just a short part of their day to concentrate on their worries with their list in hand. Keep that time period limited, say 20 minutes or so, and then have them resolve to think less of their fears the rest of the day.

Work to improve your patient's quality of life. You can do this by:

- Assuring good nutrition
- Reducing substances such as nicotine, caffeine, and alcohol
- Encouraging exercise and constructive activities
- Promoting rest breaks and good sleep habits
- Instituting sessions for relaxation therapy (meditation, massage, deep breathing)

Depression

Many people with anxiety disorders also suffer from depression. Since depression makes anxiety worse (and vice versa), it's important to have strategies to treat both conditions. In a collapse, things may be so bad that everyone is depressed to one degree or another. This is understandable, and is referred to as "situational depression". Their circumstances are what have made them depressed, not some misfiring of neural cells in their brain as in some other cases. Some depression is cyclical, relating to, for example, a woman's menstrual cycle or the time of the year. Like anxiety, there are a number of symptoms that are commonly seen in various combinations:

- Feelings of hopelessness or inadequacy
- Apathy
- Change in Appetite
- Weight loss or gain
- Irritability (common in depressed men)
- Exhaustion

- Reckless behavior
- Difficulty concentrating on tasks
- Aches and pains (without clear physical cause)

Severe cases of depression are marked by inability to get out of bed in the morning and even thoughts of suicide. Various medications known as "antidepressants" are available on the market; these include Prozac, Zoloft, and Paxil, among others.

Unfortunately, they will be unlikely to be in your medical supplies unless a member of your group already suffers from chronic depression. As such, you must look to alternatives.

Vitamin supplements like B12, Folic Acid, Tryptophan, and Omega-3 antioxidants may be effective in some sufferers. St. John's Wort has been used with some success, but is not to be used on pregnant women or children). As with anxiety, you, as healthcare provider, will have to depend on your counseling skills to aid your patient.

In situational depression as will be seen in a collapse situation, you would return to many of the techniques used to treat anxiety:

- Assuring good nutrition
- Reducing substances such as nicotine, caffeine, and alcohol
- Encouraging exercise and constructive activities
- Promoting rest breaks and good sleep habits
- Instituting relaxation techniques (meditation, massage, deep breathing)

Additionally, it will be especially important to make sure your people cultivate supportive relationships with each other. People who are depressed often feel very alone. You must work to foster a sense of community; this with provide strength to your emotionally weakened members. Make sure to accentuate the positive, even in the little things. Encourage each member of your group to share their feeling with the others. Group meetings for this purpose will encourage communication and bonding in the survival group.

You might have read about Post-Traumatic Stress Syndrome (PTSD). This condition affects many who are exposed to stressful events like sexual assault, combat, or natural disasters and can last for years. Oftentimes, the patient will re-experience the event mentally and become agitated and sometimes uncontrollable. Anger, insomnia, decreased work performance, and apathy are common manifestations. Although anxiety is a component of PTSD, anti-anxiety medications do not seem to help as much as anti-depressants. Follow the treatment guidelines previous discussed for depression.

The success of your survival group will depend greatly on your ability to spot emotional issues before they deteriorate. Once out of control, they will damage the cohesion necessary to succeed in an adverse environment. This ability will be as important to develop as any specific medical skill in a collapse.

STOCKPILING MEDICATIONS

+ + +

Accumulating medications for a possible collapse may be simple when it comes to getting Ibuprofen and other non-prescription drugs. It will be a major issue, however, for those who need to stockpile prescription medicines but don't have a relationship with a physician who can or will accommodate their requests. Antibiotics are one example of medications that will be very useful in a collapse situation. Obtaining these drugs in quantity will be difficult, to say the least.

The inability to store antibiotic supplies is going to cost some poorly prepared individuals their lives in a collapse situation. Why? Well, there will be a much larger incidence of infection when people have to fend for themselves and are injured as a result. Any strenuous activities performed in a power-down situation, especially ones that most of us aren't accustomed to, will cause various cuts and scratches. These wounds will very likely be dirty. Within a relatively short time, they can begin to show infection, in the form of redness, heat, and swelling.

Treatment of such infections, called "cellulitis", at an early stage improves the chance that they will heal quickly and completely. However, many rugged individualists are most likely to "tough it out" until their condition worsens and the infection spreads to their blood. This causes a condition known as sepsis; the patient develops a fever as well as other problems that could eventually be life-threatening. The availability of antibiotics would allow the possibility of dealing with the issue safely and effectively.

The following advice is contrary to standard medical practice, and is a strategy that is appropriate only in the event of societal collapse. If there are modern medical resources available to you, seek them out.

Small amounts of medications can be obtained by anyone willing to tell their doctor that they are going out of the country and would like to avoid "Travelers' Diarrhea". Ask them for Tamiflu for viral illness before every flu season, and Amoxicillin, Doxycycline and Metronidazole for bacterial/protozoal disease. This approach is fine for one or two courses of therapy, but a long term alternative is required for us to have enough antibiotics to protect a family or survival group. Thinking long and hard for a solution has led me to what I believe is a viable option: Aquarium antibiotics.

For many years, I was a tropical fish enthusiast. Currently, we are growing tilapia as a food fish in an aquaculture pond.

After years of using these medicines on fish, I decided to evaluate these drugs for their potential use in collapse situations. A close inspection of the bottles revealed that the only ingredient was the drug itself, identical to those obtained by prescription at the local pharmacy. If the bottle says FISH-MOX, for example, the sole ingredient is Amoxicillin, which is an antibiotic commonly used in humans. There are no additional chemicals to makes your scales shiny or your fins longer. Here is a list of the products that I believe will be beneficial to have as supplies:

- FISH-MOX   (Amoxicillin 250mg)
- FISH_MOX   FORTE (Amoxicillin 500mg)
- FISH-CILLIN   (Ampicillin 250mg)
- FISH-FLEX   (Keflex 250mg)
- FISH-FLEX   FORTE (Keflex 500mg)
- FISH-ZOLE   (Metronidazole 250mg)
- FISH-PEN   (Penicillin 250mg)
- FISH-PEN FORTE   (Penicillin 500mg)
- FISH-CYCLINE   (Tetracycline 250mg)
- FISH-FLOX   (Ciprofloxacin 250mg)
- BIRD BIOTIC   (Doxycycline 100mg) - used in birds but the antibiotic is, again, the sole ingredient
- BIRD SULFA   (Sulfamethoxazole 400mg/ Trimethoprin 80mg) also used in birds

I understand that you might be skeptical about considering the use of aquarium antibiotics for humans in a collapse. Those things are for fish, aren't they? Yet, if this is the case, then why are all of the above antibiotics also commonly used on humans? More importantly: Why are these antibiotics in the exact same DOSAGES that are used in humans? Why would a guppy require a dosage of FISH-MOX FORTE that would suffice for a 180 pound human adult? It is my opinion that they are manufactured in the same way that "human" antibiotics are made; I don't have proof that this is true, but I suspect that they might even come from similar batches.

These medications are available without a prescription from veterinary supply stores and online sites everywhere. They come in lots of 30 to 100 tablets for less than the same prescription medication at the local pharmacy. If you so desired, it appears that you could get as much as you need to stockpile for a collapse. These quantities would be close to impossible to obtain from your physician.

Of course, anyone could be allergic to one or another of these antibiotics, but it would be a very rare individual who would be allergic to all of them. There is a 10% chance for cross-reactivity between Penicillin drugs and Keflex (if you are allergic to penicillin, you could also be allergic to Keflex). Doxycycline, Metronidazole, Tetracycline, and Ciprofloxacin would be safe to take for those allergic to Penicillin.

This one additional fact: I have personally used some (not all) of these antibiotics on my own person without any ill effects. It's important to note that I am speaking primarily about aquarium antibiotics, as some dog and cat medications also include other chemicals and are not just the antibiotic.

For medications that treat non-infectious illness, such as cholesterol or blood pressure drugs, you will also need a prescription. These medications are not available in aquarium supply houses, so how can you work to stockpile them?

You may consider asking your physician to prescribe a higher dose than the amount you usually take. Many drugs come in different dosages. If your medicine is a 20 milligram dosage, for example, you might ask your doctor to prescribe the 40 mg dosage. You would then cut the medication in half; take your normal dosage and store the other half of the pill. It's very important to assure your physician that you will continue to follow their medical advice and not take more medicine than is appropriate for your condition. Your success in having your request granted will depend on the doctor.

Others have managed to obtain needed prescriptions by indicating that they are traveling for long periods of time out of the country or telling their physician some other falsehood. I can't recommend this method, because I believe that dishonesty breaks the bond of trust between doctor and patient. Consider having a serious discussion with your healthcare provider. Describe your concerns about not having needed medications in a disaster situation. You don't have to describe the disaster as a complete societal collapse; any catastrophe could leave you without access to your doctor for an extended period.

If we ever find ourselves without modern medical care, we will have to improvise medical strategies that we perhaps might be reluctant to consider today. Without hospitals, it will be up to the medic to nip infections in the bud. That responsibility will be difficult to carry out without the weapons to fight disease. Accumulate equipment and medications and never ignore avenues that may help you gain access to them.

Alternative therapies such as herbal supplements and essential oils should be stockpiled as well. Honey, onion, Silver, and garlic have known antibacterial actions; be sure to integrate all medical options, traditional and alternative, and use every tool at your disposal to keep your community healthy. If you don't, you're fighting with one hand tied behind your back. Remember that traditional medicines and even essential oils will eventually run out in a long term collapse. Begin your medicinal garden now and get experience with the use of these beneficial plants.

I would like to take a second to voice my concern over the apparently indiscriminate use of antibiotics in livestock management (what I call Agri-Business) today. 80% of the antibiotics manufactured today are going to livestock, such as cattle and chickens. Excessive antibiotic use is causing the development of resistant strains of bacteria such as Salmonella, which can cause a type of diarrheal disease in humans. Recently, 36 million turkeys were destroyed due to an antibiotic resistant strain of the bacteria. Over 100 people wound up in the hospital as a result of eating contaminated meat.

Consider patronizing those farmers who raise antibiotic-free livestock; this will decrease the further development of resistant bacteria, and thus the antibiotics you've stockpiled will be more effective.

HOW TO USE ANTIBIOTICS

✚ ✚ ✚

Antibiotics are used at specific doses for specific illnesses; the exact dosage of each and every medication is beyond the scope of this handbook. It's important, however, to have as much information as possible on medications that you plan to store, so consider purchasing a hard copy of the latest Physician's Desk Reference. This book comes out yearly and has just about every bit of information that exists on a particular drug. Online sources such as drugs.com or rxlist.com are also useful, but you are going to want a hard copy for your library. You never know when we might not have a functioning internet.

The Desk Reference lists medications that require prescriptions as well as those that do not. Under each medicine, you will find the indications, which are the medical conditions that the drug is used for. Also listed will be the dosages, risks, side effects, and even how the medicine works in the body. I don't have to tell you that this is a large book! It's okay to get last year's book; the information rarely changes much from one year to the next.

It's important to start off by saying that you will not want to indiscriminately use antibiotics for every minor ailment that comes along. In a collapse, the medic is also a quartermaster of sorts; you will want to wisely dispense that limited and, yes, precious supply of life-saving drugs.

Liberal use of antibiotics is a poor strategy for a few reasons:

Overuse can foster the spread of resistant bacteria, as you'll remember from the salmonella outbreak in turkeys recently that made so many people ill.

- Potential allergic reactions may occur that could lead to anaphylactic shock (see the section on this topic earlier in this book).
- Making a diagnosis may be more difficult if you give antibiotics before you're sure what medical problem you're actually dealing with. The antibiotics might temporarily "mask" a symptom, which could cost you valuable time in determining the correct treatment.

You can see that judicious use of antibiotics, under your close supervision, is necessary to fully utilize their benefits. Discourage your group members from using these drugs without first consulting you.

There are many antibiotics, but what antibiotics accessible to the average person would be good additions to your medical storage? Here are my recommendations for drugs (also available in veterinary form without a prescription) that you will want in your medical arsenal:

- **Amoxicillin**   250mg/500mg   (FISH-MOX, FISH-MOX FORTE)
- **Ciprofloxacin**   250mg/500mg   (FISH-FLOX, FISH-FLOX FORTE)
- **Cephalexin**   250mg/500mg   (FISH-FLEX, FISH-FLEX FORTE)
- **Metronidazole** 250mg (FISH-ZOLE)
- **Doxycycline**   100mg (BIRD-BIOTIC)

- **Ampicillin**   250mg/500mg (FISH-CILLIN, FISH-CILLIN FORTE)
- **Sulfamethoxazole**   400mg/**Trimethoprim**   80mg (BIRD-SULFA)

Additional useful antibiotics are **Azithromycin** and **Clindamcyin**. There are various others that you can choose, but these selections will give you the opportunity to treat many illnesses and have enough variety so that even those with Penicillin allergies will have options. Cephalexin is not one of these options, as it can sometimes cause a reaction in Penicillin-allergic individuals.

Let's discuss how to approach the use of antibiotics by using an example. Amoxicillin (Aquarium version: FISH-MOX, FISH-MOX FORTE, AQUA-MOX): comes in 250mg and 500mg doses, usually taken 3 times a day. Amoxicillin is the most popular antibiotic prescribed to children, usually in liquid form. More versatile and better absorbed than the older Pencillins, Amoxicillin may be used for the following diseases:

- Anthrax (prevention or treatment of Cutaneous transmission)
- Chlamydia Infection (sexually transmitted)
- Urinary Tract Infection (bladder/kidney infections)
- Helicobacter pylori Infection (causes peptic ulcer)
- Lyme Disease (transmitted by ticks)
- Otitis Media (middle ear infection)
- Pneumonia (lung infection)
- Sinusitis
- Skin or Soft Tissue Infection (cellulitis, boils)
- Actinomycosis (causes abscesses in humans and livestock)
- Bronchitis
- Tonsillitis/Pharyngitis (Strep throat)

This is a lot of information, but how do you determine what dose and frequency would be appropriate for what individual? Let's take an example: Otitis Media is a common ear infection, especially in children. Amoxicillin is often the "drug of choice" for this condition.

First, you would want to determine that your patient is not allergic to Amoxicillin. The most common form of allergy would appear as a rash, but diarrhea, itchiness, and even respiratory difficulty could also manifest. If you see any of these symptoms, you should discontinue your treatment and look for other options. Antibiotics such as Azithromycin or Sulfamethoxazole/ Trimethoprim could be a "second-line" solution in this case.

Once you have identified Amoxicillin as your treatment of choice to treat your patient's ear infection, you will want to determine the dosage. As Otitis Media often occurs in children, you might have to break a tablet in half or open the capsule to separate out a portion that would be appropriate. For Amoxicillin, you would give 20-50mg per kilogram of body weight (20-30mg/kg for infants less than four months old). This would be useful if you have to give the drug to a toddler less than 30 pounds. A common child's dosage would be 250mg and a common maximum dosage for adults would be 500 mg. Luckily, these dosages are exactly how the commercially-made medications (even in veterinary equivalents) come in the bottle. Take this orally 3 times a day for 10 to 14 days (twice a day for infants). All of the above information can be found in the Physician's Desk Reference.

If your child is too small to swallow a pill whole, you could make a mixture with water (called a "suspension"). To make a liquid, crush a tablet or empty a capsule into a small glass of water and drink it; then, fill the glass again and drink that (particles may adhere to the walls of the glass). You can add some flavoring to make it taste better. Do not chew or make a liquid out of time-released capsules of any medication; you will wind up losing some of the gradual release effect and perhaps get too much into your system at once. These medications should be plainly marked "Time-Released".

You will be probably see improvement within 3 days, but don't be tempted to stop the antibiotic therapy until you're done with the entire 10-14 days. Sometimes, you'll kill most of the bacteria but some colonies may persist and multiply if you prematurely end the treatment. In a collapse, however, you might be down to your last few pills and have to make some tough decisions.

For your patients with penicillin allergies, consider stockpiling Doxycycline, Ciprofloxacin, Tetracycline, Metronidazole, Azithromycin, Clindamycin or Sulfamethoxazole/Trimethoprim. These drugs belong to different pharmaceutical families and shouldn't cause a Penicillin allergy to erupt.

EXPIRATION DATES

✚ ✚ ✚

A question that I am asked quite often and to which my answer is, again, contrary to standard medical recommendations (but appropriate where modern medical care no longer exists) is: "What happens when all these drugs I stockpiled pass their expiration date"? The short answer is: Not a heck of a lot.

Since 1979, pharmaceutical companies have been required to place expiration dates on their medications. What does this mean? Officially, the expiration date is the last day that the company will certify that their drug is fully potent. Some believe this means that the medicine in question is useless or in some way dangerous after that date. This is a false assumption, at least in the vast majority of those medicines that come in pill or capsule form.

Studies performed by the Food and Drug Administration revealed that 90% of medications tested were acceptable for use 8-15 years after the expiration date. The FDA tested over 100 medications, prescription and non-prescription, and continues to study the issue today. The exceptions were mostly in liquid form (some pediatric antibiotics, insulin, among others). These lose their potency very soon after the date on the package. One sign of this is a change in the color of the liquid, but this is not proof one way or another.

Recently, a program called the Shelf Life Extension Plan evaluated a number of FEMA-stockpiled medications; these were mostly antibiotics that had been stockpiled for use in natural disaster and had passed their expiration dates. They found that almost all medications in pill or capsule form were still good 2 to 10 years after their expiration dates. As a result of these findings, even the government has changed their stance on expiration dates. During a recent flu epidemic, the SLEP authorized a 5 year extension for the use of expired Tamiflu, a drug used to prevent and treat Swine Flu and other influenzas.

Surprisingly, few other extended use authorizations have been approved for the other medications, even though such authorization would be helpful for millions of people preparing for tough times. Another disturbing fact: The information from the study is no longer available to the general public, as the website that originally published it now requires a special access code to enter. Despite this, you can try to obtain a back copy of *The Journal of Pharmaceutical Sciences*, Vol. 95, No. 7, July 2006, where you will find a summary of the SLEP data.

It is true that the strength of a medication could possibly decrease over time, so it is important that your supplies are stored in a cool, dry, dark place. The effective life of a drug usually is in inverse relation to the temperature it is stored at. In other words, a drug stored at 50 degrees Fahrenheit will last longer than one stored at 90 degrees Fahrenheit. Storing in opaque or "smoky" containers is preferable to clear containers. Humidity will also affect medications, and could even cause mold and mildew to form, especially on natural remedies such as dried herbs and powders.

Planning ahead, we must consider all alternatives in the effort to stay healthy in hard times. Don't ignore any option that can help you achieve that goal, even expired medicine. I encourage everyone to conduct their own study into the truth about expiration dates; come to your own conclusions after studying the facts.

MEDICAL REFERENCES

+ + +

I mentioned earlier that some reference books will be necessary for any aspiring medic. A medical library will still be there in a collapse situation, even if the internet, television, and other media are not. There are many good written resources for handling medical problems; these are but a few. The following books will be good additions to every medic's library:

Stedman's Medical Dictionary (a must for any medic)

Gray's Anatomy for Students (yes, the television show's title was taken from this book)

The Physician's Desk Reference (comes out yearly, tells you indications, dosages, and risks of just about every medicine)

The Merck Manual (good pocket reference on many common medical problems)

The Mayo Clinic Family Health book (exhaustive and thorough with lots of photos)

Clinical Physiology Made Ridiculously Simple by Stephen Goldberg, M.D. (all the basics)

American College of Emergency Physicians First Aid Manual (excellent first aid book)

Where there is No Doctor by David Werner
(third world medicine)

Where there is no Dentist by Murray Dickson
(third world dentistry)

A Comprehensive Guide to Wilderness and Travel Medicine by Eric Weiss, M.D. (pocket version)

Wilderness Medicine by William W. Forgey, M.D.
(outdoor survival)

Prescription for Herbal Healing by Phyllis A. Balch, CNC
(extensive herbal remedy book)

Essential Oils Desk Reference by Essential Science Publishing (exhaustive listings with photos)

Best Remedies by Mary L. Hardy, M.D. and Debra L. Gordon
(Plain English home remedies for 100 different medical problems; excellent integrative medical reference)

Principles of Surgery by Schwartz et al (for the very, very ambitious)

Tactical Medicine Essentials by the American College of Emergency Physicians (for really high-risk situations)

Varney's Midwifery (you never know when you'll need it)
If you have all these books in your medical library, you will have as much information at your fingertips as you'll need to keep your loved ones healthy in times of trouble.

YOUTUBE
VIDEO RESOURCES

✚ ✚ ✚

One of the best resources available to information seekers is the "viral" video. This phenomenon has placed a veritable library at your fingertips with regards to medical information. Even better than a library, you can actually see important medical procedures being performed, such as in my video "How to Suture with Dr. Bones". They range from a short blurb of a minute or so to a full one hour medical school lecture. The next few pages are essentially an entire second book filled with medical knowledge.

I have endeavored to find a representative video for just about every subject that I cover in this book. Different sources are listed, so that you can see the many options available for health information in all fields. The source is listed is listed in parentheses after the title of the video, along with a short comment. Search YouTube for the title listed exactly as listed. If more than one video exists with the same title, look to see what the source is.

I have to say that I don't agree with everything said on every video; do your own research and make you own decisions. The important thing to remember is that these sources are interested in what is relevant in today's modern world. Many of them end with "and head for the hospital" or "see your doctor as soon as possible". Few if any are considering a societal collapse in their presentations, so be forewarned. In any case, the videos will provide you an excellent base of knowledge from which to move forward.

01.Physical Exam-Introduction & Vital Signs (by tvmariel)
(Just one of many which show a doctor performing portions of the physical exam)

7.Medical Interview -Review of Systems (by tvmariel)
(One of various videos which show a doctor conducting an interview with a patient before an exam)

What Are Essential Oils (Anyway)? (by kennethgardner1)
(I can't verify all the claims made here; do you own research and decide for yourself)

The Cure-All Medication that Fixes Everything: Colloidal Silver! (by noeldeisle)
(testimonial and how to make it at home)

The Dangers of Colloidal Silver (by pogue972)
(a story about a man with argyria)

Jacket Stretcher Wilderness First Aid Paul Tarsitano 1 of 3
Rope and Stick Stretcher Paul Tarsitano 2 of 3
Tarp Stretcher Wilderness First Aid Paul Tarsitano 3 of 3
(all by pault1960)
(3 videos by an expert in improvised patient transport)

Carrying the Injured (1933) (by wellcomefilm)
(Amazing old video with various patient carry techniques)

Extremities Lift and Carry (Pocket Tools Training - NCOSFM) (by ncosfm)
(Quick how-to for 2-man carry)

Blanket Drag (Pocket Tools Training – NCOSFM (by ncosfm)
(Another video in an excellent series)

FIREMAN CARRY COACH
(by lesmillsspartan)
(How to perform a one-man carry)

Lice-Mayo Clinic (by mayoclinic)
(Treatment basics)

How To Remove A Tick (by tickEncounter)
(Step-by-step procedure)

Mt. Everest Dental Extraction at Base Camp (by cristenhfdg)
(Tooth extraction in an austere environment)

How to INSTANTLY CURE A TOOTHACHE at home remedy (by askmydentisttv)
(Dentist teaches you how to make temporary filling cement)

Respiratory Infection Health Byte (by livestrong)
(Basics of upper and lower respiratory infections)

Signs of Dehydration - and How to Prevent It (by nsipartners)
(Identifying water loss)

How To Treat Diarrhea (by howcast)
(General information)

Treatment for Food Poisoning - Memorial Hospital, Gulfport, MS (by gulfportmemorial)
(Important information)

How To Recognize the Symptoms Of Appendicitis (by howcast)
(How to differentiate from other problems)

Kidney and Urinary Tract Infection (by chcltd)
(Review of anatomy and infectious process)

How to Treat Hepatitis (by mahalodotcom)
(General hepatitis info)

Heat Exhaustion (by roperstfrancis)
(Symptoms to look for)

Hypothermia Treatment Scenario (by remotemedical)
(Actual wilderness video)

**Health and Safety Abroad: Altitude Sickness
(by HTHworldwide)**
(Signs to look for)

First Aid - Minor wounds standard care (by businessrecovery)
(Basics)

First Aid - Severe bleeding (by businessrecovery)
(Step by step)

How to Treat Gunshot & Knife Wounds (by sootch00)
(Just in case)

**The Emergency Bandage (aka The Israeli Bandage)
(by PerSysMedical)**
(Best trauma bandage)

Celox Trauma Gauze (by sammedical)
(Useful for heavily bleeding wounds)

Quikclot Demonstration (by peacemakerdill)
(Not for the squeamish)

How To Suture With Dr. Bones (by drbonespodcast)
(Learn how to put stitches into a pig's foot)

Surgical Debridement (by nucleusanimation)
(Removing dead tissue from a wound)

**Adventure Medical Preventing and Treating Blisters
(by jamestowntv)**
(Treatment process using certain brand name items)

First Aid Tips: How to Treat a Burn in the Wilderness (by ehow)
(Fire captain discussing burn injuries in the wild)

Burns: Classification and Treatment (by nucleusanimation)
(All the degrees and basic treatment explained)

Black Widow spider bite - Day 3 (by varvelle)
(Classic appearance shown)

Anaphylactic Shock (by harpergriffin)
(Definition and live scenario)

Dermatology Treatments : How to Diagnose Skin Rashes (by ehowhealth)
(Some common skin rashes explained)

Cellulitis and Treatment (by facingdisability)
(How to identify)

Symptoms of Tension vs. Migraine Headache (by fyinowhealth)
(List of symptoms of each)

Sprains and Strains (by universityhospitals)
(Quick overview)

Sprains Fractures and Dislocations (by uctelevision)
(Full 1 hour medical school lecture with lots of great info- first 8 or 9 minutes include an easy quiz)

Thyroid Disease- Health Connection (by muschealth)
(Describes high and low thyroid conditions)

Diabetes Overview (by answerstv)
(Comprehensive discussion)

Understanding High Blood Pressure (HBP #1) (by healthguru)
(All the facts in plain English)

Chest pain vs. heart attack - ask the doctor (by wptvnews)
(Different causes of chest pain)

Dr. Oz - What causes acid reflux? (by sistagirl488deleted)
(TV doctor describes how it occurs)

Understanding Epilepsy (Epilepsy #1) (by healthguru)
(Why seizures happen)

Understanding Arthritis (Arthritis #1) (by healthguru)
(Osteoarthritis and rheumatoid arthritis overview)

Healthbeat - Kidney Stones (by koattv)
(Advice to avoid recurrences)

Gallstones Health Byte (by livestrong)
(Causes, types, symptoms)

How To Perform the Heimlich Maneuver (Abdominal Thrusts) (by howcast)
(Excellent demonstration)

CPR Training Video New 2010 / 2011 Guidelines - Preview Safetycare Cardiopulmonary Resuscitation (by safetycareonline)
(Excellent preview but not a substitute for a full course)

Eye Care & Vision Problems : How to Get Rid of Bloodshot Eyes (by ehowhealth)
(Discussion of eye allergies)

Conjunctivitis - Pink Eye (by drmdk)
(Question and answer session with an eye doctor)

Anterior Nasal Packing.MPG (by ausafakhan)
(Good procedure to know)

Ears 101 : How to Relieve an Ear Ache (by ehowhealth)
(Common infections and treatment)

Prenatal Care: Early Pregnancy Visits (by marchofdimes)
(Explains prenatal care and shows an actual visit)

Top of Form

Bottom of Form

Birth of Baby (Vaginal Childbirth) (by prenateperl)
(Animated presentation of a normal birth)

5 Minute Vaginal Birth Of An Actual Live Human Fetus Baby ~The Circle Of Life Begins.flv (by 917sunlib)
(A real live birth!)

Anxiety Overview (by answertv)
(All the basics)

Signs, Symptoms, and Treatment of Depression (by nimhgov)
(Again, all the basics)

GLOSSARY OF MEDICAL TERMINOLOGY

✚ ✚ ✚

ABRASION:	area of skin scraped off down to the dermis
ABSCESS:	collection of pus and inflamed tissue
ACID REFLUX:	Pain and burning caused by stomach acid traveling up the esophagus
ADRENALINE:	name for epinephrine outside the U.S.
AIRWAY:	breathing passage
ALLERGY:	exaggerated physical reaction to a substance
AMNIOTIC FLUID:	liquid inside the pregnant uterus
AMBU-BAG:	CPR breathing unit (brand name)
ANALGESIA:	pain relief

ANAPHYLAXIS:: hypersensitivity to a substance due to antibodies after an initial exposure

ANAPHYLACTIC SHOCK: life-threatening organ failure as a result of hypersensitivity to a substance

ANGINA: heart pain caused by lack of oxygen

ANTIBIOTIC: substances that kill bacteria in living tissue

ANTIBODY: substances produced by the body that respond to toxins

ANTICOAGULANT: substances that stop clotting

ANTIEMETIC: substances that stop vomiting

ANTIHISTAMINE: drugs that relieve minor allergies

ANTIINFLAMMATORY: substances that limit inflammation

ANTISEPTIC: anything that limits the spread of germs on living surfaces

ANTISPASMODIC: decreases blood vessel constriction

ANTIVENIN: substance that inactivates snake or insect venom

ANTIVIRAL: substances that kill viruses

APPENDICITIS: inflammation of the appendix

ARTERY: blood vessel that carries oxygen to the tissues

ARTHRITIS: inflammation of the joints

ASCITES:	fluid accumulation in the abdomen
ASPHYXIANT:	substance that deprives the body of oxygen
ASPIRATION:	inhalation of fluids into the airways
ASTHMA:	shortness of breath caused by a narrowing of airways, often due to an allergic reaction
ASYMPTOMATIC:	without signs or symptoms
ATHEROSCLEROSIS:	blockage of the coronary arteries
AVULSION:	tissue torn off by trauma
BAG VALVE MASK:	CPR breathing apparatus
BANDAGE:	wound covering
BETADINE:	iodine antiseptic solution
BILE:	fluid found in the gall bladder
B.R.A.T. DIET:	diet used to treat dehydration consisting of bananas, rice, applesauce and dry toast
BRONCHITIS:	inflammation of the airways
BRONCHUS:	main respiratory airway
BRUISE:	injury that does not break the skin but causes bleeding due to damaged blood vessels
CAPILLARY:	tiny blood vessel that connects arteries to veins throughout the body

CARDIAC:	relating to the heart
CARTILAGE:	fibrous connective tissue found in various parts of the body, such as the joints, outer ear, and larynx.
CATARACT:	a clouding of the lens of the eye
CELLULITIS:	inflammation of soft tissues
CHIN-LIFT:	CPR technique that improves airflow
CHOLECYSTITIS:	inflammation of the gall bladder
CHOLELITHIASIS:	gall stones
CIRRHOSIS:	chronic liver damage
CLOSED FRACTURE:	broken bone that does not break the skin
COLLAPSE SITUATION:	circumstance where modern medical care no longer exists for the long term
CONCUSSION:	loss of consciousness caused by trauma to the cranium
CONJUNCTIVITIS:	inflammation of the eye membrane
CORNEA:	clear covering over the iris
COSTOCHONDRITIS:	chest pain caused by inflammation of the rib joints
CPR:	cardio-pulmonary resuscitation
CROWNING:	late stage of labor when the baby's head start to emerge from the vagina

CURETTAGE:	scraping dead pregnancy tissue from the uterus after a miscarriage
CYANOSIS:	blue color caused by lack of oxygen
DEBRIDEMENT:	removal of dead tissue from a wound
DEHYDRATION:	loss of body water content
DERMATITIS:	inflammation of the skin
DERMIS:	deep layer of the skin
DIABETES:	disease in which the body fails to produce enough Insulin to control blood sugar levels (type 1) or is resistant to the Insulin it produces (Type 2)
DIAGNOSIS:	Identification of a medical condition
DILATION:	the act of making more open
DISCHARGE:	drainage from a surface or wound
DISINFECTANT:	substance that kills germs on non-living surfaces
DISLOCATION:	traumatic movement of a bone out of its joint
DISTAL:	away from the torso
DIURETIC:	substance that increases urine flow
DRESSING:	wound covering

DUODENUM:	part of the bowel after the stomach
DYSENTERY:	dangerous diarrheal disease
ECLAMPSIA:	seizures caused by elevated blood pressures during a pregnancy
ECTOPIC PREGNANCY:	pregnancy that implants outside of the womb
EDEMA:	fluid accumulation
ELECTROLYTES:	elements found in body fluids
ENDEMIC:	native to an area or species
EPIDERMIS:	superficial layer of the skin
EPILEPSY:	convulsive disorder
EPINEPHRINE:	hormone used to treat severe allergic reactions (known as adrenaline outside the US)
EPISTAXIS:	bleeding from the nose
ERYTHEMA:	redness due to inflammation
ESOPHAGUS:	tube that runs from the back of the mouth to the stomach
ESSENTIAL OILS:	highly concentrated liquids of various mixtures of natural compounds obtained from plants.
EXPECTORANT:	substance that loosens congestion
FRACTURE:	a broken bone
FROSTBITE:	frozen tissue, usually in extremities

GALL BLADDER:	organ near the liver that stores bile
GANGRENE:	death of tissue due to lack of circulation
GASTROENTERITIS:	inflammation of the stomach/intestine
GINGIVITIS:	inflammation of the gums
GLAND:	organ that produces hormones
GLUCOSE:	blood sugar
GRAND MAL SEIZURE:	generalized convulsion in epileptics
HEARTBURN:	chest pain caused by stomach acid
HEAT STROKE:	symptoms caused by overheating
HEIMLICH MANEUVER:	action taken to remove foreign object from the airways
HEMOGLOBIN:	red blood cell component that carries oxygen to the tissues
HEMORRHAGE:	blood loss
HEMORRHOID:	varicose vein near the anus
HEMOPTYSIS:	coughing up blood
HEMOSTATIC AGENT:	substance that stops bleeding
HEPATITIS:	inflammation of the liver
HERNIA:	weakness in the body wall
HISTAMINES:	substances formed in allergies that cause physical symptoms

HIVES:	bumpy red rash caused by allergies
HORMONE:	substance produced by a gland that affects body functions
HYDRATION:	addition of water to the system
HYGIENE:	cleanliness as health strategy
HYPEROPIA:	farsightedness
HYPERTENSION:	high blood pressure
HYPERTHERMIA:	heat stroke or heat exhaustion
HYPERTHYROIDISM:	condition caused by high thyroid levels
HYPHEMA:	bleeding into the white of the eye
HYPOGLYCEMIA:	low blood glucose levels
HYPOTHERMIA:	syndrome caused by heat loss
HYPOTHYROIDISM:	condition caused by low thyroid levels
IMMOBILIZATION:	prevention of movement
IMMUNITY:	protection against a disease
IMPETIGO:	skin infection with weeping sores
INFARCTION:	death of heart tissue due to lack of oxygen
INFLAMMATION:	reaction to injury characterized by redness, swelling, discharge, pain and heat
INFLUENZA:	viral respiratory illness

INTEGRATED CARE:	treatment using different medical methods
INTOXICATION:	state of being poisoned
INTRAVENOUS:	inside the vein
IRIS:	colored portion of the eye
IRRIGATION:	forceful application of fluid to a wound to clean out debris, blood clots, and dead tissue
IRRITANT:	substance that causes inflammation of tissue
ISCHEMIC:	lacking oxygen due to circulatory failure
JAUNDICE:	yellowing of the skin and eyes due to liver malfunction
KETOACIDOSIS:	life-threatening condition related to failure of blood glucose control
KILOGRAM:	2.2 pounds
LACERATION:	penetration of both skin layers by injury
LARYNX:	the voice box
LASIK:	laser surgery to correct vision
LETHARGY:	extreme fatigue or drowsiness
LIGAMENT:	supportive tissue that connects bones
LITER:	0.264 gallons
LOCALIZED:	isolated to an area

LYMPHATICS:	drainage system for body fluids
MENINGITIS:	inflammation of the brain/spinal cord
MENSTRUATION:	periodic blood flow from the uterus
MIGRAINE:	headaches caused by vascular Spasms
MISCARRIAGE:	early pregnancy loss
MOLESKIN:	protective material for blisters
MYOPIA:	nearsightedness
NEUROLOGIC:	pertaining to the nervous system
OPEN FRACTURE:	broken bone that pierces the skin
OPTHALMOSCOPE:	instrument used to look into the eyes
OTITIS:	inflammation of the ear
OTOSCOPE:	instrument used to look into ear canal
OVARY:	female organ that produces eggs
PALPATION:	to feel with the hands
PALPITATIONS:	sensation of dread caused by a rapid heart rate
PATHOGEN:	something that causes disease
PEDIATRIC:	pertaining to children
PELVIC:	pertaining to the bones that provide support for legs and spine
PEPTIC:	relating to stomach acid

PERCUSSION:	to tap on the body to identify hollow and solid areas; for example, when searching for a tumor.
PETIT MAL SEIZURE:	epilepsy characterized by loss of awareness without generalized convulsive behavior
PHARYNX:	the throat
PHLEBITIS:	inflammation seen in varicose veins
PHLEGM:	mucus discharge from the respiratory tract
PNEUMONIA:	an infection of the lungs
PNEUMOTHORAX:	free air in the lung cavity affecting breathing
POTABLE:	safe to drink
PRE-ECLAMPSIA:	pregnancy-induced hypertension
PROGNOSIS:	likely outcome of a medical condition
PRONE:	lying face down
PROPHYLAXIS:	preventative measures
PROXIMAL:	closer to the torso
PROTOZOA:	microscopic organisms that sometimes act as parasites
PULMONARY:	relating to the lungs
PRESSURE POINTS:	areas where pressure on blood vessels stops bleeding to distal areas
PRURITIS:	itchiness

PULMONARY:	relating to the lungs
PUS:	inflammatory discharge caused by the body's response to infection
PYELONEPHRITIS:	inflammation of the kidney
QUADRANT:	body area divided into quarters
REBOUND:	pain elicited by pressing, then made worse by releasing the pressure on a part of the body
REFLUX:	acid traveling up the esophagus
RELAPSE:	recurrence of a disease's symptoms
RENAL:	relating to the kidneys
RESPIRATORY:	relating to breathing
RHYTHM METHOD:	method of determining fertile periods by tracking menstrual cycles
SALINE:	salt water solution used for IV fluids and irrigating wounds
SEBORRHEA:	oily, itchy rash on scalp and face
SEDATION:	to relax or put to sleep
SEIZURE:	convulsion
SHOCK:	life-threatening syndrome caused by multiple organ failure or malfunction
SOFT TISSUE:	muscle, tendons, ligaments, skin, fat
SPRAIN:	damage to a ligament caused by hyperextension

SPHYGNOMANOMETER: instrument used to measure pressure

STERILE: free of germs

STERNUM: breastbone

STETHOSCOPE: instrument used for listening to heart, lungs, and for evaluating blood pressure

STRAIN: damage to a muscle or tendon

STROKE: brain hemorrhage with paralysis

SUBCUTANEOUS: under the skin

SUPINE: lying face up

SUSPENSION: a drug mixed in a liquid

SUTURE: wound closure with needle and thread

SYNDROME: collection of symptoms

SYSTEMIC: condition affecting the entire body

TACHYCARDIA: elevated heart rate

TENDON: connection of a muscle to a bone

THERMOREGULATORY: related to body temperature

TINCTURE: plant extract made by soaking herbs in a liquid (such as water, alcohol, or vinegar) for a specified length of time, then straining and discarding the plant material.

TINNITUS: ringing in the ears

TOURNIQUET:	item that uses pressure to stop bleeding from a wound
TRAUMA:	injury caused by impact
TRIAGE:	to sort by priority
TUMOR:	a growth in or on the body
TYMPANIC MEMBRANE:	eardrum
ULCER:	damage to the wall of the skin, stomach or intestine due to pressure, acid or disease
ULTRAVIOLET:	invisible light waves that damage skin or eyes
UMBILICAL:	relating to the "belly button"
URTICARIA:	allergic rash
UTERUS:	womb
VARICES:	enlarged and dilated veins
VASCULAR:	relating to blood vessels
VEIN:	blood vessel that carries de-oxygenated blood back to the lungs
VERTIGO:	dizziness
WHEEZING:	high pitched noises heard while breathing during an asthma attack

CONTACTS

+ + +

DOCTOR:_____

DENTIST:_____

FIRE DEPT:_____

POLICE:_____

GROUP MEDIC:_____

GROUP MEMBERS:_____

_____

_____

_____

_____

_____

_____

_____

_____

_____

_____

NOTES

NOTES

NOTES

CONTACTS

NOTES

NOTES

NOTES

THE BEST MEDICAL KIT FOR THE SURVIVAL
MEDIC IS RIGHT HERE!

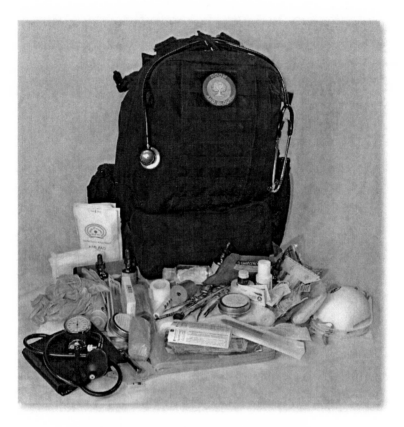

THE ONLY KIT THAT COMBINES
CONVENTIONAL AND NATURAL
MEDICINE

THIS KIT WILL ALLOW YOU TO TREAT:

MINOR TRAUMA	DEHYDRATION
MAJOR TRAUMA	FRACTURES/SPRAINS
BURNS	BLEEDING WOUNDS
DENTAL PROBLEMS	INFECTIONS
	AND MUCH MORE!
	OVER 500 ITEMS

COMPONENTS AVAILABLE SEPARATELY AND IN MODULES TO FIT YOUR BUDGET

NOW AVAILABLE AT WWW.DOOMANDBLOOM.NET ALONG WITH MANY OTHER USEFUL ITEMS

INDEX

✚ ✚ ✚

CPSIA information can be obtained at www.ICGtesting.com
Printed in the USA
LVOW13s2303160514

386210LV00001B/96/P